Fine Bird Books
1700–1900

NEDER-
LAND-
SCHE

VOGELEN.

III Deel.

Fine Bird Books
1700–1900

By

SACHEVERELL SITWELL
HANDASYDE BUCHANAN

and

JAMES FISHER

WITH A FOREWORD BY
S. Dillon Ripley

THE ATLANTIC MONTHLY PRESS
NEW YORK

First published in Great Britain in 1953 by William Collins

Published simultaneously in Canada
Printed in Japan

Library of Congress Cataloging-in-Publication Data

Sitwell, Sacheverell, 1897–1988
    Fine bird books, 1700–1900 / by Sacheverell Sitwell, Handasyde Buchanan, and James Fisher; with a foreword, S. Dillon Ripley.
    Bibliography
    Includes index.
    ISBN 0-87113-285-0
    1. Ornithological literature—History—18th century. 2. Ornithological literature—History—19th century. 3. Natural history literature—History—18th century. 4. Natural history literature—History—19th century. 5. Natural history illustration—History—18th century. 6. Natural history illustration—History—19th century. I. Buchanan, Handasyde. II. Fisher, James, 1912– . III. Title.
QL672.5.S57 1989   89-6480   508—dc19

Design by Ann Harakawa Inc.

The Atlantic Monthly Press
19 Union Square West
New York, NY 10003

First printing

FINE BIRD BOOKS: 1700–1900
was designed by Ann Harakawa and Hideshi Fujimaki, New York.
The text type is Bembo set on the Mergenthaler Linotron by
Trufont Typographers, Inc., Hicksville, New York.
The four-color separations, printing, and binding were done by
Dai Nippon Printing Company Limited, Tokyo, Japan.
The paper is 106-pound Espel Matte.

———

PLATE 1
[FRONTISPIECE]
*Cornelis Nozeman commissioned 250 elaborate illustrations
for* Nederlandsche vogelen *(Amsterdam 1770–1829). The Hoopoe, Bullfinch et al
of this half title make an artificial, yet charming, composition.
Jan Christian Sepp, elder and younger,
drew and etched the plates.*

———

PLATE 2
"The Cock Hoopoe" illustrates Eleazar Albin's
A Natural History of Birds *(London 1731–38), the first British bird book with colored plates.
It grew out of his vocation of painting
private collections of natural history objects. Albin's daughter Elizabeth
drew and colored many of the plates.*

The Cock Hoopoe.

CONTENTS

NOTE TO THE NEW EDITION

THIS VOLUME GUIDES US THROUGH an extraordinary body of art and science. It documents a period when these two strands of culture were tightly interwoven; a time when the natural sciences spawned the most artful expression of the printer's craft ever achieved. Through its superb visual record and its comprehensive bibliographic catalogue, *Fine Bird Books: 1700–1900* provides collectors with an unparalleled introduction to the great natural history books and prints.

The Bibliography, not limited to cataloguing a single library or collection, nor being a strictly scientific compilation, encompasses the breadth of two centuries of exquisite colorplate books with the collector in mind. The field is not confined to the giants of the era, such as John Gould and John James Audubon; it includes more obscure but no less superb works such as Descourtilz's *Oiseaux brillans du Brésil* (plate 31), of which fewer than ten copies are known to exist. The Index leads the reader to the scattered contributions of individual authors, artists, and printmakers, from the rare excellence of Dietzsch to the accomplished prolificacy of Keulemans in the late nineteenth century. Thus *Fine Bird Books* is perhaps the greatest single guide to these prints, allowing collectors, both avid and casual, to become better acquainted with the books and prints they own or would like to own.

We have added to Sacheverell Sitwell's original text Handasyde Buchanan's Appendix to define the language of connoisseurship, which allows a collector to know and discuss prints with precision. We are grateful to publisher Weidenfeld and Nicholson for permission to reprint this section as well as Buchanan's enlightening Introduction to his own book, *Nature into Art*. As a reflection of the increasing interest in the field, we have been able to double the number of titles in the reference bibliography, all books published since *Fine Bird Books* appeared in 1953.

We were prompted to republish this volume because, although *Fine Bird Books* is quoted extensively in the catalogues of auction houses, dealers, and museums, it is largely unavailable to the private collector. The large size of the original edition (14″ × 20″) confines its use to the floor or the dining table, and libraries often limit its circulation to a rare book reading room. From time to time the original edition (limited to 2,000 copies) appears in a book dealer's catalogue for around $1,000.

The editors are pleased to make Sitwell's text and Fisher and Buchanan's scholarly bibliography widely available in a convenient and well-illustrated format. *Fine Bird Books* is a unique authority. It combines the expertise of naturalist and man of letters Sacheverell Sitwell, renowned ornithologist James Fisher, and London book dealer Handasyde Buchanan. This constellation results, perhaps, in a certain anglophilia, but those familiar with the original edition will note that we have illustrated works from a greater diversity of sources to more accurately reflect the overwhelming contributions of European artists and printmakers. Indeed, many of the greatest engravers and printers in London arrived there from the continent with their techniques fully mastered.

Revisions to the text are limited to the clarification of Sitwell's often casual references to authors and titles. Notations of several factual errors appear as Editor's notes (a–g) appended to the Notes. The List of the Plates offers the latest provenance of the fifty-two plates illustrated in full color. A look through the list reveals the variety of collections from which we have photographed fine examples of colorplates for our illustrations.

The editors wish to thank all those who have helped prepare this book, but particularly the librarians, curators, and rare-book dealers who made their collections, time, and support so readily available. Graham Arader and Donald Heald, renowned New York dealers of fine colorplate books, opened their galleries to us and gave valuable counsel on our selection of images. The New York Public Library was an extraordinarily rich source of material and assistance, and we especially thank Bernard McTigue, curator of the Arents Collection, and John Rathe of the Rare Book Room for their constant cooperation and support. We are also indebted to Sotheby's, which made important books available to us from the collection of H. Bradley Martin. Hirschl & Adler Gallery and Karen Clarke at the Watkinson Library of Trinity College made available their fine examples of Audubon prints. Stanley Crane at Pequot Library opened his doors on the works of Daniel Elliot. Valerie Wheat at the library of the American Museum of Natural History facilitated our access to its complete collection of the works of John Gould. We also appreciate the interest and research afforded us by Cornell University, McGill University, the University of Kansas, and Yale University. We are grateful to Robert Lorenzson, who photographed most of the prints, for his superb skill and keen appreciation of the subject.

Finally, the editors wish to thank Elizabeth Braun, without whose expertise, inspiration, and unflagging energy this book could not have been produced. Her love of fine colorplate books and her attention to detail are evident on every page of this volume. She was tireless in her search for the best possible examples of each plate we have illustrated, and her captions and List of the Plates attest to her exacting scholarship. She also took pains to emend the text and bibliography where errors or the scholarship of the past thirty years called for it.

THE EDITORS

FOREWORD

OF ALL THE BOOKS on birds that I have had the pleasure of collecting, few have fascinated me as much as *Fine Bird Books: 1700–1900*. Originally published in Britain by Collins & Von Nostrand in 1953, it is, itself, a fine bird book, beautifully printed and designed by George Rainbird and Ruari McLean of London. The printing of the illustrations is, by twentieth-century standards, exceptional; the paper splendid; the letter-press type, Bembo, one of my favorites; the format, folio, fully up to portraying the great oversize works treated; and the binding good. The original volume, now rare, was a wonder for its time which will live on in memory and, as on this occasion, in a splendid revised edition.

The work is undoubtedly one of Sir Sacheverell Sitwell's most charming and erudite, and it is curious that so little mention of the volume is made in reference to the accomplishments of this, the youngest of the Sitwell siblings. Sir Sacheverell's essay reveals a comprehensive understanding of bird life and a full acquaintance with the world of ornithology. It is difficult for me not to assume that Sitwell was far more than an amateur in the current sense. He was, instead, an amateur in the earlier sense of someone who, while not employed in his profession, has a special understanding of it and much practice in it. And, I may add, an obsession coupled with the means to sate it.

His older brother, Sir Osbert Sitwell, said of Sacheverell when he was but a young boy: "With an intelligence already highly developed, he set himself, out of school, with an energy and intensity that were remarkable, to amass knowledge—but of course the sort of knowledge he wanted to amass." Fortunately, his chosen interests—history, art, architecture; high culture in all its manifestations—embraced as well the natural sciences, particularly as practiced in the eighteenth and nineteenth centuries, when art and science were more closely allied than they are in our own century.

The study of the history of science seems to lag these days, I am afraid, because lack of time and perhaps a lack of understanding of the importance of history itself seem to prevail. The tradition of writing well about birds has lost its appeal. Today, there are many monographs on families of birds, but the style of writing therein betrays the conventional university or curatorial backgrounds of their authors. It implies a Ph.D. in the matter of the science itself, not in the matter of writing or of good English style. This is to be deplored, for good writing should accompany good scholarship at all times, as it does so brilliantly in *Fine Bird Books*.

Surely Sitwell loved birds, and in his affection for them and his almost musical prose he expresses his love in an ineffable way, a delight to the reader in science as well as to the collector of beautiful books.

The bibliography of the whole family of finely illustrated bird books—the central purpose of this book—is an excellent one and part of the standard literature in ornithology. I wish that we could describe it more accurately; as, perhaps, a kind of dictionary of wonder. For a work performed so arduously and so brilliantly as to leave no opportunity for improvement in subsequent generations is a monument to those who have been in the foreground of this mysterious, often unrewarding and compulsive profession. I would be loath to describe Handasyde Buchanan and James Fisher's bibliography to *Fine Bird Books* as anything but a fascinating source of perennial delight.

Sitwell's choice of Buchanan, the bibliophile, and Fisher, the ornithologist, to compile the bibliography was a stroke of genius. Fisher provided the perfect foil to Sitwell. An idiosyncratic man who did much for introducing to ornithology the same sort of literary erudition which Sitwell espoused, he also did much to broaden interest in the pursuit beyond academic bounds. By the time that Sitwell chose Fisher to work with him on *Fine Bird Books*, Fisher had become perhaps the most popular figure in English ornithological circles, along with Sir Peter Scott, whom he accompanied on several ornithological expeditions.

Fisher had a wide variety of experience, having switched his studies from medicine to zoology during his postgraduate years. As an editor of Collins's New Naturalist series of monographs, he wrote on many aspects of British natural history. This involved him more and more in the popularization of his subject. A brilliant lecturer, a captivator of audiences large enough to challenge his own physical size, he forged a bridge into the present day, when ecology and the environment are recognized fields of scientific study.

Buchanan, for his part, was the quintessential bibliographer. For years the proprietor of Heywood Hill, the venerable London bookstore, he was for decades a leading scholar and a champion of the great illustrated natural history books. His *Nature into Art*, published in 1979, did much to fuel the current appreciation for the volumes he had catalogued twenty-five years earlier in his collaboration with Fisher and Sitwell.

The birds depicted in *Fine Bird Books* will never be painted better than by the artists and artisans whose extraordinary works are recorded in Buchanan and Fisher's bibliography. Like the books that illuminate them, many of these birds are incomparably rare. Some are extinct, others in danger of extinction owing to the miseries of development that we have imposed on ourselves and our descendants. As tropical forests disappear, the great tundra lakes of central Asia are drained, and plagues engendered by pollution wreak havoc on temperate forests, the chance of seeing such wonders of creation diminish. We can only deplore their passing, but at the same time live on in the glory rendered by such a publication.

S. DILLON RIPLEY

Quercus, anpatius; Ilex Marilandica
Folio longo angusto Salicis: Ray: Hist:

Willow Oak.

Picus maximus rostro albo?
Largest White Bill'd Woodpecker.

T. 16.

INTRODUCTION

Handasyde Buchanan

THE SCOPE OF THIS BOOK is the period from about 1700 to 1900 or a little earlier, and its aim is to show a selection of the best illustrations from old natural history books with coloured plates, together with an account of these books and their creators, which represent what might be called the golden age of the natural history book. It is not intended to be a complete history of books in this period, but rather a personal choice from among the best examples. The majority of these books were about birds and flowers, although insects are, indirectly, well represented since almost all books about them are, from the point of view of their plates, in effect flower books.

At the beginning of our period—the time when books with coloured plates were first produced—the pictures were taken from copper-plate engravings, and coloured by hand. This method was used from 1700 until about 1830 when that type of illustration was outmatched by the aquatint, the mezzotint and the stipple engraving, often printed in colours. This was the finest hour of colour printing. Around 1830 the lithograph appeared, which involved printing from a stone instead of a copper plate; it was still, however, coloured by hand. But towards the end of the nineteenth century the chromolithograph, in which the colour came directly from the stone and was not applied by hand, had won the battle. Of course it made natural history books grow steadily cheaper, and was the parent of all later flower, bird and animal plates, but these illustrations lack the individual artistry that made the earlier ones fascinating and unique, and the pleasure of looking at the pictures as works of art has gone. An account of the differences between these various processes, and how each was done, appears at the end of the book, on page 171. However in the 1950s a number of superbly produced, definitive books were published, all with bibliographies and fine reproductions of plates, such as *Great Flower Books* and *Fine Bird Books*. I contributed to most of them. Now these books have themselves become treasured, collectable items.

During the eighteenth and nineteenth centuries certain countries were at the top of what might be called the natural history book league, and this is perhaps the place to say who they were, when and why. The Dutch came first because they were the earliest explorers—Tasmania, for instance, was originally discovered by the Dutch in the seventeenth century, and known as Van Diemen's Land. Maria Sibylla Merian's *Insects of Surinam* (Surinam being a Dutch colony in northern South America at that time) of 1705 was the best example of Dutch work, although as late as 1794 a lovely and anonymous flower book called *Nederlandsch Bloemwerk* showed that the Dutch had not forgotten how to produce

---

PLATE 3
This now extinct Ivory-billed Woodpecker illustrates
The Natural History of Carolina *(London 1731–43). Author Mark Catesby traveled in*
North America to collect natural curiosities for the Royal Society at London.
This book related his discoveries through 220 hand-colored etchings and was the largest,
best illustrated natural history book of its day.

beautiful work. The Germans were active in the early eighteenth century, and J. W. Weinmann's *Phytanthoza Iconographia*, a mammoth book in folio format, comprising four volumes with 1,026 plates, is perhaps the most notable example. But from 1730 onwards the British really dominated the field with a very large number of great books.

There is, of course, one colossal exception in these years. France, with Redouté for flowers and Levaillant for birds, using stipple engravings expertly printed in colour, undoubtedly created the finest books of all between 1790 and 1830, despite competition from excellent works such as those of Thornton and Brookshaw in England. The United States—although of course it produced the magnificent Audubon—does not really enter into this particular discussion, since it must be remembered that Audubon's gigantic masterpiece, *The Birds of America*, was actually printed and published in London.

One interesting and sometimes confusing point is that some famous books are known by the author's name, and not by that of the artist. Redouté, the greatest of all French flower book artists, has his name on almost all the books with which he was associated—Redouté's *Roses*, Redouté's *Liliacées*, and so on—though not always as the principal. Levaillant, however, whose name appears on most of the great French bird books of that same period, was a naturalist who travelled far, but never to my knowledge drew any of the pictures for his books—almost all were drawn by Barraband. Dr Thornton was the author of perhaps the most splendid of all English flower books, popularly known as *The Temple of Flora*, but whose real title is *New Illustration of the Sexual System of Linnaeus*. Of the justly famous plates which illustrate this book only one, the Roses, was drawn by Thornton himself. Books are sometimes known by the artist's name, and sometimes by the name of the author of whatever text they may contain. A number of different activities were involved in producing a book, and although some tasks were often performed by the same person, it was quite possible for an explorer to provide the specimens, which would then be written up by someone else, illustrated by a professional artist, engraved by another hand, and perhaps hand-coloured by a whole team of people. All this explains the plethora of credits which are often to be found at the foot of natural history plates. The abbreviations used by artists, engravers and printers are given on page 175.

Although this book is only intended to cover printed books with coloured plates, it is worth saying a word or two about the original watercolours. Some artists were admirably served by their engravers and printers—despite Audubon's immense talent as a bird artist, for instance, *The Birds of America* would be less of a masterpiece were it not for the skills of Robert Havell. Other artists, however, were treated less well than they deserved, and so, perhaps unjustifiably from the artist's point of view, their books are considered less good. But all natural history artists are best judged by their original work, and anyone who has the opportunity of seeing the watercolours for *The Birds of America* at the New York Historical Society, or Georg Ehret's *vélins* (paintings on vellum) at the Victoria and Albert Museum and the Library of the Royal Botanic Gardens, Kew, will be well rewarded for the effort.

The part played by the great Swedish naturalist Linnaeus (1707–78) cannot be underestimated. He made an enormous contribution to natural history by tabulating a completely new system of classification for plants and animals. Before Linnaeus classification had been a somewhat haphazard affair and lacked any sort of standardization. The most commonly followed system for plants had been that of Tournefort, who based his distinctions on the shape of the corolla. Linnaeus, on the other hand, defined his categories by the sexuality of plants—a system that scandalized the prurient morality of the Victorians, who felt that young girls in particular should not be exposed to such grossness! In his *Species Plantarum* of 1753, and *Genera Plantarum* (1737; fifth and most important edition, 1754), Linnaeus divided plants, after examination of their male sexual organs, into 24 classes, which in turn, he subdivided into orders *vis-à-vis* their female sexual organs. The names were derived from the Greek— lilies, for instance (as illustrated in Mrs Bury's *Hexandrian Plants*), which have six stamens, are in the class 'Hexandria' (from the Greek words for 'six' and 'male') and of the order 'Monogynia' (from the Greek for 'one' and 'female'), since they have only one style. Linnaeus was an imaginative man and did not lack a sense of humour: he described the class Polyandria (many male organs), which includes the poppy, as 'Twenty males or more in the same bed with the female'.

While this book is concerned with the art and beauty of the natural history book rather than with its botanical or zoological merits, a number of expeditions—and subsequently books—were undoubtedly embarked on as a direct result of the availability of this relatively simple and foolproof system of classification, and lovers of old natural history books have good cause to be grateful to Linnaeus.

We have, of course, reached a stage today when no one but a fool would bet on the value of any book, because of inflation. But it is worth having a look at the past in this connection. *The Temple of Flora*, which was listed in 1890 catalogues at £20 (!), was on sale for £100 when I started as a bookseller in 1930. When I returned after the Second World War and found that the price of everything had escalated, it was then £500. By 1965 (it is now very scarce in the right state and in good condition) that price had shot up to £4,000–5,000. It may now be £12,000 or more; good copies rarely, if ever, turn up.[a]

The value of a book depends on so many different reasons—date, size (book sizes are dealt with on page 176), number of volumes and plates, intrinsic beauty, scientific merits (this is perhaps less important than it should be, and someone from a more scientific background than I should say whether this is true or not); but ultimately on its scarcity. There are from six to ten copies of Samuel Curtis's *The Beauties of Flora* in existence, and indeed it is likely that no more were printed. This folio volume, published between 1806 and 1820, has only ten plates. It is in effect priceless.

Not all the books described or illustrated here really merit the epithet 'great'. But they are all of the highest quality—in other words, their printed plates are among the best ever produced. The texts in these books are frequently poor, even non-existent, or merely what we would now call extended captions. Many of them were produced over a long period, as single plates, and were thus clearly meant to form picture books or to be framed—either for their decorative qualities, or for their informative value, as when describing a newly discovered animal or plant. All the plates reproduced in this book are intended to be enjoyed as things of beauty.

The Dodo.

Geo. Edwards, Sculp: A.D. 1757.

294

FINE BIRD BOOKS

Sacheverell Sitwell

TO MOST HUMAN BEINGS, and all persons of sensibility, something of mystery and of magic attaches to the tribes and nations of the birds. It is because, to the mystery of so many schools of flight performing in so many differing styles, there are added the magic and beauty of birth from the egg-shell. Little wonder if in pagan religions there have been sacred birds! The soaring of the eagle and condor on patrol above the air-chasms in the mountains comes from the egg-shell, alike with the rainbow birds that are as a shower of flowers in flight. The difficult 'lift' of the swan from off the level waters, and the slow, 'monitoring' and flapping flight of the wild swans all are born of the egg-shell, as are the swallow, the bird-of-paradise, the fighting cock. It is difficult to relate together the satyr tragopan, the sunbird, or the halcyon, the raven, the hoopoe, and the woodpecker, except that all come of the egg-shell. All are born of that immaculate matrix, of that shell of china.

I do not think there could be a more marvellous experience pertaining to these mysteries than to walk, as I have done upon a spring evening, in a heronry. It is one of the biggest remaining heronries in this country, not far from the banks of Dee. Large numbers of the birds (I heard them numbered at as many as seventy or eighty couples) had nested high in the trees that stand in a long wood beside some marshy ground which leads down to the river. The trees were in young leaf, but not enough to hide those airy cradles. No sound of bird, and nothing odd or peculiar, until you had come a few steps into this sacred grove, until, perhaps, the outer world was lost to you, and you only saw the trees. There were little streams or water-channels through the blackish mud, and here at a tree-foot the ground was strewn with pieces of blue egg-shell that were like shards of broken china. More and more of the broken egg-shell, blue and transparent, paler white, within, so that it was as though one wandered by some celestial kitchen-midden where the stork-kings threw down their cups of porcelain, once used; and then an entire egg, chipped and broken, with the yellow ichor spilling from it, when, as though to some signal, the whole heron-nation rose into the air and clapped their wings. They made off to the river in ungainly flight; raising their legs awkwardly, like under-carriages beneath them, and one would have thought not a heron was left upon the nest. But it was only the male birds that took alarm, and the hen birds still rode their nests.

It was now that standing at the tree-foot looking up, more of the blue egg-shell fluttered down from the next tree, as though it were broken porcelain of the consistency of air, and paper-thin; while leaning nearer to the tree-stem, seeing the nest high up among the topmost leaves, there came down a

PLATE 4
George Edwards illustrated Gleanings of Natural History
(London 1758–64) with etchings of the exotic, the familiar, and the extinct such as this Dodo.
It is a continuation of his earlier A Natural History of Birds *(1743–51),*
whose plates he etched in the same format. Edwards's decorative figures were copied
by textile, porcelain, and other artists.

faint but unmistakable tapping sound, and as it tapped, a fragment of the blue porcelain, no bigger than could be taken up in the fingers and cracked between my nails, fluttered down and fell from my shoulder upon the leafy floor. It was the fledgling heron tapping with its own beak inside the egg-shell, breaking its own way out from the egg into the world, and the beak and wings of the mother-heron could be seen, sitting upon her nest. As well, there was the chattering of the young heron already hatched, high above, the two or three 'day-old' heron chicks; and now the male herons flew back from their fishing-grounds along the river and noisily came down as near to their nest as possible or even perched upon an edge of it, high in the branches. The whole wood was, once more, a metropolis of the herons. Their droppings lay thick upon that leafy floor.

There is this about the herons. One stork standing in a field brings a whole landscape into the Orient. One stork's nest upon a chimney, in Alsace, in Spain, in Denmark, tells us that the storks flew above mosque and minaret to get here, and on their return will cross the Mediterranean into Africa. But the heron is native to our meres and rivers. The heron knows the hemlock and the willow-herb, the antlered oak tree and the hanging wood. He fishes where the collier comes with rod and line late in the afternoon when the light is waning, and the Salvation Army band is heard practising from far away. I am thinking of a particular lake in Derbyshire where there has always been a pair of herons, within sound of the collieries and the main railway line; and there are lakes and rivers all over the country where herons live in summer and winter for, of course, they are not migratory like the storks. The herons on their long legs stand sentinel above their fishing-grounds on summer evenings; early in the morning when the dew is upon the grass; and while the mist closes in on a November night. In pairs, mostly, or in small hamlets; but there are the heron towns, few in number, and this was one of them, perhaps the most popular of all, where I walked upon that April evening while the gnats were in a late hour of their lives and nothing else stirred but the clapping wings and noisy beaks of many hundred herons.

The only parallel adventure I have had in my own life to this visit to a heronry was in the Danube Delta, in Roumania. In point of landscape this is a region as little like the Western World as any shores descending to the Yellow Sea. Large portions of it are a swamp of willow trees, as tall as oaks, but only fifteen to twenty years old, growing with their roots in shallow water, their limbs serving for perch and display ground to so many aquatic birds, in such variety, that in retrospect they become like the over-populated, artificial branches in Gould's twenty-four glass cases of humming-birds, that master-piece of the taxidermist's art and mirror of the mid-Victorian Age, originally shown in a special building in the Zoological Gardens during the year of the Great Exhibition of 1851, and now relegated, forlorn and rather moulting, to the dusty corridors of the Natural History Museum at South Kensington.[b] Lower down the Danube the landscape opens into the Black Sea; and it was here in the great heat, with mirages playing on the horizon, that we saw certain low islands raised but a few inches, like green dairy meadows, in the tideless waters. Far away, white cities gleamed and sparkled, as though it was the Orient of domes and minarets, much as the walls and domes of Kairouan when you approach that holy city out of the Tunisian sands. But it was nothing of the sort. Those were white pelicans, towns of white pelicans camped upon the islands, packed closely, bird to bird, and covering the entire surface, but it was late, we were far out in the Delta, and adventured no nearer to the pelican cities.

Similar experiences, vastly greater in scope and degree, and in comparison to which the two just related are as the stutterings of a mere tyro, show the way that nature has opened her secrets, reluctantly, or in indifference, to the ornithologist. Expeditions, such as that undertaken[1] by Mr Peter Scott to find the breeding ground of Ross's Goose, in the Perry River region in the centre of the Arctic coast of Canada, would have been utterly impossible of achievement until the present time. In the result, this rare goose,[2] computed to number no more than two or three thousand individuals in the world, which winters in the Sacramento and San Joaquin valleys in California, and of which the first nest was only found in 1942, has been reached by aeroplane. The landscape of lakes and islands which this nation of snowy birds inhabits for a few weeks only in the Arctic summers has been seen for the first time by European eyes. That strange region, with its wandering Eskimos and sparse flowers and the wonderful purity of its light, has been fascinatingly described. Is the mystery any nearer solution of what factors determine a whole race of birds, living in community together, to move so punctually between summer and winter quarters that can be precisely pinpointed upon a map? We cannot tell. The secrets of bird migration, of how they find their direction, and of what prompts them in their choice of particular localities, are only beginning to be unravelled.

But it is towards these larger aspects of ornithology that future discoveries are converging. The wonder of the naturalist as he first beholds a bird's plumage is on the wane. There can be but few more birds to discover. It is for this reason that the great Bird Books are of the past. They attained their climax of grandeur and perfection a little later than the Flower Books. It is not easy to understand why this was so. For, in fact, more flowering plants have been brought back by botanists and introduced into our gardens during the first half of this century than in all the rest of time together. We have to conclude that it was the earlier, more formal flowers, that lent themselves for coloured illustration. I think this is true of the eighteenth century Flower Books, as it is of Pierre Joseph Redouté, Dr Robert Thornton's team of draughtsmen, Robert Sweet, and Mrs Jane Loudon, and the others. The 'natural' school of gardening, from William Robinson to Farrer, and from the rhododendron collectors and hybridists to the Alpine gardeners, will leave few painted relics of its glories. They are not communicable on paper. But the Great Bird Books of the nineteenth century came just in time to record the era of bird exploration, the gorgeous and formal livery of the birds lent itself to drawing in colour, and the destructive rise in costs which now makes any enterprise of the kind a practical impossibility had not begun. We shall see that Bird Books continued in scarcely diminishing splendour till the turning of the century. The technique, it is true, was chromolithography in all its garish hues and colours. But how else render the parrots and the lories? As for the birds-of-paradise, Richard Bowdler Sharpe's *Monograph of the Paradiseidæ* did not appear until 1898. This is, indeed, the last of the great Bird Books.

The most beautiful early drawings of birds are from the hands of Pisanello (c. 1399–1455). There are coloured drawings by him of hoopoes, herons, kingfishers, eagles, owls, and falcons (in the Louvre). They are the sketches for details in his paintings or his medals, and no drawings could be more beautiful or painstaking. He made five drawings of a magpie upon one sheet of paper; and of five doves

Der VIII.ten Hauptart
I.te Abtheilung
I.te Platte.

Der Schuffut oder Uhu,
Bube, Noctua maxima,
Le grand Duc,
f. Chaffeton f. grand Hibou

93.

1.fuß 10.Zoll.

and six kingfishers upon the same sheet of his sketchbook. Storks and cranes had a particular attraction for Pisanello. There are fourteen of these birds upon one page. His medal of Alfonso of Aragon (1449) has a group of eagles perched on rocks, upon its reverse side, to match the eagle profile of the King of Aragon and conqueror of Naples. Those many persons who love Pisanello's 'The Vision of St Eustace', with the saint riding in an enchanted wood of hares and stags and greyhounds and storks or herons on the wing; and his 'Madonna with St Anthony the Hermit and St George', the latter, a young knight with frizzed, fair hair, wearing a fleeced coat beneath his armour, and that wide-brimmed white hat with a feather stuck gaily in the crown (both paintings in the National Gallery, London); or who admire his medal of John VIII Palaeologus in the curious headgear with a domed crown almost like the Papal tiara and odd, projecting peak, in front, that was prerogative of, and peculiar to, the Basileus of Byzantium; should know that the earliest and most beautiful of Bird Books could be assembled from Pisanello's sketch book in the Louvre, alone. In the following century, Albrecht Dürer's celebrated watercolour of a dead jay seems more of an inquest than a work of art. But if I am correct in thinking that John James Audubon may have been inspired to paint his 'Meadow Lark', the most detailed of his plates, by seeing Dürer's drawing of 'The Cornfield' in the Albertina, what might not Dürer have achieved could time be reversed, could he have seen Audubon's huge folios, and had the whole immense field of colour reproduction in aquatint or lithography been open to him, who was the master of engraving upon wood or copper, but had to content himself with black and white.

It is, perhaps, an oddity that the Dutch seventeenth century produced no Bird Books. In the paintings of Melchior d'Hondecoeter, types of Houdans, Polands, Duckwings, Campines, and probably one or two now extinct strains of domestic fowls are to be distinguished, as well as many breeds of tame pigeons. There were painters, too, like Jan Weenix, who specialised in pictures of dead game. The situation is the same in the case of the flower painters. Cornelisz De Heem, Mignon, and later, Jan Van Huysum, Rachel Ruysch, and all the host of Dutch flower artists left a multitude of works behind them, but, obviously, they saw themselves as painters and not botanists. It was Crispin de Passe, of a famous family of engravers, who produced the *Hortus Floridus* (1614); and it is perhaps significant that Maria Sibylla Merian, who published her splendid work on the flowers and insects of Surinam (Dutch Guiana), in 1705, came, too, of a well-known family of engravers. Briefly, the point is that the school of Dutch flower painters produced no Flower Books, and neither did Hondecoeter, or the other Dutch bird painters, produce a Bird Book.

The 'primitive' of the coloured Bird Books, and the earliest artist to have his etchings reproduced within the covers of this present volume, is the Englishman, Mark Catesby. He was born in 1679, and in 1712 went to America where he stayed seven years, studying botany. Later, he made a

PLATE 5
Vorstellung der Vögel in Teutschland *(Berlin 1733–63)*
illustrates wild birds like this Owl, as well as hybrid domestic fowl.
Author Johann Leonhard Frisch and his sons
took thirty years to produce this book, which illustrates their bird collection.

second visit to the American colonies, settling at Charleston, South Carolina, but at a period previous to the Georgian buildings for which that town is famous. Coming home in 1726, he studied etching on purpose to make the illustrations for his own works and began the publication of his *Natural History of Carolina, Florida, and the Bahama Islands*, five years later. Birds were only one of the interests of Mark Catesby, and he was at least as curious about flowers or the coralline structures of the Bahaman reefs. His is a beautiful book, with a decided American interest as being one of the earliest works to portray the birds and flowers of North America, but it would be as idle to pretend that it is among the greatest Bird Books as it would be to compare his flower paintings to the magnificent drawings upon vellum of Georg Dionysius Ehret (1708–1770) who was one of the most superb botanical draughtsmen there has ever been. There is the tendency for Mark Catesby's birds to perch upon a conventionalised tree trunk in the manner of most of the eighteenth century ornithological plates. It is a mannerism that becomes monotonous, and that persists through the work of George Edwards, William Hayes, and until Audubon made all earlier ornithological works look uninformed and artificial. But, in fact, botanical drawing up to this point was in advance upon the delineators of birds. More skilled hands were at work depicting flowers, and the era of the great Bird Books was still to come.

Until a deeper degree of competence comes into ornithological illustration there is more of entertainment, as of aesthetic pleasure, in the unsophisticated draughtsmen of old Dutch or German books on birds. Our plate 1 from Cornelis Nozeman's *Nederlandsche Vogelen* is so utterly artificial in conception and execution that it makes a very virtue of its weakness and becomes an ornament of the age of Rococo. Belated, at that, for it did not appear till 1770, but it is a work of 'Confucian' Holland when the Dutch, like flies in amber, lived in a provincial vacuum and were left over from another age. 'Owl' (pl. 5) from Johann Frisch's *Vorstellung der Vögel in Teutschland* (1733–63), is more delightful still. It has a whole section of domestic fowls, and I daresay the reality was as curious as the printed image. For in all probability it was only in the hands of the English fanciers of a hundred years ago that Gold- and Silver-laced Polands, and Gold- and Silver-spangled and Pencilled Hamburg fowl in all the elaboration of their exhibition strains, were brought into perfection. What we see in Frisch are their wild, uncouth forebears. There are tufted and top-knotted fowls as fantastic in mien and plumage as the 'African King' who attends the Derby. These are, clearly, ancestors of the Polands and identical with the Paduan fowl of Aldrovandi.[3] Other domestic fowl in Frisch are a Bloodwing Pyle, and one of that breed with feathers blown in all directions, called Frizzles. The draughtsman who drew the plates keeps his excitement and naïveté in front of all these birds. He even gets down to them and draws them from their own level so that, in the plate, the cock-bird struts menacingly towards you as large as one of the masqued birdmen of the Venetian Carnival. Frisch's owls are in a class to themselves, owing to the various techniques he practises to portray their plumage. This he expressed by a wonderful range of dots and dashes, of criss-crosses and hatchings. For the feathers of one particular owl he seems, like one or two painters of our day, to be making a drawing with his typewriter. His ducks are, perhaps, a lesson in how to give importance to the humble bird that floats upon the stream and waddles, ridiculously, upon the bank.

Frisch's highly amusing Bird Book, it must be remembered, is contemporary with the compositions of Bach and Handel. It has its qualities, like many lesser things that belong to a great age. The Englishman, George Edwards, is another of the 'primitives', for he was born in Essex as early as 1694, one year, incidentally, after the Dodo was last seen or heard of. It was earlier in the century (in 1638) that Sir Hamon Lestrange as he 'walked London streets, saw the picture of a strange fowl hung out upon a cloth,' and went to see it. That was the Dodo in the Strand. Sir Thomas Herbert, visiting Mauritius in 1628, had written 'Her visage darts forth melancholy'. That sadness (as though doomed), and the freakish awkwardness of the flightless pigeon, are all in Edwards's plate which, for that matter, is a faithful copy of contemporary drawings of the Dodo (see pl. 4). Others of the early Bird Books, such as Peter Brown's *New Illustrations of Zoology* (1776) and Hayes's *Portraits of Rare and Curious Birds . . . in the Menagerie . . . at Osterley Park* (1794–9) it may be suggested at this point, are charming and delightful, but whether in point of accuracy or as works of art they are of little more importance than the series of birds produced by Samuel Dixon of Dublin, who invented a process by which he made relief pictures of birds out of some form of composition, and then coloured them. Hoopoes, or Golden and Silver Pheasants by Samuel Dixon, make pretty decorations; and such is, perhaps, the aesthetic level of Brown or Hayes. It is pathetic to read, in the Advertisement to *Portraits of Rare and Curious Birds*, of Hayes's large family, 'all under his roof, and dependant on his labour, and having only a precarious income, determinable upon his decease'. The hand-colouring of the plates was the work of no fewer than seven of his family. But the letterpress in this book is as informing as the coloured plates. What could be more endearing than to read: 'They seem to possess a superior understanding . . . and are more docile, kind, and sincere in their attachments. This amiable disposition was particularly manifested in the subject of my plate, for its fondness, affectionate attention, and attachment to the person that had the care of it was beyond expression'—and then to turn to the 'subject' of the plate, and discover it to be a most beautiful, Red-crested Cockatoo! While considering the publication of his work, Hayes 'had frequent permission to consult a most respectable character in the neighbourhood, and it was this gentleman who, seeing some specimens of their juvenile performances, was pleased to consider them as convincing proofs of early genius, which was worthy of cultivation'. Several of the best coloured plates in my own copy of *Portraits of Rare and Curious Birds* are signed, in green ink, 'Matilda Hayes'. Can she have been the eldest daughter of that hard-worked family?[c]

Xaviero Manetti's *Storia Naturale degli Uccelli* (1767–76), published in Florence, is a bigger affair altogether, in proof of which 'Wood-Duck' (pl. 7) of our reproduction is taken from plate 179 of the original. It is a work in six huge volumes, and was perhaps the finest Bird Book issued to date, and one of the most sumptuous publications of the Italian eighteenth century. (It was not a contribution to Ornithology!) But Italy's painters and architects were almost at an end. Even the fine books, now, were English or French. For the whole of the century Italy has little more to show than the pretty engraved vignettes of the Venetian *Settecento*. But Manetti in this enormous work from Florence is forerunner of the great ornithological works of the future. His plates are larger and better engraved and more splendidly coloured than those of his predecessors. The birds are no longer perched upon sham

branches. There is an endeavour to show them in their natural surroundings, and not either in the aviary or stuffed and set up on an artificial tree.

We are nearing a time when voyages like those of Captain Cook in the South Seas, or the great French navigators, would be properly equipped scientific expeditions with trained naturalists and zoologists on board, and even, on occasion, painters to make drawings. Captain Cook took William Hodges with him on his second voyage, and John Webber upon his last journey, but their concern was more with landscape and with the natives. William Hodges, in particular, made paintings of the coast scenery and war canoes of Tahiti, pictures in which you get the new light of Pacific islands never seen before by European eyes. Lord Macartney had William Alexander with him on his embassy to Pekin, when he was received in audience by the aged Emperor Kien Lung living in his palace at Jehol, but this careful draughtsman only made incidental observations upon birds or flowers. His chief concern, and it is understandable, was with this strange world of enchantment which he reached just before it was too late and turned to dross. It is of interest that one of the most beautiful plates from Hayes's *Portraits of Rare and Curious Birds* is of the 'Great Crowned Indian Pigeon', and the description reads that 'these birds are natives of the Molucca Isles, in the Indian seas, under the line, and found in great plenty in New Guinea, from whence they were taken to the Isle of Banda, where they are called by the Natives Bululu, and by the Dutch Kroon-Vogel . . . A pair of these birds were presented to Lady Ducie, and kept for some time in the menagery' . . . This is within little more than a decade of Captain Cook's first journey, and at a time when New Guinea was as much an object of mystery as it remained until our own times.

The next stage will be reached when naturalists, themselves, start off upon long journeys. François Levaillant is typical of this new development. His *Histoire Naturelle des Oiseaux d'Afrique* (1796–1808) in six volumes, with its 300 plates printed in colour and retouched by hand, is one of the first works of the naturalists who travelled in order to see and study the birds in their proper environment. In the course of that, Levaillant's adventures, edifying and unedifying, make good reading. At moments, his English translator, making apology to the 'Noble Lord' of his dedication, has to say: 'My Lord, modesty forbids that I should continue'. This is generally in reference to Levaillant's Hottentot mistress, Nerina, who could be apostrophised as the steatopygous Venus, a sort of Hottentot Venus Callipyge. Levaillant hunted the lion and leopard in his court suit of 'Blue-Boy' silk, with white gloves, ostrich-plumed hat, and lace ruffles, to show his respect for those noble animals. He named a beautiful cuckoo, Klaas's Cuckoo, after Nerina's brother, and one of the most wonderful of the South American trogons, the Nerina Trogon, after the Hottentot Venus and solace of his travels. Jacques Barraband (1767–1809) drew the plates for Levaillant's *Histoire Naturelle des Perroquets* (1801–05), *Histoire Naturelle des Oiseaux de Paradis* (1801–06) and *Histoire Naturelle des Promerops* (1807–16); as also, for

---

PLATE 6

*The Natural History of Carolina (London 1731–43) is the first colorplate book
about North American birds. Artist-naturalist Mark Catesby
taught himself etching to produce plates such as "Heath Hen."
Catesby's text asserts that his amateur prints are more accurate than prints
made by artisans who reinterpreted a naturalist's drawings.*

Anatra d' Estate. ══════════ Anas Estiva.

All'Ill.mo Sig.re Dottore Orazio Traversari Medico a Cervia.

Latreille's *History of Insects*. Barraband had studied in the Gobelins tapestry works, had painted on Sèvres porcelain, and decorated the dining-room at St Cloud. So Levaillant is not to be numbered among the bird painters.

The whole world, now, slowly opens as a field of investigation for the naturalists. It was a process which began in the last thirty years of the eighteenth century, was only retarded by the French Revolution, and even received fresh impetus from the Napoleonic Wars. After he had made himself Emperor, it was a part of Napoleon's deliberate policy to initiate a series of magnificent publications that would vie with those undertaken to the orders of Louis XIV. These were sent as presents to crowned heads, men of science, and learned bodies, in evidence of the splendours of the Empire. In this manner many glorious books came into being; and it is in this light that we should see Redouté's *Les Liliacées* and his two works on the flowers of Empress Josephine's gardens at La Malmaison. The works of Levaillant owe their sumptuous character to the same impetus. His *Histoire Naturelle des Perroquets* is, unwittingly, a part of the glories of Napoleonic France; even if it has to be remarked that a portion only of the world of parrots was known to him, for the forests of New Guinea and the eucalyptus and pepper groves of Australia were still virgin soil, as they were to remain until John Gould set forth for Australia a quarter of a century later, in 1838. It was only then that the ranks of parrots were inspected in their bright regiments. In the same way, Jean Baptiste Audebert's book with the truth-telling title, *Oiseaux Dorés ou à Reflets Metalliques* (1802), is subject to the same criticism. Its plates, heightened with gold, and so finished that they are little less than hand-illuminated engravings, make this one of the most beautiful books of its era (see pl. 13). But the birds are drawn too small, and mostly to the same size. Audebert can have seen only a few living birds-of-paradise, and the majority are drawn from skins. It is the gold reflections of the plumage that render the book unique and wonderful. But the whole evidence was not available to Audebert; the full flights of squadrons of 'les oiseaux à reflets metalliques' were only reviewed towards the middle or end of the nineteenth century.

The 'Nicobarica Pigeon' (pl. 17) from Coenraad Jacob Temminck and Florentine Prévost's *Les Pigeons* (1809–43), suggests enquiry along other lines.[4] This work has plates by a Dutch lady, Madame Antoinette Pauline Knip, to whom the Empress Josephine stood patron. It is to be said, at once, that the system of hand-colouring in this book is little suited to the body of the engraving, which is done in stipple.[d] In any case, by their very nature, aquatint and lithography are a better medium for Bird Books, since their 'grain' does not to the same degree obtrude and show through the colour. Hand-coloured plates, of which the body is in stipple, nearly always look as if their colouring had been the work of children. The French process of engraving had, by now, much improved upon that of the earlier Bird Books, but perhaps this stricture holds true of all books, French or English, until the appearance of

PLATE 7
*Xaverio Manetti et al produced one of the most striking eighteenth-century
bird books. Ornithologia methodice (Florence 1767–76) conveys 600 hand-colored etchings
including this animated Wood Duck.
The lack of anatomical information conveyed by the etched lines is partially compensated
for by the delightful personalities of the subjects.*

MERGUS SERRATOR, Foemina.

Audubon. He is, to the other bird artists, as Dürer to the wood engravers who came before him. Audubon did not, however, aquatint his own plates: we shall see that this was mainly the work of Robert Havell, Jun., of a famous family of engravers, so that the greatest Bird Books, those of Audubon in aquatint and of Gould in hand-coloured lithography, were the work of Englishmen.

Madame Knip's pigeons are too wooden, despite the beauty of their hand-coloured feathering.[e] Bird Books, up to this moment, are still inferior to Flower Books, as can be seen by comparing *Les Pigeons*, admittedly one of the finest works of its day, to almost any work with plates by Redouté, to Duhamel du Monceau's *Traité des Arbres Fruitiers* (1807–35), or to the incomparable Pierre Poiteau and J. Antoine Risso's *Histoire Naturelle des Oranges* (1818–20), with its golden and speckled globes and moon-like gourds depicting every known form of orange or citrus fruit. Madame Knip's plates are large and handsome, none the less. Her concern is with wild pigeons, though a few of the more curious domestic forms are included. Another work, by Pierre Boitard and Corbie, *Les Pigeons de Volière et de Colombier* (1824), is a disappointment. Here is a subject that has never been treated as it could be, and now it is too late. Pigeons are one of those races of birds in which the hand of man has run to fancy, as it has in flowers, the other instance being with the races of domestic fowls.

·But the pigeon fantasies have not been exploited. There was, here, a theme to last a minor painter for his lifetime. The two races alone of Oriental Frills and German Toys are as the roses and lilies, or, as the Montagues and Capulets, for rivalry. Having written elsewhere, and at length, of many of these pigeons, and composed special episodes upon the Modena Pigeon and the Oriental Frill or Turkish Frilled Pigeon, I must be content with drawing attention to the varieties of German Toys that are figured in the book named in my footnote,[5] for in the mention of this one race alone, in its ramifications, there is evidence for what could have been.

But an eagle hovers over the pigeon lofts.

Could there be a sight more awe-inspiring than the descent of an eagle upon a lawn that is alive with Fantail Pigeons? It was in my mind when I was in Spain during August of 1951, in the heat of the Mediterranean, near the golden littoral of Tarragona, the 'aprica Littora' of the Romans and all night long there was a thunderstorm, loud boomings, like huge artillery low in the heavens, wind and tremendous rains early in the morning, and a torn and ragged sky, and when the rains stopped towards mid-day we saw some great birds hovering over the stone pines of the Parque, as though arrived from a distance and looking where to settle, and they still hovered and came nearer, and at last went down out of sight, and we were told they were eagles come down from the mountains after the storm. We went out, later, into the wood and could not find them.

But I was thinking, already, of this book, and the arrival of the eagles had something wild and

---

PLATE 8
This female merganser illustrates Cornelis Nozeman's
Nederlandsche vogelen *(Amsterdam 1770–1829). The artist has posed the duck*
with its bill open and silhouetted against the paper,
thus showing the distinctive serrations which enable it to catch fish.

untamed about it, as when you go along a rose-hung lane and meet the Gypsies. Eagles are eaters of carrion and birds-of-prey. I imagined the eagles coming down upon a lawn of Fantail Pigeons. I thought of that fateful day when the Turkish Conquerors rode into San Sophia and found it full of the women and children of the Greeks, and of all citizens who did not bear arms; and the Turks slew all whom they could slay, and took away the rest into slavery. So do civilisations perish. And I began thinking of the Fantail Pigeons, that are Indian by origin, like *bayadères* and temple dancers, and were the toys and playthings of turbaned kings. Fantails have been known with as many as forty-two slats or feathers in their tails, but thirty-six is the more usual number; white fantails which roll themselves into a ball, curved back, with heads below their breasts, like a snowy globe dancing upon a pair of feet, and with the two wing-vanes on either side to steady them, that trail along the ground with a particular sound.

Into such an assembly of Fantail Pigeons the eagle would come down as among a flock of snowy lambs. The pigeons are defenceless and would die without a fight. Their end comes as suddenly and violently as when a fox gets among the chickens.

A wanton slaughter; but this whole episode is only written to draw further attention to the lack of any considerable work on all the various breeds of domestic pigeons. It is a gap, and a big one, in the series of great Bird Books. The reason must be that pigeons were too low in the Victorian social scale. There are only a few books with coloured plates by the artist Harrison Weir (1824–1906), who was better at poultry than at pigeons; and a big book with coloured plates by Ludlow,[f] a Birmingham artist (d. 1916), a master in little, in his way, but he, on the contrary, drew pigeons better than poultry, and the irate admirers and *aficionados* of the cockfight accused him of depicting their Blood-wing Pyles and Silver Duckwings to look like Pouter Pigeons. Perhaps, too, there could be an understandable impatience for tame pigeons on the part of lovers of the Golden Eagle!

The Birds of Prey tread, forlorn and melancholy, and not a little frightening, in their high cages. One is reminded of famous exiles and prisoners of war; Schamyl, Abd-el-Kader, Toussaint l'Ouverture; not to mention Napoleon looking out to ocean from the rock of St Helena. The essence of such imprisonment is that it should be among an alien race. Such conditions are fulfilled wherever Birds of Prey are in captivity. In all the annals of war and crime there can be few sights more terrible than to see them pace their cages, or look fixedly into the sky. Anyone who has crawled up a mountain side in Sutherland, near to the precipice edge, in order to see the nesting place of a Golden Eagle, must have sympathy for such a warrior, and soaring spirit, when in prison.

It is said, how truly or not I do not know, that the Golden Eagle builds its nest facing the North. Is not the curve of the eagle's beak a synonym for the countenance of a conqueror, whether in war, or in any of the territories of the lonely spirit? The eagle is not lapped in luxury; the satrap pleasures are not written on its lean features. To the eaglet there is more of pride and dignity attaching than to any other animal except the lion cub, which has the eyes of the lion, and in bearing and movement is the son or daughter of a king. The child of the great soldier (i.e., Napoleon) was called *l'Aiglon* (the eaglet), and the meaning would not have been the same had he been called the cygnet (the swan's son), or the vulture's son. The only creatures in the animal kingdom that share something of its spirit are the game cock and the fighting bull. More likely than not the eagle's nest would look out upon the iron North.

But there is a bird that looks fiercer still. Perhaps there is no such expression of natural ferocity to be met with anywhere, among men or animals, as upon the features of a Malay Fowl. This ugly breed, which rather resembles game cocks, but is not closely related to them, is seldom seen out of Southern Cornwall, where for some reason there has long been a cult for them. I have kept them myself, and speak, therefore, from experience. In character, they are cowardly bullies. A Victorian writer says of them: 'I am not aware of any varieties of fowls so cruel, oppressive and vindictive as the Malays . . . From their great strength, they are able to inflict severe injury on their opponents, frequently treading them down, and then actually tearing them to pieces'. Their facial characteristics are very distinct and peculiar. The head is 'long and snaky, and the eyes are bright, fiery red, to accord with the restless, vindictive expression of the face. They have heavy, overhanging eyebrows, which give a most cruel, harsh expression. The beak is more curved and hooked than in any other breed of poultry, still further adding to the fierceness of their look. The plumage is short, hard, and of extraordinary lustre, of strong elastic feathers, hard and metallic; and the Malays walk as though encased in whalebone armour from the effects of cold'. But it is above all in that harsh, cruel expression of the beak and eye that the Malay Fowl is of a race to itself.

Fierceness and martial valour, not of the mean sort, are to be found among the hawks and peregrines, bird mercenaries who have taken military service against their kind. They are a part of the maze of chivalry, and to read of them is to be seduced into a satellite world of old terms and defunct meanings, which extends in history from Moghul Emperors and Princes to living Emirs of Transjordan and Arabia, and from the book on hawking, *De Arte Venandi cum Avibus*, written by Frederick II *stupor mundi* ('world weary') early in the thirteenth century when he returned from his Eastern travels to his octagonal Castel del Monte which stands on a barren hill in Apulia, looking out over the distant Adriatic, to the Dutch falconers of Valkenswaard, a village on the Dutch frontier near Bois-le-Duc, who have practised their craft from the Middle Ages to the present day. No wonder that the bibliography of falconry, a work of utmost fascination, and one combining poetry with erudition in proportions not often shaken up and seldom tasted, should end with a glossary that gives more than six hundred technical terms of falconry in the seven principal languages.[6]

The Greenland Falcon in hood (pl. 36) comes from the *Traité de Fauconnerie* of Hermann Schlegel and A. H. de Wülverhorst (1844–53), and is one of the more splendid bird drawings. Joseph Wolf, the draughtsman, had a particular propensity for sea birds of prey. There is a positive menace in turning from the 'Greenland Falcon' to the ducks and other birds of innocence that enhance our pages. Did I not write that an eagle was hovering over the pigeon lofts? The *Traité de Fauconnerie*, too big, unfortunately, to be read with pleasure, being, itself, of Dutch publication, gives a great deal of most curious information concerning the falconers of Valkenswaard. They worked, more particularly, with Iceland Falcons, which detail brings a fascinating but minor history into motion. It appears that the Kings of Denmark, beginning from late in the sixteenth century, sent a special ship every year from Denmark to Bessastadur, the old capital of Iceland, carrying huntsmen from Norway whose duty it was

to snare the Iceland Falcons that were only to be found among lava or basalt crags, near to the deserts in the centre of the island, or nesting on cliffs that looked down on to the frightful sea. These falcons were given as presents by the Kings of Denmark to other kings and princes all over Europe, and the custom was only discontinued when the Royal Mews at Copenhagen were closed owing to the wars of Napoleon in 1803.

There are huge pictures by a Dutch painter at Herrenhausen that form the most complete document of the sport of hawking and show it as practised by the ancestors of our Hanoverian Kings.[7] All the apparatus of hawking is given in detail, including the curious device of the cadge or brancard, a wooden frame like a tray or door with slats of wood across it, carried strapped to the shoulders, with six hooded falcons perched on it, and a man, the cadge-bearer, walking in the middle of it. Why these paintings have never been reproduced or described in any book, German or English, must remain a mystery! To look at them with the *Bibliotheca Accipitraria* which is of convenient size, in hand, and when opportunity offers to turn over the twelve huge coloured plates of the *Traité de Fauconnerie*, would be to understand in theory, as from the armchair, all that can be learned about the sport of hawking. The scenery of these paintings is the sandy heath round Hanover. The Greenland Falcon is nearly related to those falcons from Iceland that had, so to speak, their regimental depôt in the Royal Mews at Copenhagen, and intermarriage and geographical proximity make it more than probable that those are Iceland Falcons that we see in the paintings at Herrenhausen going forth to battle with the Elector Ernst-August, father of our George I.

Other and earlier sources of supply for this ancient and princely sport were no less curious. Another race of falcons was snared and hunted during the Middle Ages in Albania, whence were partly stocked the mews of the Kings of Aragon, and those of the Sforza and Visconti, tyrants of Milan. Yet another race came from the Isola di San Pietro, the 'Insula Accipitrum' of the Romans, off the southern coast of Sardinia.[8] Gyr-falcons, such as those of Greenland and Iceland, were not the only birds employed for hawking. There were Peregrines, Hobbies, Merlins, Goshawks and Sparrow-hawks. Gyr-falcons caught on the sandy flats of Lithuania were sent as presents by the Grand Masters of the Teutonic Order. Several 'convoys' of the Baltic falcons reached Henry IV of England from this source, together with the bodies of three gigantic aurochs taken in the Lithuanian forest. This is recorded in the *Tresslerbuch* or *Diarium* of daily expenses of the huge monastery of Marienburg, the headquarters of the Teutonic Knights, under date 1399–1409. The Lithuanians, at that date, were still pagan and had Druids as well as aurochs in their forests.[9] The last auroch died in Poland in 1627, and gold- or silver-mounted aurochs' horns were favourite presents from Grand Masters of the Teutonic Order. Thus fabulous are the history and circumstances of the sport of falconry. But it is a subject, all told, which has an intrinsic

---

PLATE 9
Thomas Pennant classified The British Zoology *(London 1761–66)*
by illustrating birds exemplifying a particular genus. For example, this nattily etched out
Heron illustrates "Division 2 Water Birds, Section 1 with Cloven Feet, Genus 1 Herons."
Peter Mazell etched this plate after the watercolor by Peter Paillou.

poetry of its own, of the same alloy as that attaching to a game of chess, or to a pack of tarot cards, and no less romantically alluring than the art of tauromachy, or the diaspora of Gypsy lore.

The rare figure among bird painters, whom we are now nearing, wore, of his own determination, the Romantic halo. The 'American Woodsman', as he liked to be known, may be, within his limitations, the most considerable painter that the American continent, North and South, has yet produced. But two other factors, his genius apart, make Audubon pre-eminent. He had studied every bird that he delineated, with hardly an exception, in its natural background, and every bird is reproduced, lifesize, in its natural dimensions. It is for this last reason that he undertook publication in so enormous a format.[10] There are 435 plates in the first edition of Audubon's *Birds of America* (1827–38); and reproduction of just one of them in its actual size, were there an aquatinter alive who could undertake it, would cost something approaching a thousand pounds in money at its present value. Had an Ostrich or an Emu been among the *Birds of America*, Audubon would, quite likely, have increased the dimensions of his folios to include it. What would have happened, one wonders, had Audubon undertaken the birds of New Zealand and felt constrained to paint a picture of the extinct Moa, which was eleven feet six inches in height, or even, according to some authorities, thirteen or fourteen feet tall? The legs of the Moa, thick as a steel girder, reached to higher than the heads of the Maori warriors who hunted it, while the eggs of this flightless monster were ten inches long by seven broad. Or, nearer to Audubon's intentions, for it is a bird of the Americas, he might have had to widen the lateral format of his elephant folios in order to include the Condor Real, or King Condor of the Andes, guarded, so the Peruvian Indians tell, by the ordinary white-necked condors, who bring him food, a pure white bird measuring, according to Humboldt, as much as twenty to twenty-five feet across its wings; and Humboldt adds that, according to his information, not more than twenty-five of the bird-leviathans were in existence![11] Quite apart from such romantic possibilities, Audubon is unique among bird painters.

J. J. Audubon was born on Santo Domingo in 1785, the natural son of a French naval officer, turned planter, and a *créole de Saint-Domingue*. He visited France, stayed at Nantes, and worked for a few weeks in David's studio. At eighteen years old he was sent to a farm belonging to his father, near Philadelphia. He married, took up the study of ornithology, moved inland to Kentucky, and then southward to New Orleans. In 1826 he sailed for England, met Thomas Bewick and Sir Walter Scott, was lionized in London and Edinburgh for his handsome appearance, dandified manner, breath of nature, and the anecdotes that he told, and arranged for publication of his *Birds of America* from the latter city. The work was sold by subscription in parts of five plates at a time, but after the first ten plates had appeared, the colourists employed by the Edinburgh firm of Lizars failed him, and Audubon continued publication in London. All the remaining plates were aquatinted by R. Havell, father or son, but in greater number by the latter. The total cost of the volumes worked out at £187.10s., and it came out in less than two hundred complete sets, though as many as a hundred subscribers defaulted in the later issues. It has been calculated that a total of three hundred impressions may have been taken of the earlier plates. Perhaps it should be added here that Robert Havell, Jun., on completion of the *Birds of America*, sailed for the United States, in 1839, and set up his home on the left bank of the Hudson River (not far from where Audubon passed his last years), dying eventually at a great age, in 1878.

During the eleven years that the *Birds of America* was being published (1827–38), Audubon travelled in Europe to make the acquaintance of ornithologists and collectors, and to collect subscriptions.[12] He also returned several times to the United States to secure new specimens, making expeditions to the Carolinas and Florida in 1831 and 1832, to Labrador in 1833, and to Texas in 1837. At the same time he wrote the text to go with the plates, calling it his *Ornithological Biography* (Edinburgh 1831–39). When all was completed he returned to America, and issued the octavo miniature edition of his *Birds of America* from Philadelphia; but the plates were lithographs and not aquatints, and of inferior workmanship. A further sixty-five plates depicting the birds of Western North America were added to his octavo edition, making 500 plates in all. An artist of ceaseless energy and industry, Audubon then started his researches on the smaller mammals and completed seventy-six of the one hundred and fifty plates (lithographs) of the *Viviparous Quadrupeds of North America* (1845–48). His animal paintings are not perhaps sufficiently appreciated, for this, too, is a work of tremendous scope; but Audubon's health was failing, and he died in New York City in 1851.[13]

The poetry in Audubon is because he was working in the wilderness. No painter before him had penetrated into Florida or Louisiana. His were the first eyes of observation to see Texas, or to paint the ice-floes and rocks of Labrador. He worked in North and South Dakota while these states were still virgin soil, only roamed by Indians; and travelled by boat and on foot up and down the Ohio and the Mississippi, watching and working in the rice swamps and the cotton groves. In 1842 he made his only journey to the Great West, beyond the Mississippi to the head waters of the Yellowstone; but he never saw even the distant outline of the Rocky Mountains, or reached to the Pacific. Yet an entire new continent lay open to him. Perhaps it is impossible for anyone in our century to realise quite what is meant by this limitless freedom and invitation to adventure. The Eastern seaboard of the United States had been settled for two centuries, from Connecticut and Massachusetts down to the Virginias and South Carolina. Many parts, even of these States, were still the backwoods; while the deep South, Alabama, Georgia, Florida, South Carolina, with its aristocratic leanings and its black slaves, drifted along in the possibility of becoming to the other States of the Union what Andalusia is to the rest of Spain. There were French settlers in Louisiana, and a few Mexicans in Texas (which, in any case, did not become a State of the Union until after Audubon's life work was done), but during the period 1820–40 civilisation ceased at the Mississippi. The whole West opened beyond that, and when we think how little the natural history of even the long inhabited States had been studied, it will be agreed that such a vast field for investigation has never, before or since, been opened to the naturalist.

At that time, let us remember, a little green and yellow parrakeet with scarlet cheeks, the Carolina Parrakeet, was even found in New York State. Audubon is often at his best in these smaller, more homely subjects; in the lovely plate of Baltimore Orioles nesting in a flowering tulip tree; in his Goldfinches perching on dark blue thistles; in his drawing of the Meadow-Lark (pl. 23) in a background of bamboo-like leaves and the yellow flowers of *Gerardia flava*, a work that hints, as I have written

Coq hupé.

elsewhere, at Audubon's knowledge of Dürer's marvellous watercolour of 'The Cornfield', in the Albertina, at Vienna. Every lover of Audubon will have his favourites, and there will be many admirers of his Woodpeckers; a wonderful study of the Pileated Woodpecker, with fiery crest just like a *Kniphofia* or red-hot poker, noisily chattering and quarrelling on a dead tree stump which is festooned with the blue raccoon grapes; or other Woodpecker plates with as many as nine, or more, different Woodpeckers upon a leafless tree.

Nevertheless, it is in his huge plates, as we would expect, that Audubon is unsurpassable, though a few of these may have become too familiar through reproduction. He was in time to watch the Scarlet Ibis while it nested in Florida; and his Snowy Heron on look-out in the Carolina ricefields dwells in a pristine world and hardly heeds the hunter's gun. His Flamingo, in characteristic attitude, serpentine head and neck swaying just above the water, stands in all the improbability of its long neck and bowing shoulders, dyed deep in the *rose Pompadour* of Boucher's tapestries, for the flamingo inspires and inhabits a *chinoiserie* all its own, helped, not hindered, by the Latin patronymic bestowed upon it by the ornithologists. The flamingo towns in the Camargue, in the delta of the Guadalquivir, in the Rann of Kutch, are no less among the wonders of the world if we think of them as cities of the Phoenicoptera! The Roseate Spoonbill is an apparition of another order, an angelic version of the spoonbilled demons in paintings by Hieronymus Bosch; and in Bosch's nightmares where every detail has a symbolic significance those must have a particular meaning of their own. There is a spoonbill archer in his *Inferno*, which forms the right hand panel of his great tryptych in the Prado (and before that it hung to better purpose in the Escorial). I can write of this demon from long knowledge, having known him since I first went to Spain in 1919. He is one of the demons coming out of the fires of hell; only two or three inches high in the painting, with spoonbill head and a man's body, cloaked, rather as if he were a pantomime demon wearing cloak and spoonbill all in one piece; his long bow on his shoulder, but all blanched and of a horrible pallor, like that of the worms of the vault who burrow in the black soil, or those fish that have lived for so many millenniums in the water of underground caverns that they have lost their sight and colour. But Hieronymus Bosch, who hardly left his native town of S'Hertogenbosch (Bois-le-Duc), may well have seen or heard talk of a spoonbill for they nest in Holland to this day. The Roseate Spoonbill is a rose-petal sister to the flamingo, as far fetched in fantasy as the duck-billed women of the Congo, and wearing by way of feminine caprice a brimless green jockey cap! Thus, the spoonbill, seen and discussed as though it is a human being. With the flamingo, scarlet ibis, snowy heron for companions, and a pelican for fair weight, the wildest fantasies would fall short of the truth.

It has been suggested that the landscape backgrounds in the 'Roseate Spoonbill' (pl. 26) and other plates are not the work of Audubon, but are due to George Lehman, a Swiss painter who went

---

PLATE 10
Comte George de Buffon catalogued the animate world
in his 44-volume Histoire naturelle générale *(Paris 1749–1804).*
A special set of illustrations to the ten ornithology volumes was edited by Edme Daubenton
and called Planches enluminées *(Paris 1765–81).*
It featured 973 colored bird etchings by François Martinet, such as "Coq hupé."

Le Faucon Pelerin mâle.   *Accipiter Peregrinus mas.*   *Sparviere Pellegrino maschio.*

Maddalena Bouchard sculp.

with Audubon to the Carolinas and Florida in 1831. If this is true, probably the same hand painted the views of North American towns that are often seen in the distance in his plates of waterfowl. The East Battery at Charleston, for an example, appears low down across the marshes in his Long-billed Curlew; and there could be a whole collection of early views of American sea-coast towns drawn from Audubon. Such small derogations of detail in no way diminish the stature of Audubon, or the achievement of his huge volumes. Neither does it detract from him that the aquatinting of his plates were done by Robert Havell; any more than the knowledge that the Japanese woodcuts were engraved on the blocks of cherry wood by other and professional hands, with names that are ignored, or never mentioned, can make it otherwise than that Hokusai or Hiroshige are the masters of their art. Who but Audubon, himself, could have painted the sea shells in his plates of sea birds? There are rosy shells on the lonely sand in his Pectoral Sandpipers, in his Ivory Gull, and Sabine's Gull; Cabot's Tern stands over the cracked armour of a lobster; Forster's and Trudeau's Terns have sea shells near them; the White-rumped Sandpiper, in terms of porcelain, has a whole dinner service at its feet.

Audubon was at his greatest in the *bayous* of the Mississippi, and in his sea birds; as though his imagination took fire in the Creole landscapes of his childhood, and in an Arctic that he conceived of, having never known it, as a poetical Baffin Land. The prairie, it is obvious, did not interest him. If you would see that, it is to be found in George Catlin's *North American Indian Portfolio* (1844), a marvellous work of its kind because of its drawings and descriptions of the Redskins. But there is not one Red Indian in Audubon. Behold him, though, among the ice floes! His plate of five sea birds, including the Ancient Murrelet, Crested Auklet, and Rhinoceros Auklet shows him in his vein. Or did another hand paint the ice floes for him? No lover of Audubon will be willing to believe this. It is probable, owing to the inaccessibility of this quintet of birds, that they were painted from dead specimens; and it is to be noted that the Arctic scenery of Audubon has a theatrical air to it, and even a hint of the nautical drama. He has been influenced, too, by the aquatints in early Arctic Books of travel. At the same time, with far-seeing vision, Audubon was trying to create the background of that Northern wilderness where the birds nest, which has only been seen by naturalists within the last few years.

The bright colours of the Arctic sea birds attracted Audubon. He painted the King Eider, which Mr Peter Scott with his long experience calls the most beautiful of all its race, with its black and white body that is the base or ground for its 'make-up', cinnamon neck, and mask of rose-red and green. Others of the birds have clowns' masks: Steller's Eider, a white mask, shadowed green as though by the gas lights of the old pantomime; one or two ribbony feathers lined with blue, not standing straight up in the air like the three feather stumps glued to Grimaldi's forehead, for those were the stalks of feathers, the clown had cut the filaments away, but straggling, more like the long, sad feathers in

PLATE 11

Maddalena Bouchard captures this Peregrine Falcon
in a supremely gallic shrug as a generic small brown bird attends.
Her Recueil de cent-trente-trois oiseaux *(Rome 1771–83) has no text,*
but the etchings are titled in French, Italian, and Latin.
The border recalls the gold edging of the painted menageries
made for aristocratic naturalists.

Nellie Wallace's cap; a yellow belly; and wings of white and green. The Atlantic Puffin is one more of the clowns of a perpetual Boxing Day; but the Tufted Puffin wears a parrot's mask in order to be the parrot of the cold seas, and has a curving beak and long wispy plumes that are comically prolonged eyebrows. To the Harlequin Duck, which so nearly resembles a clown's mask in its head colouring that no one could fail to be reminded of the pantomime, Audubon has been less responsive, although it is the most painted of the Arctic clowns. Perhaps he was disappointed in its antics, or could only paint the dead bird when the living clown was fled.

Another division of his sea birds are those depicted, with no background, plunging down into the sea. They are the most original of all his paintings, for no one had attempted anything of the sort before. Indeed, on being shown one of them without warning it would be hazardous to guess the painter's name, more especially if told that it dated from the eighteen-thirties. The birds to whom Audubon has accorded this dramatic treatment are the terns. The Roseate Tern, the Arctic Tern, the Common Tern, the Gull-billed and the Least Tern, all are plunging downwards, or rising in a parabola from the heaving wave. What a long way he has advanced in simplification from the Meadow-Lark! Yet he was, in fact, practising these different styles of painting at the same time. But the terns are his greatest bird pictures. He had to think of a means of expressing all their characteristics in the flash of a moment as they hurled down, headlong, from the leaden sky. This had not the 'long exposure' of his other subjects.

It is always a sensation, in looking through the huge folios, to open at the sea birds and search among them till you find the terns. For there is nothing in ornithological painting to match the Arctic birds of Audubon. But, indeed, there is nothing in the world of fine books quite like the first discovery of Audubon. The giant energy of the man, and his power of achievement and accomplishment, give to him something of the epical force of a Walt Whitman or a Herman Melville. The *Birds of America* is a heroic undertaking; and that one man should have endured the hardships and ardours of so many long and lonely journeys, painted the pictures, written the text, and contrived the publication upon so gigantic a scale, puts him among the immortals. There, upon the library shelves, he is in dusty company. Audubon's *Birds of America* is one of the most valuable books in the world. But who comes to look at him? In the library in Holland where there is a copy, his huge volumes lie undisturbed for months on end. But Audubon is the greatest of bird painters; he belongs to American history, and as a writer he described things that human eyes will never see again.[14]

After Audubon, a new period begins. At plate 39 is a pair of the game cocks of old England. It may be unexpected in a Bird Book to find a set of fighting cocks. As a rule, the professional gladiators are excluded. Never before, it is probable, have they crowed their way among the scarlet ibises and birds of paradise. But here they stand in their bright colours, as flaunting as matadors, as brilliant as the toreros in their spangled suits and capes. Here are the game cocks, not trimmed for battle, but 'put out to walk', in lustrous plumage as when lording it among their hens.

This warrior caste, trained and bred for fighting for a hundred bird-generations, are displayed here in their splendour, but at the moment of their fall. For cock-fighting was made illegal in Great Britain in 1844. The golden age of cocking was in the 1820's and 1830's. After that date their decline was so swift that they were in danger of extinction, and no one now living has known them in their glory. The strains were only kept going in the hands of certain amateurs. Many are lost and will never be seen again. This small painting gives some idea of the compact brilliance of their feather. For but few paintings exist of game cocks; though there is always the hope that an album of drawings of the bird warriors, by an unknown hand, may turn up one day. It was a lore to itself. Here again, there was enough material to last a minor painter for his lifetime.

All of these breeds, or nearly all of them, were in decline after the fateful year of 1844; and I have written, already, that there is nothing in history to compare with the sudden extinction of these warriors except the abolition of the Samurai in Japan. Some of the strains lingered in the hands of but one fancier. The two wars, and especially the last war, have been their death blow. But they are still to be met with in Cumberland and the north of Lancashire, and in a few unlikely places. A fascinating but small literature exists upon cock-fighting, and this is, perhaps, the moment to draw attention to American books upon the subject, with especial reference to *Game Fowls: their Origin and History*, by J. W. Cooper, M.D., published by the author, a 'Shady-breasted ruffian', if ever there was one, at Westchester, Pennsylvania, in 1869. For he gives a list of breeds and strains before the American Civil War. He opens with two horrific coloured plates of a Strychnine ready for battle and a Tartar cock in feather; but the tone of this rather horrifying work with its undercurrent of drink and viciousness is given when the author remarks of the 'Old Jacksons', a breed of great celebrity in about 1830, that they had the reputation of fighting better when they had lost both eyes. The recollections of this unpleasant individual go as far back as 1820, and one can almost hear the slangy talk and drawling accents of his accomplices and foes. In fact, with the help of a little imagination, there are the characters in his book for a long novel, or a film.[15]

What would have happened, it is amusing to conjecture, had Dr Cooper and some of the fraternity arrived one day at Charlotte Street, Bloomsbury, the residence of John Gould, the Victorian 'bird man' of all time? Without too great a strain on probability, one can see the Yankee Doctor, cheroot in mouth, in strange boots (they would be sure to be strange!), a light suit and a 'ten-gallon' hat, getting out of a four-wheeler, and lifting the crates of birds on to the doorstep; a Strychnine cock, three Tartar hens, and a trio of Baltimore Top-Knots. This is no more than what Dr Cooper sent as a present for 'Censor', the 'well known London correspondent of *Porter's*, now *Wilkes', 'Spirit of the Times'*, in 1859. For Gould's enormous ornithological works were published from his house in Charlotte Street; it was here that his artists and lithographers and small staff of colourists were employed; and it is probable that no house that ever existed had as many dead birds delivered on its doorstep over so long a stretch of years. Gould lived here for forty years, from 1840 when he came back from Australia until his death in 1881. Birds were sent to him from every part of the world; and in the text accompanying his plates he so often expresses himself as being in perpetual expectation of new arrivals from collectors on far shores. It was there that the humming-birds and birds of paradise reached Gould for so many years on end, but it is safe to say that it would never have occurred to the Victorian ornithologist to have paintings made of the various strains of game cocks, any more than one could expect the botanists who collected wild

plants in China in the beginning years of this century to show an interest in the auriculas or tulips of the hand-loom weavers of Lancashire and Cheshire, or in the gold- or silver-laced polyanthus, artisans' flowers which were to those counties what peasant arts or peasant costumes are to other European lands, and which in those very years were at the climax of their beauty, soon to decline and be forgotten. We may be certain that Dr Cooper with his Tartars and Strychnines, and his Baltimore Top-Knots, would have met with short reception and been turned away.[16]

The writer has personal knowledge of four of these six colours [see note 16]. G. Ferguson's *Illustrated Series of Rare and Prize Poultry* (1854), from which our plate 39 is taken, also illustrates the Black-crested White Poland: opposite number, as it could be called, to the White-crested Black Poland of our illustration. To this variety (white, with black top-knots), a curious history attaches. For they have now entirely died out of the world, and were seen for the last time almost exactly a hundred years ago. One writer states that the last seen specimen of the genuine race appears to have been a hen found by Mr B. P. Brent, at St Omer, in 1854. The 'party' owning this hen said they were still to be found in Brittany: Mr R. Palmer Williams, of Dublin, 'a gentleman who has paid great attention to the history of the different varieties of crested fowls', writes (in 1873): 'This breed, up to about thirty years ago, was to be had in some parts of Ireland, as I have been informed by friends who knew it well. It died out as the result of the Famine . . . A few years after this time, I heard of the breed, and tried to procure it; and having heard that it was to be had at Bordeaux, I went specially for it, but was informed that there, as well as at Paris, the breed was no more to be met with; so that it would appear that about the same time it vanished everywhere. The parties who last had the Black-crested White in Ireland were the descendents of the French Huguenots at Portarlington and Maryborough, which would lead me to expect the breed came from France, if not from Holland'. Shortly before the 1914 War, one breeder reported he had re-created this lost race, but no more was heard of it.

It is irresistible to quote the no less curious history of the Sultans, another crested breed described in old poultry books. There is a charming colour plate of a pair of these white paragons, by Ludlow, in Lewis Wright's *The Illustrated Book of Poultry* (1880). For Sultans were all-white birds, with white feathered boots and top-knots. They were introduced into England by Miss Watts, in January, 1854. They were sent to her by a friend in Constantinople, who described them as 'bellissimi galli bianchi', and 'arrived in a steamer chiefly manned by Turks'. The Turkish name for them was Serai-Taook, or fowls of the Sultans, and they were said to be favourites in harems. But Miss Watts never succeeded in getting any more birds from Turkey: She describes them as 'abundantly decorated, with full tail, abundant furnishings, boots, vulture hocks, beards, whiskers, and full round Polish crests'. Another breeder in Ireland, who secured a hen through a lady who had been given one by the 'captain of

---

PLATE 12

James Bolton's Harmonia ruralis *(Stannary, Scotland 1794–96)*
instructed ladies in the wild habits of their cage birds. The etchings are minutely drawn and
show the benefit of field study, for Bolton poses this Song Thrush with a food plant.
He encouraged owners of pet birds to supply wild food,
and to keep cages and water "clean and sweet." Each bird plate is paired with one featuring
the bird's intricately built nest.

Le Parkinson mâle. Pl. 14.

a vessel in the Mediterranean', writes of them as 'lively without romping, with a cheerful chatty voice'. Sultans, after the lapse of nearly a century, were still described and advertised in the *Feathered World Year Book* for 1937; but when I wrote to a lady living in Wiltshire, who bred them, in 1941, I was informed she had only a few old and sterile birds in her possession, and knew of no others. It may be that there are still Sultans in the United States. If not, we must take it that they are extinct, and another curious private history is ended.

But having seen birds on the doorstep, we will enter Charlotte Street in their stead. This is the house of the greatest figure in bird illustration after Audubon. Every room is full of the bodies of birds; there are bird skins on every table; and every spare foot of space is given over to the lithographic presses and the hand-colouring. At various times Gould had different artists working for him; for example, Edward Lear[g] of *The Book of Nonsense*, perhaps the best of all bird painters, who found him difficult, and quarrelled with him,[17] but chiefly, William Hart. The rough sketches were always drawn by Gould, himself, and were drawn on stone by Hart or Henry C. Richter. Hart also made finished paintings of about forty plates of the *Birds of Great Britain*. Hart began working for Gould in the summer of 1851, making the designs for the monograph on Humming-Birds, which Richter drew on stone, and colouring the metallic portions of the plates. He was at this work for fifty years, for it was Hart who after Gould's death made the watercolour drawings for Bowdler Sharpe's *Monograph of the Paradiseidae*, the last of the Great Bird Books, which was not completed till 1898. The state of confusion in Charlotte Street can be gauged when it is known that on Gould's death in 1881, Messrs. Sotheran, the booksellers, bought from his executors the copyright and the whole remaining stock of his works and found themselves in the position of having to remove many hundreds of parcels, weighing upwards of thirty tons, from Charlotte Street to the basement of their shop. Some of these parcels Messrs. Sotheran did not open and examine until fifty years had passed, with the result that many hundreds of original drawings for his various publications came to light, including plates for unpublished works that were in preparation, and a roll containing a number of the double-sized plates of the 'Resplendent Trogon'. In this way, a plate which had to be folded, and only appeared in the first edition of Gould's *Monograph of the Trogons*, in 1838, came to light again after the passing of nearly a hundred years, and in colours which were as fresh as new.[18]

It is often argued as a reproach against Gould, and in favour of Audubon, that Gould was a 'closet-naturalist' working in his London home, that he never saw the birds in their natural surroundings and did not know their habits, and that he was not even the draughtsman of his own plates. He always, however, as we have seen, made the rough outlines of the drawings, which in early days, until her death, were completed by his wife; or by Edward Lear who drew, particularly, the owls and cranes.

PLATE 13
In Oiseaux dorés ou à reflets métalliques *(Paris 1800–02),*
artist Jean Audebert and ornithologist Louis Vieillot combined talents.
The watercolor model for "Le Parkinson"
was provided by Sydenham Edwards, an Englishman best known for botanical prints.
Color-printed engravings such as this were used
to great advantage by Levaillant [q.v.].

Le Perroquet Jaune écaillé de rouge. Pl. 137.

Barraband pinx.   De l'Imprimerie de Langlois.

Later, the finished drawings were the work of H. C. Richter, or of W. Hart or of Joseph Wolf. Gould, however, directed the whole of these enterprises, and from his first work to his last they bore the imprint of his character. When the monograph on the birds of paradise was published, after Gould had died, it appeared as a natural supplement to the forty-three huge volumes of his works, and being the work of his own artists and colourists bore the same character even without the direction of his guiding hand. Therefore, unless the whole series from 1832 to 1898 are 'automatic' publications, appearing independently of any directing force, they are due to one person, and that individual is Gould.

Neither is it true that Gould never studied any of his birds in their natural habitats. Born in 1804, the son of one of the Royal gardeners at Windsor Castle, and having made a youthful hobby of bird stuffing, he was in 1827 appointed taxidermist to the newly formed Zoological Society of London. His first publication *A Century of Birds from the Himalaya Mountains* appeared in 1832, but no publisher would risk undertakings on so large a scale as he was planning, and henceforward Gould was his own publisher. His next work was the *Birds of Europe*, in five volumes (1832–37), containing the enormous number of 449 plates, most of them by his wife, but a few by Edward Lear. We will leave aside, for the moment, his monographs on the toucans and on the trogons, two of the most beautiful of his works, which were appearing during these very years, in 1834 and 1838, for these, certainly, were undertaken in the home, not in the field. But having begun publication of his *Birds of Australia* in 1838, and completed two parts only, he came to the conclusion that it was impossible to continue the work from England, cancelled the two parts which had come out, and set sail for the Antipodes. There he remained for two years, adding no fewer than three hundred new species to the handlist of Australian birds. The work came out eventually in eight volumes, with nearly seven hundred plates.

After Gould's return to England it was the huge scope of his projected works, more than anything else, that made it a necessity for him to stay at home. He had begun publication of his monograph on the humming-birds, and he explains in his preface that this was only practicable from a city which had the amenities of London or of Paris. No one living naturalist could be expected to follow the humming-birds, many of them no bigger than a bee, into their haunts in Central and South America. There had to be a headquarters into which all reports came, and where work was slowly progressing after sifting and analysis of so many travellers' tales. This was exactly what Gould accomplished in his home in Charlotte Street, and his *Monograph of the Trochilidae, or Family of Humming-Birds*, in five volumes and Supplement, the most stupendous of tropical publications, came out over the years 1849–87, with 418 hand-coloured plates. A new technical process, which was the result of long experiment, had to be invented in order to portray their metallic plumage. 'Members of the genus *Augastes*', he writes in the introduction to this huge enterprise, 'are conspicuous for the shining, metal-like masks with which their faces are adorned, the *Aglaectines* have the lower part of their backs clothed in armour-like feathers, the brilliancy of which must be seen to be understood, but, which, strange to say, is only apparent when viewed from the back; for if looked at in the direction of the feathers, none of these hues are perceptible' . . . And he apostrophizes 'for ornament only, the crests of *Cephalepis* and *Orthorhynchus*; the beards of *Ramphomicron* and *Oxypogon*; the ear-tufts of *Petasophora* and *Heliothris*; the elegant appendages to the neck of the *Lophornithes*; and the singular, plume-like tail-coverts of *Chalybura*, which in their structure of snowy whiteness strangely remind one of the corresponding feathers of the Marabou Stork'. In order to illustrate the wide range of the humming-birds over the North and South American continents Gould tells how *Selasphorus rufus* goes as far North as Sitka, in Alaska (then Russian territory); how humming-birds are found on Juan Fernández, an island in the Pacific Ocean belonging to Chile, but not on the Galapagos; and that Captain King observed *Eustaphanus galeritus* 'flitting about among the fuchsias of Tierra del Fuego in a snowstorm'. How many times, he concludes, have ignorant persons not assured him that humming-birds are to be found in England, sending him, in argument, a *Macroglossa stellarum* (Humming-Bird Moth) that they have captured in their gardens! Since, for many more of us, this momentary illusion when one of these wondrous insects hovers in the throat of the fox-glove, some August evening, may be the nearest approach we ever have in our lives to the true humming-birds, we will open the huge volumes of his *Monograph of the Trochilidae*.

The *Trochilidae* opens with two plates of Sickle-bills, green thrush-like humming-birds with long forked tails, in whose shape of body you can see that the nearest relations to this entire family are the swifts. There follow some lovely Hermits, a Train-bearing Hermit, in particular, a bird-ballerina like a water-wagtail that could be transformed in enchantment into a fairy bird that dances on a drop of dew; but it is fair to say that in this first volume the latent beauties of the nation of humming-birds are but hinted at, and not explored. Soon after the beginning of volume 2 there is an explosion of colour in the form of the Crimson Topaz (*Topaza pela*) with golden, auriferous throat, crimson wings and long sickle tail, a humming-bird which Gould writes that his friend and patron, Mr Loddiges of Hackney, said on several occasions must be the most beautiful of its entire race, and that nothing lovelier would ever be found. But the Fiery Topaz, from Cayenne and Surinam, of the next plate, discovered after his friend's death, is more molten still, and its metallic colours ring upon the page. Close upon this burning apparition comes the Chimborazian Hill Star, found only in the crater of that Ecuadorian volcano, and nowhere else in the world, a humming-bird shaped like a swift or a swallow, for its blue wings are curved like a swallow's wing, and it has a snow-white breast. There ensue the family of Mangos, in lovely colourings; and, then, the Black-capped Humming-Bird of which the plumage, with gorget and mantle, resembles a horned lizard transformed into a bird, and is reminiscent in colour and in silhouette or outline, as it sits upon the branch, of the Sickle-bill, or *Epimachus* Bird of Paradise; and the second volume ends with some Wood Nymphs, humming-birds which have two long tail-ribbons as though in emulation of birds of paradise.

We are among the Coquettes, that have crests like jays, in volume 3, but this in only a rudimentary statement of the marvels of fantastic adornment that they have invented for their own delight. Some have simple crests, if the crest of the jay is ordinary, but the great Crested Coquette (*Lophornis regulus*) has dots of bronzy metallic green at the tips of the feathers that compose its crest; while another of the family, the Spangled Coquette (*Lophornis reginae*), has each feather or filament of its crest surmounted by a ball-like dark bronzy green spangle, for there is no other word for it, giving the effect of a sparkling stage tiara. The hen, as in so many of the humming-birds, has a beauty of her own, but would not be guessed as the female to this popinjay. Near to the Coquettes there come the Racket-tails, which have evolved those peculiar tail ornaments upon the same principle as the birds of paradise. We shall see that the King Bird of Paradise (*Cicinnurus regius*), with crimson body only six inches long, so small that it could be mistaken for a humming-bird, has the same two wire-like tail feathers ending in little, metallic-green rackets. A moment later we have reached the Thorn-tails, with tails of blue and white, splintered or tapered, and spike-thin. One of the Thorn-tails has a headdress of two long hair-like plumes, little thicker than that, erect upon the crown of its head, but slightly curved in ornament, giving to it a most curious appearance as of a horned humming-bird; and the next fantasy of this little fairyland of glittering invention is a Thorn-tail that has thought of crossing its long tail-feathers so that they are like the handles of a pair of garden secateurs. For the pruning of what lovely but lilliputian flowers! When we come to the Calypte, with head glowing ruby, and trained mantle, wearing adornments of metallic lilac, Gould remarks of its fiery colours that he has noticed that the more metalliferous the land of origin of a humming-bird the more metallic are its hues, that there must be a reason for this, but that he is at a loss to account for it! And to confirm his theory there follow immediately the Rufous Flamebearer, the Little, and the Broad-tailed Flamebearers, flashing like meteors, their lapping plumes compact, seemingly of burnished metal.

We are now far advanced into the hinterland of these miraculous transformations and inventions. The Wood Stars are in a little world to themselves of smallness, with short wings and sometimes with no tails. The Shear-tails in their molten iridescence, and to lilliputian scale, keep something of the pterodactyl. Now comes a humming-bird as sensational as the Crimson Topaz. It is called *Loddigesia mirabilis* (after Gould's friend in Hackney) and has crossed disks upon its tail feathers, as if its range of flight could be no further than from flower to flower. We have to think of it not only posed in stillness on a spray of flowers, but hovering, or rather flickering, with a metallic quivering of all its feathers, and a shaking of those tail ornaments so difficult to keep unentangled and not caught upon leaf or petal, and that must vibrate or rattle as though they are a pair of fairy sistrums. Even now, the wonders of this volume 3 of the *Trochilidae* are not exhausted. The White-booted Racket-tail enters, followed by more Train-bearers; there is the Blue-tailed Sylph (*Cyananthus cyanurus*), and a Green-tailed, not less lovely; the Comets, or *Cometes*, with green-gold metallic wings, the Sappho Comet with a crimson tail; Sunbeams and Helmet Crests.

Plover Crests, another family, have a few plates to themselves at the beginning of volume 4. There are Sun Gems, with white breasts, long tails, and scarlet ornaments, the shape of fans, behind their ears. And there are Violet Ears, including *Coruscans*, the chequered Violet Ear; Sword Bills;

Le Perroquet Aourou-couraou Pl. 110

Barraband pinx.t De l'Imprimerie de Langlois.

Heliangelus, the Sun Angel, in metallic gorget, with ruby-topaz throat; Puff-Legs, with white muffs upon their legs; Sapphires; and Emeralds, ending with one which perches on a Victoria Regia waterlily. The Supplement, appearing after Gould's death, but embodying his recent researches and bringing the subject up to date, has some lovely later discoveries; Warszewicz's Rainbow, cinnamon-coloured, with green mantle; a Purple Snow-cap; a Little Wood Star, smallest of all the humming-birds, and no bigger than a hornet; a Blue-throated Helmet Crest; Salvin's Coquette, and the Roraima Coquette, which has a pair of throat ornaments, fancifully shaped, and spangled in green and gold with eyes like those in peacocks' tails.

In our description we have taken no account of Jacobins, humming-birds in blue-green and white, which, owing to their arching bodies and long tails, hover at the flowers like swallows with four wings; of *Heliothrix*, a green and blue family of humming-birds shaped like swifts or martins; of *Helianthea eos*, golden star-fronted; of *Heliomaster*, or Star Throat, that is like a sharp-billed thrust; of the Coloured Crowns which are blue-necked, with azure crowns, and green-and-white-spotted bodies like linnets; of *Eustephanus*, like a green-spotted thrush, with white and green fantail, found only on Juan Fernández, the island of Robinson Crusoe; or of the Hooded Vizor-bearer with green and gold metallic-shining beard, and a pendant, locket-like touch of crimson at the extremity of that. They, and many others, will be found in those enormous volumes; but I pause only where, looking through them often and again, I have found myself taking out my pencil to make notes. The humming-birds are so beautiful in themselves that the ecstasy of delight into which they throw one should not let it appear that the *Trochilidae*, in aesthetics, is other than among the most beautiful of Victorian illustrated books; or of those, at least, that have hand-coloured lithographic plates. To argue more than that would be equivalent, in other context, to saying that Audubon was a greater artist than Albrecht Dürer. The *Trochilidae*, nevertheless, is an incomparable catalogue and compendium of beauties. The humming-birds are depicted, wherever possible, darting or hovering near their appropriate flowers. There are sprays of orchids, for which collectors of the last century risked their lives in the forests of Guatemala, in the Andes, or on the Amazon, that are hardly less gorgeous than the humming-birds. Or those shown swaying on a bough of bright blue *Ceanothus*, portending that the bird comes from the new El Dorado of California. I can never part from the *Trochilidae*, and close the huge volumes, without wishing that the range of these little birds was not confined to the Americas. What further wonders,[19] were they but found in the Himalayas, in Nepal and Burma and Yunnan, wherever live the Peacock and Fireback Pheasants, and the Satyr Tragopan! If only there could be humming-birds in New Guinea; and a millennium ago there had been an emigration of birds of paradise from Papua, alike to the craters of Chimborazo and Cotopaxi, and the head-waters of the Amazon! In short were humming-birds and

---

PLATE 15

Some of the parrots in François Levaillant's
Histoire naturelle des perroquets *(Paris 1801–05) look like portraits, not scientific illustrations.*
Levaillant's text points out that the symmetry of
yellow markings on "Perroquet Aourou-couraou" is atypical of the species.
Artist Jacques Barraband thus portrays an individual bird,
not a scientific illustration representative of the species.

birds of paradise like the race of trogons in both hemispheres? Such are idle fancies. All in all, the *Trochilidae* of Gould is his masterpiece, and must ever remain a feast of beauty and a source of wonder.

It is time for a brief consideration of Gould's other works. His *Birds of Europe*, in 5 volumes 1832–37, is remarkable for the owls and cranes drawn by Edward Lear. But most of the plates were drawn and lithographed by Mrs Gould, after his own sketches and designs. The most popular of his works is always likely to be *Birds of Great Britain*, published in five volumes from 1862 to 1873. The plates, as stated before, were drawn on stone by W. Hart and H. C. Richter after the designs of Gould, Joseph Wolf, and the two lithographic artists themselves. There are lovely pictures of the homeliest of British birds; while fantasy and accuracy working hand in hand have full play in the fresh-water grebes and mergansers; the Horned Grebe, the Great Crested Grebe, the Red-breasted Merganser, and the Buffle-head. The Horned Grebe has green velvet cheeks and a fox's mask; the Red-breasted Merganser, a white collar and green feathery crest; the Buffle-head, a green mask and a white cockade; the Hooded Merganser, a white cockade, high and fan-shaped, trimmed or edged with black. Perhaps Gould, in his enthusiasm has, so to speak, waived passport formalities and opened the frontiers too wide. For a bird blown ashore in a storm is hailed as a visitor to Great Britain; and according to that rule every foreigner who has ever been to England is an Englishman.

So we come to his *Birds of Australia*, in eight huge volumes with nearly 700 plates, a work done, as we have seen, from personal observation, for Gould explored Bass's Straits, Van Diemen's Land or Tasmania, South Australia, and New South Wales. Leadbeater's Cockatoo (pl. 42) is reproduced from this, of a purpose, for in its rose-petal loveliness it is so much softer than the glittering army of the parrots. It is in volume 5 that those comedians enter with their shrill voices and bright colours, fifty-four in all, with ten more in the Supplement;[20] and later, there are the Bronze-wings or Ground Pigeons, that imitate the plover in shape and habits, laying their eggs upon the sand. There is the Harlequin Bronze-wing; and others with breasts of rosy lilac and metallic spangles upon their golden green, cupreous, or deep blue wings. Some of the Fruit-eating Pigeons are most beautiful. *The Birds of New Guinea* in the inevitable five enormous volumes, is the last of Gould's great publications, intended to supplement his Australian birds. It has, as we would expect, some birds of paradise, of which more later; and in volume 3 there are some pretty scarlet honey-eaters or honey-suckers. In the next volume nine plates of pittas or ant-thrushes are pre-eminent, including the Necklaced Pitta from Borneo, wearing no less than a blue necklace upon its scarlet chest. Gould, writing of it, says that it reminds him more than anything else of the necklace of shells (*Elenchus irisodentis*) which the Tasmanian women used to wear as he saw them years ago, before they became extinct from the face of the earth. There are also a wonderful Red-breasted Kingfisher (*Tanysiptera*) with a long tail composed of a pair of plumes; and the Port Moresby Racket-tailed Kingfisher, a wonder of the air, as beautiful as the blue meteor, and rival to the humming-birds and birds of paradise.

Gould's *The Birds of Asia* (1850–83) in 7 volumes, has, again, some lovely kingfishers, and there are ten wondrous trogons in the first volume. There are sunbirds; no fewer than nineteen pittas; twenty-two woodpeckers; and an addition of fifteen parrots to Gould's century of those bird-comedians, including three Racket-tailed Parrakeets of surpassing beauty. The Amherstian Pheasant appears in splendour with the variegated leaves of a pair of ferns to enhance and point its beauty. Why did not Gould attempt a *Birds of Africa*? The *Toucans*, the *Trogons* (many of them American), the *Partridges of America*, add up to a considerable total of American birds, and there can have been little point in devoting further labour to what had already been accomplished by Audubon upon so magnificent a scale. It must always be regretted that Gould never directed his attention to the African birds. Such beautiful subjects as the bee-eaters (*Meropidae*)—and how many other birds—awaited him?

But the scale of Gould's accomplishment is huge enough. Opening his *Odontophorinae, or Partridges of America* (1850), an exceptional work for it is illustrated modestly with but thirty plates, we alight, at once, upon Masséna's Partridge, from Mexico, of which Gould remarks that 'the male is rendered exceedingly conspicuous by the singular disposition of the markings of the face, which are very strongly contrasted, and forcibly remind one of the painted face of the clown in a pantomime'. It is a partridge with black and white mask, and a black and white spotted breast. There are the Blue Pies of Hindustan, in six varieties, in his *Birds of Asia*; the spotted and lunated wagtails or forktails of the Himalayas, pied black and yellow; the fly-catchers and red honey-eaters of his *Birds of Australia*; and the green cat-birds of New Guinea, with black, white, or yellow breast markings. The mention, however, of the bird mask and peculiar markings of Masséna's Partridge brings one back for a last moment to his parrots. Impossible not to envy the naturalist who, working for so many years on the humming-birds, could yet be impresario for those gorgeous comedians perching upon boughs of the eucalyptus or the pepper tree; or for their second or supporting company, using that term in theatrical language, of the painted lories, not forgetting the lesser and innumerable, though not less glorious, parrakeets. Although I have mentioned it before in another place, I cannot refrain from repeating what Gould says of Leadbeater's Cockatoo, that 'its rose-coloured wings and glowing crest might have embellished the air of a more voluptuous region'. Of the Rose-breasted Cockatoo which is scarcely less beautiful, Gould remarks, 'I have seen it as tame in Australia as the ordinary denizens of the farmyard, enjoying perfect liberty and coming round to the door to receive food in company with the pigeons and poultry, among which it mingled on terms of intimate friendship'. This was, of course, in early days in Australia, considerably more than a hundred years ago. The Yellow-bellied Parrakeet was eaten in pies at every table; while the Adelaide Parrakeet was as common as sparrows in the London streets. The painted masquers flew down in hundreds out of the eucalyptus trees at milking-time. How wonderful to have to your achievement, for he contrived all, if he did not execute it, such an army of parrots as well as all the fairyland of humming-birds!

A pair of Gould's most lovely works, his monographs on the toucans (1833–35) and on the trogons (1836–38), I have kept for discussion until now. Both are early works. In terms of aesthetics, one is fantastic, and the other beautiful. These two families of birds could not be in deeper contrast; they could almost be illustrations of the good and evil principles. And the evil, as one is taught when young, are clothed in garish colours. The toucans, with their enormous beaks, have gone in for unimaginable transformations of their basic colours; their eyes, even, vary from bright blue to red. The beaks can be

black, with an upper edge of pale straw yellow, or the beak is crimson red with a black dividing line. But sometimes the bill is green, olive green; or the lower bill, a bright blue with green shadings. There are the toothed toucans, with toothed bills; and the aracaris, smaller, pocket toucans; including the Many-banded Aracari, with yellow breast dashed or tigered scarlet, and two broad belts or bands of black; culminating in the preposterous Curly-crested Aracari, tigered with 'half-moon' flecks or crescents, and with a ridiculous crest of curled metallic feathers of the consistency of metal shavings. Trogons, in contrast, are purely and absolutely beautiful; with red or green breasts, mostly, but others are yellow-breasted. Nearly all the trogons have barred tails of black and white. There are eared trogons, like the 'Mephisto' pheasants; the Beautiful Train-bearer and the Shining Train-bearer; but most lovely of all is the Resplendent Trogon or Quetzal, dwelling in deep seclusion in the highlands of Honduras. The robe of Montezuma is supposed to have been formed from its long tail feathers, suggesting that up to the time of the Spaniards it had a wider habitat. At times, under poetical licence, I have imagined the Aztec Emperor wearing a summer robe of rose pink flamingo feathers from the islands, or a summer mantle woven from the scarlet ibis, keeping the green quetzal plumes for a Mexican winter. It is when looking at such a beautiful plate as this (pl. 33) of the Resplendent Trogon, that one senses the stillness of the dead bird stuffed upon the branch and misses, in Gould, its life habits and the story of its love-making: these have only recently been discovered by Dr Wolfgang von Hagen. From legends connected with it, as much as from stories of the Red Indian warriors in their crests of war-eagles' plumes, are derived all notions that the primitive inhabitants of the Americas were dressed in feathers. Their feathered appearance in early books and tapestries is due, in little, to the Resplendent Trogon.

The monographs on the humming-birds and on the trogons are marvellous enough, but it could be argued that the *Monograph of the Paradiseidae* (birds of paradise), 1891–98, is the climax to Gould's life work. He included many of them in his *Birds of New Guinea*; but many new species were discovered after his death in 1881, and it fell to Dr Bowdler Sharpe, who completed others of Gould's projects, to compile the great work on the *Paradiseidae*, which is the last of the Fine Bird Books. Nevertheless, as we say, it is Gould's posthumous attempt upon this most glorious of all the families of birds.[21] The variation in these miraculous beings has been a source of endless argument between scientists, and it was once stated in all seriousness that many of the most beautiful are but hybrids. Certainly there are hybrids among the birds of paradise; but also it may be equally true that not only their strange courtship rites, but even the fabulous and far-fetched inventions of their fantasy, in which they excel all other living creatures, may be evolved as a measure of racial purity in order to keep within their families and not interbreed and hybridise. If this is so, it suggests that there may be another and more profound instinct, resembling a conscience, in the birds of paradise that directs them in the sense

PLATE 16

*Marie Jules-Cesar de Savigny prepared the ornithology section for the report on
Napoleon's Egyptian campaign. The large atlas volume to* Système des oiseaux de l'Egypte
*(Paris 1810) has 14 color-printed engravings.
This stunning Golden Eagle was engraved and etched by Bouquet
after the painting by Jacques Barraband.*

that human beings are swayed by a majority of public opinion, even contrary to their own desires. Such instinct, in view of their lovely fantasies in personal adornment, the female in acquiescence to the male, has to be credited with what can be nothing other than an aesthetic sense as powerful as that which inspires men to poetry, to compose music, paint pictures, or to be architects. If we were certain of what instincts prompted human beings at a certain stage of their development to form themselves into tightly bound communities ruled by Draconian laws, apparently for the very purpose of developing the most peculiar formalities of costume, as in many peasant villages, we would be nearer an understanding of the secret motives of the humming-birds and birds of paradise.

The typical, or even basic member of this family, is the Greater Bird of Paradise (*Paradisea apoda*). Half-a-dozen skins of this bird were brought to Europe from the Philippines as long ago as 1522, the occasion being that voyage of Magellan when he rounded Cape Horn and gave a name to the Pacific Ocean. The Habsburg Charles V, in fact, was given the birds of paradise in the same years that he was sent golden objects belonging to Montezuma and to the Incas of Peru. This particular tribute came to him as a present from the King of Bataan, in the Moluccas. Chinese merchants had been trading in those seas for many centuries, by which means bird of paradise plumes from New Guinea were brought to Cambodia and worn by the Kings and builders of Angkor. Not that the junks of the Chinamen sailed as far as New Guinea, but the centre of the trade was in the Moluccas. Bird of paradise plumes were worn, also in the headdresses of the Turkish janissaries in the pantomime ritual of the Old Seraglio. The only country in the world where they are still worn as part of the Royal insignia is in Nepal, where four or even six plumes of the Greater Bird of Paradise wave from the diamond encrusted headdresses of the King, the Rajah Prime Minister, and members of the Rana family. We ignore, in saying this, the ignoble massacre of birds of paradise for women's headdresses which disgraced the last decades of the nineteenth century, when as many as 50,000 plumes reached the milliners and hat-makers of Paris in a single year.

For a long time the legend persisted that the Greater Birds of Paradise lived in the air, always turning towards the sun like flowers, and only alighting upon the earth to die. This was because the birds reached Europe without feet or wings, owing to the method employed by the Papuans to dry the skins. The typical Greater Bird of Paradise is found in the Aroe Islands, off the South coast of New Guinea, and is a bird about the size of a dove or crow. Birds of paradise, in fact, are thought by many people to be nearly related to the crows. It is a coffee-brown bird, with yellow head, and metallic green throat. Its plumes, which form its glory and have for so many centuries imperilled its existence, are fawn and yellow in colour, and when the bird is in flight they float behind it like a flowing train. In display, however, the plumes are lifted and thrown backward, giving the impression of leaping like a

---

PLATE 17
Les pigeons *(Paris Vol. I: 1809–11; Vol. II: 1838–43)*
contains sophisticated, intense color-printed engravings, as seen in "Columba nicobarica."
The artwork is that of Antoinette Knip,
and the authors of the first and second volumes are
Coenraad Temminck and Florent Prévost.

fountain spray. A pair of long wire feathers, of which the aesthetic possibilities seem to have eluded this bird's imagination, flow from its tail. Two or more cockbirds upon a branch, displaying, must be like a vision of celestial cancan dancers. There are six subvarieties of the Greater Bird of Paradise, distinguished by grey dove breasts, dark breast cushions, and bright red, orange, or deep crimson cancan plumes. The Lesser Bird of Paradise resembles the Greater, structurally, in basic colours, and general principles of ornamentation; but one of its cousins, the Red Bird of Paradise (*Paradisea rubra*), from Waigeo Island off northern New Guinea, has developed that pair of tail wires into corkscrew twists of metalled ribbon, like metallic seaweed. The front of its head, moreover, has two horns which are covered with 'bright green scaly feathers', the colour of sunlight shining upon green moss. Another cousin, the Emperor of Germany's Bird of Paradise (*Paradisea gulielmi*), hangs upside down in courtship, an acrobatic performance in which it emulates one or two other birds of paradise, and which will be noticed later.

The Twelve-wired Bird of Paradise, not one of the true birds of paradise but a rifle-bird, is about as big as a starling. It is the only one of its family to live among the sago palms and mangrove swamps along the coast. Perhaps this bird and the Blue Bird of Paradise of the mountains are the most dazzlingly fanciful and improbable of the entire race. It has three special ornamental peculiarities; a wonderful breast shield of velvety black feathers with a green iridescence, which, in courting, erects stiffly, and forms a green-rimmed fan not quite encircling its head; yellow flank feathers like small ostrich plumes; and six wires coming from those plumes, to either side, which stiffen and become taut in courtship. The male bird in courting makes play, too, of the inside colouring of its mouth and throat which is a sharp grass-green. The hen, a little thrush-like in body, but longer and thinner, seems to bear no possible relationship to this gorgeous creature. Both sexes have vivid red feet and legs; and the hen, a brown and white barred chest.

The Six-plumed seems to follow, naturally, upon the Twelve-wired. But only verbally, for they have nothing else in common. The Six-plumed is a bigger bird than the Twelve-wired, and about the size of a magpie. The typical bird of this series, for it goes into several variations, has black, velvety plumage, a gold or silver tuft of feathers on the crown of its head, and a metallic shield of feathers on its breast darting forth bronze and green and golden lights. It has a beautiful clear, light blue eye. It has a little crest of metallic feathers on its head; and from just behind the eye spring six plumes, three to a side, each plume nearly as long as the bird's body and ending in a racket-shaped terminal, with the inevitable hint of some form of aerial transmission or reception. Further, the Six-plumed has a lustrous black cape or mantle folded at the back, or it can be thrown forward and moved round the body, spreading open like a fan or an umbrella, with that metallic path for centre, when the bird darts its six plumes to the front. To see this bird displaying is to understand the Papuan legend that the Six-plumed Bird of Paradise is a protection against thunder and lightning. One of the most beautiful variations, unknown to Gould and Bowdler Sharpe, is the Carol Six-plumed, which has evolved for itself a helmet or headpiece to match its golden brown and lilac breast-shield, and a coloured mantle or 'umbrella' of black and silky white and brown.

Another of the magical, starling-size birds of paradise is the Lesser Superb, which from its coal-black livery has invented the most fabulous transformations; a blue-green crown to its head that flashes forth metallic fires in the sunlight; a dazzling metalled breast-shield the shape of a pair of open wings; and a cape of velvety black feathers which it raises above its head. The Lesser Superb can even fly for short distances with all its ornaments open and extended, so strong is the muscular attachment for working them. Part of the display, as well, is the opening of its apple-green mouth and gullet. It has metamorphosed itself into a three-tiered, or storeyed, plumed being, flashing forth metallic fires.

The Little King Birds of Paradise have bodies no bigger than robins or sparrows and are no more than six inches long from the points of their beaks to the ends of the metallic green ornaments upon their tail wires. The species (*Cicinnurus regius*) has six variants. It is a bright glittering crimson little bird with a white belly, but an exquisite fancy and imagination have given to it a torque or collar band of emerald green, and invented a pair of false wings or pectoral fans, for courting, of a light brownish colour, each plume ending in a white bar, and tipped with iridescent, metallic green. There are a lower pair of flank fans or false wings, silky white, but lacking the iridescent green, and the little bird, in courting, lifts the upper pair in a circle behind its neck, which has the emerald torque, and stiffens the white pair below. The tail wires, which are beautifully curved, are webbed, at the end, to form disks or rackets of the same metallic green. The courting of this little creature must be among the most fascinating sights in nature. One collector tells of looking through his glasses and seeing 'a small bird rise from the top of a tree and soar into the air like a skylark. After it had risen about thirty feet it suddenly seemed to collapse and dropped back into the tree as though it had been shot'. Another tells of one phase in its courtship when 'it throws the long tail-wires forward over its head, while gently swinging its body from side to side. The spiral tips of the wires look like small balls of burnished green metal, and the swaying movement gives them the effect of being slowly tossed from one side to the other' as by a juggler. During another form of display, 'dropping under the perch the bird walks backwards and forwards in an inverted position with his wings expanded. Suddenly he closes his wings and lets his body fall straight downwards, looking exactly like a crimson pear, his blue legs being stretched out to their full length and his feet clinging to the perch. The effect is very curious and weird, and the performance . . . like that of an acrobat suddenly dropping on to his toes on the crossbar of a trapeze'.[22]

The Lonely Little King, another of the series, has its emerald green torque expanded into a pectoral shield of four times the width. Its tail feathers are a little different in structure and curved more like a lyre. The Bare-headed Little King, or Wilson's Bird of Paradise, found only on a couple of islands off New Guinea, has a cobalt blue head with the marking of a double cross on it in black feathers, a sulphur yellow mantle, glittering green pectoral shield, and its lyrelike tail feathers are steel blue. In courting it makes play of its 'shot' colours . . . 'the feathers of the face give the effect of black velvet when the pile is pressed; the breast, owing to the position of the incidence of the light seems black, with red reflections . . . As the beak is opened the feathers of the head are moved to cause them to assume their normal glossy intense black, which contrasts vividly with the light green of the mouth. Quite

suddenly the bird retracts the head and neck, elevating the breast and expanding the "shield", which is now seen to be bright green'. The Exquisite Little King, figured in Iredale, is so rare that only a dozen specimens have been secured in seventy years, and its habitat is still quite unknown. It has tail feathers of 'bright shining metallic oily green', metallic blue feathers at its throat, a bright green breast shield with a blue border and green lights in that, and brownish green breast-fans or false wings. The Magnificent, too, is related to these. It wears a heavy green metalled gorget, with shining blue feathers under it, brilliant blue tail wires without disks, and a yellow rug of beautifully trimmed feathers which it moves and flashes as a cape. It has pale blue claws; and displays upon prepared dancing floors from which it has stripped all the dead twigs and leaves.

The ornamental device of breast-fans or false wings among birds of paradise is best seen in the Sickle-bills, which are of dragon or pterodactyl outline perching on the branch. In support of this, the soft feathers of their faces have metallic-like tips and look like scales, and the primary tail feathers are dagger-pointed at their ends. They have tails as much as two feet long to 'brake' their flight; and collectors have described them rising up in ecstasy in their display and falling like a stone just to recover themselves before they reach the ground. It must be imagined that the false wings have their part to play in this. Meyer's Sickle-bill, at the first glimpse, is the uncoloured pattern or prototype of the Sickle-bills. There are accounts of this bird preparing or dressing itself for display, each plume of its false wings being 'arranged' by 'its long slender bill . . . for at the supreme moment, each feather must fall perfectly into place'. Even this monochrome among the Sickle-bills has violet reflections in its lower pair of fans, while the upper show purple, the tail 'shot' with purple and the head blue-green. But the Greater Sickle-bill is King-dragon of its race; the 'dagger-pointed' plumes under its tail marvellously suggestive of the scaly belly of the flying lizard or pterodactyl, and its two series of breast-fans giving it the appearance of having four false wings. The Red-billed has a mantle or lower pair of false wings of Isabella colour, each plume fringed with metallic violet, while the upper pair are lilac-violet, if smoothed, but give off golden reflections when the 'pile' is raised the other way. In display, this bird makes two semi-circles round itself. The White-billed has only one pair of false wings, and a green breast in place of the lower, but these are kingfisher blue, with coppery-red and black tips to them, and are shaped like the 'wings' of flying fish.

Still more peculiar and far-fetched ornaments are yet to be described. Wallace's Standard-wing, found only on Batjan and one or two other islands in the Moluccas,[23] is said by some authorities not to be a bird of paradise at all, but to belong to the far distant friar birds of Australia. It is ashy-olive in colour, in Wallace's words, with a lovely breast-shield of metallic green; but it has two pairs of long white plumes springing at right angles from its shoulders, which it can lay along its body, and raise into

---

PLATE 18

This orange confection, "Coq de Roche," appears in all
his brilliant plumage via the printmaking medium of color-printed engraving.
The best engravers accurately reproduced Jacques Barraband's watercolors
for Histoire naturelle des oiseaux de paradis *(Paris 1801–06).*
Author François Levaillant buoyed his lavish bird books on the patronage
of those whose fortunes were made under Napoleon.

36

White-headed Eagle.

the air at will. The Standard-wing, as figured in Iredale, waving each pair of the white plumes alternately up and down, looks like a bird pretending to itself that it is a helicopter. The collector is to be envied who, not long ago, saw some thirty cockbirds of this extraordinary race displaying and flying round with these erected white feathers in a forest in the Moluccas. The Enamelled, or King of Saxony's Bird of Paradise, is, if anything, more fabulous still in its peculiar ornamentation; and so rare that no specimens have ever been taken alive, and nothing is known of its habits. In this instance, some authorities say that it is not a bird of paradise but a bower bird. A little bird, about as big as a robin, it has a yellow chest, and a velvety black back shading into brown. From just above its eye spring two long streamers, trailing backwards more than twice the length of its body. Or, in fact, they can be as much as two feet long. These streamers are described as being like strips of celluloid in texture, and are strung with plaques, or small squares or flags of regular shape, enamelled light blue on the outside, and white or dull brown on the inner. It is, probably, the most fantastic adornment in the whole of nature, but it is to be qualified, as in the case of Wallace's Standard-wing, with the proviso that both birds have almost exceeded the canons of beauty. It must remain a mystery how many millions of years, or how short a time, has been devoted to their adornments. This latter bird with its light blue enamelled streamers, has an air of being engaged in some form of propaganda, or electioneering. It is peculiar rather than beautiful, and lacking in the poetical logic which is so instinctive in other birds of paradise.

There is yet the possibility that there are other birds of paradise to be discovered in the mainland of New Guinea, or the adjacent islands. The Ribbon-tailed has only been known since 1935, though there were stories of it some years before. Its home is in an inaccessible area deep in the interior, and it was only in 1948 when a landing ground was laid out nearby, that living birds were flown to an aviary in Australia. This is a bird, therefore, never figured by Gould or Bowdler Sharpe. It is a dark rufous black or brown, with a green throat, and the pair of immense tail feathers, two feet long, are tipped with black. Collectors have said that these long plumes 'make flicking sounds' as the birds, which are weak in flight and only go from bough to bough, trail them through the air.

Perhaps the most fabulously beautiful of all birds of paradise is lacking in the metallic glitter of the others. It has no note of gold or copper in its plumage; no metalled under-reflections, or flashes of ruby or emerald in the changing light, or according to the way in which the bird, itself, varies the texture of its surfaces. Instead, it is of a different colour pattern from that of all others of its family; and is precisely that colour which, looking at the entire race in all its wondrous transformations and adornments would, else, be lacking in them. It is the Blue Bird of Paradise (pl. 52) called after the Crown Prince Rudolph who met his death in the hunting lodge at Mayerling. This, again, is a bird the size of a thrush or starling. It displays upside down, like an acrobat swinging from a trapeze, and its

---

PLATE 19
Alexander Wilson wrote the first systematic account
of birds of the United States, American Ornithology *(Philadelphia 1808–14).*
Wilson's drawings, such as this Bald Eagle,
were engraved by Alexander Lawson, and show each feather in great detail.
It was Wilson who inspired the young Audubon to embark
on his own monumental publication.

whole appearance is designed for that. During these moments, the Blue Bird of Paradise from the head upwards is clothed in a mantle of bronzy green, the colour of some night skies, has a purple band above that, a bar of maroon-crimson like a rim of fire on a night horizon, then, the most intense violet-purple as of the awful zenith, and all the surrounding splendour of its fans of deep blue feathers. The two tail-wires, without ornament, make a pair of arcs above that. This display of the Blue Bird of Paradise, which no naturalist had yet observed in the day of Gould or Bowdler Sharpe, is so entirely fantastic and extraordinary that to an imaginative mind it might suggest that the bird is exhibiting itself in a dance figure devised by Petipa for some celestial bird-dancer or *bayadère*. No lover of ballet can fail to be reminded of that 'lift' at the climax of Princess Aurora's *pas de deux* in the last act of *The Sleeping Princess*, known to dancers as the 'fish dive'. It suggests, as well, that the bird is imitating a rainbow; or even that it has heard stories of that double arch or fountain when the whales are spouting on the horizon and the moon climbs, in mystery, out of the blue immensity of ocean.

It is to be remarked that the Blue Bird of Paradise hen is a little less ordinary in appearance than others of her race and has some hint in her of the splendours of the cockbird. Yet some of the hen birds have a particular pensive beauty of their own, as though used to the wonders of the males' plumage, and no longer surprised by it. Such, indeed, is their attitude when the cockbird is displaying. They are indifferent: not interested. What is the purpose of so many and such wonderful *travestissements* and transformations? What a mystery it is to look upon the hen bird of the Red Sickle Bill, foreshadowing nothing in its thrush-like plumage, and with only the thin, hooked bill and light blue patch around its eye in promise of the changing colours of the cockbird's pectoral fans or false wings, breast-shield, and metallic mantle! All the male birds of paradise, be it noted, are here described in mature plumage, and not in the bewildering stages of their moult or immaturity. For reasons of space I have had to omit further mention of the manucodes, that are so like crows in shape, and are of a marvellous violet or purple inkiness, with varied colour reflections. Neither is there room for the bower birds, of which the stories told are almost too extraordinary to be believed. The Blue Satin Bower Bird decorates its bower with land shells, pieces of bone, bits of glass, nails, scraps of tin, various berries according to season, blue bus-tickets, on purpose to match the colour of its eyes, and bright coloured feathers; it even paints the interior of its bower, making use of flat wads of some fibrous material for brushes, which it holds in its bill, the pigment being made from charcoal mixed with its own saliva. Other bower birds are masters of a marvellous range of imitations, mimicking, almost in poltergeist manner, the voices of cats and dogs, the call of the eagle and butcher bird, the 'cry of the blue-winged Kookaburra', and closing its recital with 'the whirring noise made by the crested bronze-winged pigeon flying through the trees'.

But the Fine Bird Books are drawing to their close. It is only fair to say that Bowdler Sharpe's monograph on the birds of paradise has a close rival in that of his contemporary, American ornithologist Daniel Giraud Elliot. Elliot's monograph came out in 1873 with thirty-seven superb plates by J. Wolf,[24] a better painter in every way than Gould's assistant, W. Hart. His drawing of the Lesser Bird of Paradise basking in the fountain spray of its own golden and white cancan plumes, formed of wire-like cirrhi, 'leaping' or 'performing' in a glorious double curve; or his drawing of the Long Tailed Bird of Paradise, maned and gorgetted, and in silhouette like a 'throwback' to the flying lizard, are finer than any of the plates in Bowdler Sharpe. But Elliot's *Birds of Paradise* is premature in date. So many of the species were not yet discovered. It is for this reason that Bowdler Sharpe, with double the number of plates, bringing up the tale of exploration of New Guinea to the turn of the century, and omitting no more than two or three of the very latest finds, is more valuable than D. G. Elliot. But that author had, as it were, a private ornithological world of his own. Its inhabitants were birds of paradise, pittas, hornbills, but D. G. Elliot was not his own painter, except among the Pittas. Early in his career, in 1863, he had brought out his book on the *Pittidae, or Ant-Thrushes* with plates of a delightful, rather primitive character, after his own drawings.

The other major work of D. G. Elliot, the equal in every way to any work by Gould, is his *Monograph of the Phasianidae or Family of the Pheasants* (1872) with seventy-nine hand coloured plates after drawings by J. Wolf.[25] His plates of the Golden Pheasant, and its mutations, must always remain among the most splendid of bird illustrations. This world of the pheasants has been explored again in recent times, but never has there been so poetical a rendering of that flashing golden crest, long ocellated tail borne like a train, and cape or ruff of orange and black feathers. Below that, again, there is a mantle of metallic green and black; but J. Wolf, good bird painter that he was, has not attempted the display of the Golden Pheasant, when this bird of the crimson chest, dancing with quick steps, tautens its whole body and the ruff stiffens into a wonderful halo of concentric serpent rings of orange and metallic steel black, while, with flashing eye and brilliant crest, the cockbird makes a low hissing noise, and resumes its dance.

The Lady Amherst Pheasant is, if anything, more lovely still; a *bayadère* with emerald green head, little crown or tiara of feathers, and red crest running down into that incredible cape of white, barred with metallic black or steel blue serpent scales or meshes. It has a pure white chest, where the Golden Pheasant is bright crimson; its throat and back are greeny-blue in iridescent markings; it has four scarlet feathers to each side in its tail, which, for the rest, is long and sweeping, mottled grey and white, and barred with black. The first sight of the Lady Amherst Pheasant may convince one that it is the most beautiful bird in the world. These two birds balance and are the equivalent of each other, though the Lady Amherst is a little bigger and heavier. There are good plates of the Lady Amherst, both in Elliot and in Gould's *Birds of Asia*; but the Chinese Silver Pheasant, perhaps the best known of all, though larger, is too delicate and lace-like of effect to lend itself to drawing. Perhaps the Silver Pheasant is always at its best upon a Chinese painted wallpaper.[26] The fourth member of the family most often seen in aviaries is Reeves's Pheasant, a large bird with a white snow-head, typical pheasant-breast in large tortoiseshell markings, and an immensely long tail. Specimens of this pheasant of snow and tortoiseshell have been known with tails as much as six feet long and this, again, is a bird familiar from Chinese paintings. It is said that the long tail feathers of Reeves's pheasant were worn in the headdresses of actors playing military rôles in the old Chinese theatre. Elliot's Pheasant is another beautiful creature of red tortoiseshell and snow. Belonging to this group of long tailed birds there is, also, the blue Mikado Pheasant, not figured in either Gould or Elliot because its history goes back no earlier than 1906, when

Inhabits North America, U. States.   **WILD TURKEY.** *Meleagris Gallopavo.* 1 Male. 2 Female. 3 Young   Jas Johnston Sc.
4 Locust Tree.

two of its tail feathers were found in the headdress of a mountain tribesman in Formosa. The writer has kept one of these blue pheasants and would pay tribute to its purplish blue back and body, mottled with black, and long blue tail barred with white. Swinhoe's Pheasant, also known to the writer personally, is a Formosan bird but belongs to another group, that of the Kaleege Pheasants. Ugly rather than graceful in form, and predestined to be one of the blue pheasants, Swinhoe's has produced dark crimson scapulars, wing coverts that are fringed with metallic green, a white mantle and snowy tail feathers. It is a bird of all colours: and one is not surprised to read in Delacour that Swinhoe's on fairly frequent occasions has 'thrown' a cinnamon mutation, called *le Swinhoe havane* in French aviaries.

It is a brilliant world, this of the Monal (Impeyan) and Koklass Pheasants, its fantasy heightened into improbability by the scintillating reds and greens of the Cochin-Chinese junglefowl, ancestors to all our families of cocks and hens. Thence, we are in the territories of the Crested Firebacks, inhabitants of Sumatra, Siam, and Borneo, marvellous creatures of metallic plumage foreshadowing the peacock in crest and shape of body. The first impression is that they are peacocks in blue and rufous colourings, but without the wondrous ocellations in their tails. Vieillot's Crested Fireback is one of these blue 'phantom' peacocks; the Siamese and the Malayan Firebacks are two others with more of bronze and green metal in their plumage; but it may be that the loveliest of this race is Bulwer's Wattled Pheasant, so intent upon its 'blueness' that its wattles are a bright sky blue, its body is black with blue metallic spangles or spangled fringes to its feathers, there are some lights or reflections of crimson in its plumage, and it has a superb and wonderful white 'ballet' tail. In these same jungles there live the Peacock and the Argus Pheasants. Most beautiful of these would seem to be Ghigi's Grey Peacock Pheasant from Annam (how well-sounding are the names *Éperonnier* and *Polyplectron* in French and Latin!) giving frontal and side displays, like a true peacock, with wonderful, enormous opal ocellations in its wings and tail; and the Palawan Peacock Pheasant, from the island of that name off the north coast of Borneo, a bird with green peacock mantling and a freckled brown chestnut tail with blue-green eyes. Rarer, still, are the Argus Pheasants. These birds, in recorded instances, were sent as ritual presents by the Emperors of Annam to the Emperors of China, but little was known of them until Monsieur Delacour undertook a series of special expeditions to French Indo-China for this purpose in the years between the wars. The Malay Crested Argus, dark cinnamon brown, with little round white spots all over its body and tail, has the appearance of a tropical bird, of phoenix race, caught in a static snowstorm. But the Great Argus Pheasant is the true phoenix. This marvellous bird, whose seemingly purposeless beauties so much excited Charles Darwin, like many of the great dancers, 'looks dull and ungainly in ordinary circumstances'. In the Great Argus, unlike the Peacock, it is the wings, and not the tail, that are particularly developed. When it displays, peacock-like, it makes a rhythmical shivering of

---

PLATE 20
Thomas Brown's Illustrations of the American Ornithology of Alexander Wilson
and Charles Lucien Bonaparte *(Edinburgh 1831–35) perfects the illustrations of*
Wilson's American Ornithology *and Bonaparte's supplement to it (Philadelphia 1825–33).*
"Wild Turkey" *modifies plate 9 of Bonaparte's supplement;*
the chicks were added, virtually copied from plate 6 of
Audubon's The Birds of America, *then in the process of publication.*

PLATE LXXII.

RED NECKED GRIBE, MALE

its wing feathers, which, carried a step further in illusion than the display of the peacock, makes those eyes or *ocelli* in its wings appear to revolve and turn. In order to watch the effect upon the hen, every now and then the cockbird will poke its head through between two of the feathers, take a momentary glance, and withdraw again. 'In old males', writes William Beebe, 'shot toward the end of the breeding season, it is possible to locate this peephole by the disturbed, frayed condition of the web in its immediate vicinity. Thus,' he concludes, 'through the peephole in his living curtain, the feathered actor is able to keep watch upon his audience . . . the female, however, shows not even a momentary passing interest . . . often even turning her back upon the splendid performer'. Yet this courtship dance of the Great Argus Pheasant, with the 'trapeze' dance of the Blue Peacock, may be the most beautiful of all the sights of nature.

A peacock must be as difficult to paint as a sunrise or a rainbow. And even if classed with the pheasants to which it belongs, the Indian Peacock is so familiar a sight that it is impossible to describe it. Perhaps the Green Peafowl of Java and Indo-China, with its bigger build and richer colouring, the brighter blue of its plumage and the green metallic edging to the feathers, is the more beautiful of the two races. The strains of pied peacocks that have been established, with patches of white predominating in their plumage, are more unusual and more interesting than their congeners. And there remain white peacocks. There is no figure in classical dancing more beautiful to watch, and no effect in music more thrilling, than when a white peacock at the climax of its display runs forward, and shivering its whole body, rattles its quills together, in the same instant uttering the long drawn 'Indian' cry of the peacock. The hen bird shows no interest, but the white peacock will repeat the performance a number of times for its own pleasure, and in order to fascinate the onlookers.[27]

This marvellous race of birds has yet other wonders. There are the Eared Pheasants or Cross-optilons. According to Delacour, the Brown and the Blue Crossoptilons have been much molested in Western China for their feathers; particularly the Blue Eared because of their tail feathers which, for centuries, were worn as hat ornaments by Military Mandarins; but the large White and Grey Crossop-tilons are 'abundant and fearless', and are to be seen in quantity around the Buddhist lamaseries where they are fed. This gives their habitat, which is the high plateaus and mountain slopes of Tibet. Unlike the Crested Fireback, the Peacock Pheasants (*Polyplectron*), and the Argus, which live in the steaming jungles, the Crossoptilons are birds familiar with the rose-pink magnolia (*Campbellii*) and the rhodo-dendron. A peculiarity of the Crossoptilons is that male and female have the same plumage. In appearance they are the Mephistos of their breed. The Blue Eared, living specimens of which were only brought out of China in 1929, has red eye lobes, white upcurving ear tufts giving it the Mephisto 'look', and long tail feathers that are like lavender or smoky-blue ostrich plumes. We have to think of the

---

PLATE 21
This Red-necked Grebe appears in Prideaux
John Selby's Illustrations of British Ornithology *(Edinburgh 1821–34).*
Selby collected and mounted the bird skins,
and lovingly etched each life-size bird with peculiar, messy lines of his own design.
The strong figure drawing and inspired needle work
result in delightful prints.

Pl. 27.

OISEAU-MOUCHE SAPHO.

Publié par Arthus Bertrand.

Bévalet pinx.   *Rémond impr.*   *Coutant sculp.*

Mephisto pheasants feeding in front of Tibetan monasteries which form the only still unstudied body of architecture in the world. This image once established, it will be as difficult to disassociate the Eared Pheasants from the Tibetan lamaseries as it is to part the nomad Lapps from their antlered reindeer, of the Spaniards from their bull fights.

The Tragopans, or Horned Pheasants, are Himalayan birds. Their heads have black facial markings, and their deep red chests are as though marked or flecked with snow. It is said that they are more nearly related to partridges than to pheasants. There are five races of tragopans, and good plates of them all in Elliot's *Phasianidae*. In addition to the snow-flecked crimson or carmine of their chests they have these peculiarities; a pair of blue, fleshy horns, two or three inches long, which become erect in the moment of display; and their incredible wattles, which could be compared to a heraldic apron or lappet of multi-coloured skin, which they unfold, suddenly, over their chests, and retract again as quickly as it was spread. The Western (Black Headed) Tragopan, gaudy inhabitant of Nepal, has red cheeks with four semi-circles of blue dots below its eyes, and a flesh-pink wattle with central stem or fern branch of the same pale blue; Temminck's Tragopan, blue cheeks with patches of green, and a crimson wattle or apron, with paler blue circles of larger and small sizes, and apron edging of the same blue; the Satyr Tragopan, darker, blue-purple cheeks, with dark blue central motif on a green apron, crimson ornaments upon that, and a black velvet edging. These incredible bird hatchments, during the short moment while they are displayed, are of a marvellous effect below the bright cheeks of the bird, the black hair of its *occiput*, combed backward, and its pair of blue horns. The courtship dance of the tragopan begins with 'a slow, stately walk about the female', much resembling the *paseo*, or opening walk and promenade of the performers in a Spanish dance. The writer has had a Satyr Tragopan in his possession for several months, and never ceased to wonder at its 'breast of blood-red ruby all flecked with eyes of snow, like the "run", the spatial pattern or descent of raindrops upon a window, so regular that they seem as if punctually and meticulously renewed, thrown and spattering, burning like the fire of frost in the incredible, the martial crimson of its chest'. There is this difference between the Satyr Tragopan and Temminck's Tragopan, that the former has the snow flecks on its carmine breast outlined in black, and descending the breast more evenly in gradation, whereas Temminck's Tragopan has larger marks that are but snowflakes. The wattle of the latter, to judge from the colour plate of the lappets of tragopans in C. W. Beebe's *Monograph of Pheasants* (1918–22), may be more striking in its colour pattern, blue upon red, than the red and green and purple of the Satyr Tragopan. During the months I had one of these birds in my possession I saw the blue horns and the heraldic mantle on no more than two or three occasions, and for a few seconds only, but for long enough to see this stout built partridge, lacking the grace of the pheasant, transformed into the horned god of the Himalayas. Never could anyone who has

---

PLATE 22

*René Primevère Lesson, like John Gould [q.v.], contributed greatly
to the study of hummingbirds.* Histoire naturelle des oiseaux-mouches *(Paris 1828–30)
depicts species in jewel-like color-printed engravings
such as the dramatic "Oiseau-mouche Sapho." Artists Bévalet, Prêtre and Oudart
painted animals at the Muséum d'histoire naturelle.*

known the Satyr Tragopan hear mention of Nepal without having the momentary image in his mind of that pair of blue horns, the lappet of bright colours, and that breast of carmine flecked with snow.

D. G. Elliot brought his ornithological work to a close with his *Monograph of the Bucerotidae, or Family of the Hornbills*. The more extraordinary of the hornbills are as peculiar as the toucans; the Rhinoceros Hornbill (pl. 50), for an example, of Borneo and Sumatra, with its casque of horn curving backwards, and placed on top of and above its beak. There are the Homrai, with a double edge or brim to its casque; and the Fantee White-crested Hornbill, African inhabitant, black and white, with long 'glider' tail, and a crest like the tail of a laced fantail pigeon. The African hornbills are entirely antediluvian of appearance; culminating in Sclater's Hornbill, with beak and casque shaped short like a chopper; and a mane or crest of long, loose filaments, for they are hardly feathers, spotted with grey, and reproducing the exact shape of a maned or crested lizard. Elliot's monograph has plates by John G. Keulemans, a new name, if a late one, and that of a most prolific painter. There are seventy-three plates in this *Monograph of the Hornbills*; but Keulemans made 120 illustrations for Bowdler Sharpe's monograph on the kingfishers (1868–71); 121 for George E. Shelley's monograph on the sunbirds (1876–80); and no fewer than 149 for Henry Seebohm's monograph on the thrushes (1902). There is no difficulty in making out a quick list of 700 or 800 plates to various works by Keulemans.[28]

Here, therefore, we take leave of the greater Bird Books. There are the lesser works; Dresser's monographs on the rollers (1893) and the bee-eaters (1884–86), two lovely families of birds; and Shelley's monograph on the sunbirds. One should not fail to mention, for their beauty, the Azure Rollers of the Moluccas, and a Racket-tailed Roller from Africa that compares with those humming-birds and birds of paradise that have racket-tails. The sunbirds may be one of the five most beautiful nations of the birds; what could be lovelier than the Malachite Sun Bird, a coppery green 'self', or the Superb Sun Bird from Madagascar, pure emerald green with black wings? Shelley's yellow backed Sun Bird, from Palawan, has a metallic crown of greeny blue, a crimson mantle, and blue tail. The Negros Sun Bird of the Philippines is black-bellied, with a yellow back, a blue head, a violet-blue tail with metallic lights in it, and the rest of its plumage is a bright blood-red. There are sun birds with throats of metallic lilac, and metallic violet, and their plumage, to go with that, is an olive belly, a deep red mantle, and scarlet chest; or a yellow breast with dark brown-green wings, and with that throat of metallic violet, the 'body' of colour is a deep violet 'self'. It will be obvious that the sunbirds are as beautiful as the trogons, the pittas, the birds of paradise, and the humming-birds.

There are works of a wonderful minor intricacy such as Alfred Malherbe's *Les Picidées*; and it is pleasing to quote the rest of the title, *Histoire Naturelle des Picumninés, Yucinés, ou Torcols*, a work of which only 100 copies were privately printed at Metz in 1861–62, with hand-coloured lithographs by M. Delahaye and others. Many of the woodpeckers are conspicuous for the mock-tortoiseshell markings of their back and wings; and others have spotted or tabbied breasts like thrushes. There are sapsuckers with long thin bills like humming-birds; and Malherbe illustrates a beautiful cactus pecker that has its home in Guatemala. This work on woodpeckers, in its involved complexity, is more satisfying than the broader effects of, to take two examples, the hundred and more lithographs by Keulemans in Bowdler

Sharpe's *Monograph of the Hirundinidae or Family of Swallows* (1885–94), or the century by Keulemans in illustration to Frederick du Cane Godman, *A Monograph of the Petrels* (1907–10). A pair of last works that need mention are the *Monograph of the Scansorial Barbets* by Charles H. T. Marshall and George F. L. Marshall, and the *Monograph of the Jacamars and Puff Birds* by Philip L. Sclater. The *Scansorial Barbets* and the *Jacamars* are on a par with Dresser's *Rollers* and his *Bee-eaters*; indeed, the quartet of books, together, with Shelley's *Sunbirds* added to them, are the minor works of the school of Gould. Within a few years *The British Birds* (1918–19) of Archibald Thorburn oversteps the limits of our period and brings the long succession of Fine Bird Books to an end.

The period of precise counterfeit or delineation comes to a close. In all probability, painters of birds are more likely, in future, to concern themselves with the summer colours of the Arctic tundra where the families of wild geese have their breeding grounds. The flamingo cities will be their subject. Or they will study the flight formations, and what could be called the choreographic principles of birds upon the wing. In this connection it should be stated that some of the most beautiful descriptions of birds manoeuvering in their masses are to be found in the recent autobiography by Mr Roy Campbell. His account of the homing halcyons flying low above the milk-white waters of the evening Mediterranean; of the green and crimson lories bathing in a stream in Zululand and staining the water crimson with the pigment off their wings; or of a flock of carmine bee-eaters falling out of the heavens like a shower of roses, banking steeply, and diving down again, contain in themselves, it may be thought, not only poetry, but the future of this school of observation and this branch of painting. So the past closes its pages; and we are left with many shelves full of huge volumes which, beginning in fantasy, continue in accuracy, attain to an extraordinary degree of truth and sanity during the long nineteenth-century, and now may either expire altogether, or take to the path of poetry. Whether this will happen in our lifetimes we may never know; but can, in the meantime, take our pleasure in what is old and true.

THE NOTES

1. And yet more recently another by Mr Scott (with Mr James Fisher, my colleague in this book) to find the greatest breeding ground of the Pink-footed Goose in the central oasis of the Icelandic Desert.

2. But not the rarest goose. This is the Nene of Hawaii, of which there are perhaps only forty individuals—about a quarter of them in the Severn Wildfowl Trust's wonderful collection of water fowl at Slimbridge in Gloucestershire.

3. Ulisse Aldrovandi (1522–1609) began to publish his works on natural history in 1599, at the age of 77, and the series was only brought to a conclusion in 1668. The first edition of his *Ornithologia* bore the imprint Bononiae (Bologna), and there was a second edition from Frankfurt in 1610. He has long sections on pigeons and domestic fowl.

4. This book was a favourite of Ruskin's. His copy is in the library of the Ruskin Museum at Sheffield.

5. *Mustertaubenbuch*, by O. Wittig, with 220 watercolour paintings by C. Witzmann, published by Fritz Pfenningstorff, Berlin, N.D. (probably about 1925). The section referred to covers pp. 1–62 of the above work. I have written on the races of domestic pigeons in *Primitive Scenes and Festivals*, Faber & Faber, London, 1942, pp. 146–165.

6. *Bibliotheca Accipitraria*, by J. E. Harting, London, Bernard Quaritch, 1891.

7. These paintings were too big for inclusion in the exhibition held in London in 1952 of the treasures of the former Royal house of Hanover.

8. This island, six miles from the mainland of Sardinia, has a town, Carloforte, settled in 1736 by Charles Emmanuel III of Savoy with a colony of Genoese fishermen, whose ancestors had been established on an island off Tunis since the thirteenth century. The population of Carloforte are said still to retain their medieval Genoese dialect and costume. Their employment is tunny-fishing. Mussolini made some efforts to turn Carloforte into an Italian naval base.

9. The Lithuanians, who are not of Aryan origin, but allied ethnographically to the Turks and Magyars and Finns, were the last European people to become Christian. The still existing Polish family of Radziwill are descended from Wojszund (d. 1412), last Grand Priest or Druid of Lithuania, whose son Radziwill was baptised with the King Jagellon in 1396. Druids, it may be added in parenthesis, existed in the island of Ouessant, off Finistère, until late in the reign of Louis XIV.

10. The paper used by Audubon for the *Birds of America* is a double-elephant folio, made by J. Whatman, watermarked with the date, and measuring 39½ × 27 inches.

11. The incredulous, and those inclined to be sceptical, will find stories of the Condor Real from first-hand evidence in *Adventures in Bolivia*, by C. H. Prodgers, London, John Lane & Co. 1922, pp. 203–208; and the same author's *Adventures in Peru*, 1924, p. 69.

12. Audubon met Redouté, the flower painter, in Paris in 1828, in his studio in the rue de Seine, and showed him the first parts of his gigantic publication.

13. All of Audubon's watercolour drawings for the *Birds of America*, with the exception of three only, are to be seen at the New York Historical Society, having been bought from his widow in 1865. Several of his animal paintings are in the American Museum of Natural History.

14. In 1813, near Louisville, Audubon saw one of the great nations of the passenger pigeons flying overhead. His estimation was that it contained 1,115,136,000 birds. There are extraordinary contemporary accounts of these flights of passenger pigeons passing by for three days and nights at a time, and of their droppings falling as evenly as snow flakes with a steady sound. They were slaughtered indiscriminately. Audubon describes hunters going out into the woods, at night, with lighted cauldrons to boil down the bodies of the birds, with no time to load the guns, and having to beat them down with sticks and clubs. But this whole race of birds, as though sensing their doom began to dwindle of themselves; they were nearly extinct by the middle of the century, and the last 'expatriate' passenger pigeon died in the Cincinnati Zoo in 1914, that year of evil augury for the human race.

15. John Harris, the Cornish Cocker, says in his Memoirs, 'The American Dr Cooper fooled us nicely . . . We started off with sixty-three cocks to the 'Adelphi' at Liverpool, and there we waited six weeks en route for Denver, U.S.A.; for the stakeholder could get no deposit sent on as promised; in fact, it was simply American bluff on Dr Cooper's part. We were told after, it was just as well, for we should have probably have won our main of £1,000 easily, but never left Denver City with it, without a bullet or two trying to stop us'. This was in 1875. *Cockfighting and Game Fowl, from the note books of Herbert Atkinson of Ewelme*, publ. George Bayntum, Bath, 1938, p. 205. Herbert Atkinson (d. 1936) was a great amateur of Game Fowl, and twelve of his paintings were published as a supplement to *The Feathered World*; the best of them, a Derby Black-breasted Red, a Black Henny and a Fig-pudding.

16. In addition to the game-cocks on pl. 39 there are a pair of White-crested Polands. These birds, with their peculiar head tufts covering a curious protuberance of the skull, are to be found described and illustrated in Aldrovandi (1599) and are called by him the Paduan or Padavinian breed. They have no historical connection with Poland as a country. There are often Polands in Dutch paintings of the school of Melchior d'Hondecouter (1636–1695). The comb of this crested fowl assumes a peculiar character; it consists of two horns, forming a kind of crescent. There are bearded and beardless varieties of Polands; but the bearded are best known. Polands were very popular in Victorian times; but are seldom seen, now, except as bantams. Colours are Gold- or Silver-spangled, Pure White, Pure Black, and Buff spangled with White, or Chamois.

17. A superb example of Edward Lear as ornithological draughtsman is his *Illustration of the Family of Psittacidae, or Parrots* (1834), with large coloured lithographs of superb quality (see pl. 30).

18. Much of this information is derived from *Piccadilly Notes*, Nos. 9 and 22 (1934), a publication appearing from Messrs. Sotheran, the booksellers, then of 43 Piccadilly, and is the work of their manager, Mr J. H. Stonehouse, who joined the firm not many years after Gould's death in 1881 and remembered the circumstances attending the removal of the stock from Charlotte Street to their premises in Piccadilly.

19. This may be the moment to draw attention to a work that few except professional entomologists have ever seen. It is *Icones Ornithopterorum, a Monograph of the Bird-wing Butterflies of New Guinea*, by R.H.F. Rippon, in two volumes, with fan-

tastic illuminated frontispieces. No two copies are alike and it is conjectured that not more than thirty copies in all were completed. All were hand-painted by the author himself to subscriber's orders, and only as required, each copy taking several months to colour. This work, dealing with a race of butterflies as beautiful in their way as the humming-birds, is among the curiosities of literature, the motive behind its loving accuracy being deep religious conviction. It is sad to think that the loveliest of all the Bird-wing Butterflies of New Guinea was found after the author had died. I am indebted to the correspondent who drew my notice to this lesser marvel of the late Victorian age (1898–1906).

20. Descriptions of Gould's parrots and lories appear in *The Hunters and the Hunted*, London, Macmillan & Co., 1947, pp. 213–237; and in my *Tropical Birds*, in Batsford's Colour Series, 1948, pp. 3–7.

21. The plates from *Birds of New Guinea* were used, wherever possible, but in many instances the species were re-drawn, or drawn anew, by W. Hart, who had helped Gould in the preparation of his plates for more than forty years. I have been much helped in my remarks upon the birds of paradise by a recently published Australian book, *Birds of Paradise and Bower Birds*, by Tom Iredale, illustrated by Lilian Medland, Georgian House, Melbourne, 1950; and by an article, *Strange Courtship of Birds of Paradise*, by Dillon Ripley, with good paintings by Walter A. Weber, in the *National Geographic Magazine*, for February, 1950. For the habits and life stories of the birds of paradise, the modern authorities are indispensable. Wallace's *Malay Archipelago* (1869) is, however, still the best book to read for accounts of birds of paradise in their natural surroundings.

22. *Birds of Paradise*, by Tom Iredale, pp. 102, 103. Further quotation from p. 116. Further quoted on our pp. 47 and 49 from his p. 92.

23. Batjan, in the Moluccas, is more than two hundred miles west of New Guinea, and that distance remote from other birds of paradise. But there is a putative bird of paradise (*Lamprolia victoriae*), a little jet-black bird, much farther away than that, in the mountains of Fiji, nearly two thousand miles from New Guinea.

24. It is the same Joseph Wolf who drew the Greenland Falcon in hood of our pl. 36, from the *Traité de Fauconnerie*. His plates for that work, and for D. G. Elliot's *Pheasants* and *Birds of Paradise*, put him in the same rank as Audubon and Edward Lear as a bird-painter. J. Wolf was born at Mainz, Germany, in 1820 and died in 1899, but he did most of his work in England.

25. Two indispensable works on pheasants have been published in recent times. They are: *Pheasants, their Lives and Homes*, by William Beebe, published first of all, in a limited edition, and then with the two volumes in one, by Robert Hale Ltd., London, 1938; and *The Pheasants of the World*, by Jean Delacour, Country Life Ltd., London, 1951. This latter work, with coloured plates by J. C. Harrison, contains the sum of fifty years experience on the part of M. Delacour, who has maintained the biggest existing aviaries of these birds, and in the course of many expeditions to Indo-China has seen many of the rarest of them in their native haunts.

26. Delacour describes twelve races of the Silver Pheasants (genus *Lophura*), some of them but little known, and not yet brought to Europe or America.

27. One of the two most interesting ornithological discoveries of this century is that of the Congo Peacock (*Afropavo congense*). It was always thought that no bird of the pheasant family occurred in Africa. Dr James Chapin first saw a single feather of the Congo Peacock in the hat of a native in the Ituri Forest in the Congo in 1913. He put it away, and never forgot it. In 1936, in the Congo Museum, at Tervueren, near Brussels, he saw two mounted birds on top of a cabinet, and at once recognised them. They had been sent to the museum in 1900 by a Congo Mining Company. In 1937 Dr Chapin went, in person, to the Congo and obtained specimens. Living Congo Peacocks reached the New York Zoological Society in 1949. There is only one species of the bird, a big, 'primitive-looking' peacock, coloured green and brown and blue, but without a peacock tail (*The Pheasants of the World*, by Jean Delacour, Country Life Ltd., 1951, pp. 323–334). There is a colour plate of the Congo Peacock on p. 330. It may be imagined how much this discovery of an African peacock would have excited nineteenth century ornithologists. Another sensational discovery of our times is that of the supposedly extinct giant gallinule, *Notornis mantelli*, a giant rail native in the lake region in the southern part of the South Island of New Zealand.

28. A *Monograph of the Lories, or Brush-Tongued Parrots*, by St G. Mivart, 1896, has 61 plates by Keulemans and is, probably, his best work.

EDITOR'S NOTES

a. In the fall of 1988, an exquisite copy of Thornton's *Temple of Flora* sold in New York City for more than $200,000 (roughly £95,000).

b. Two of Gould's hummingbird glass cases are exhibited in the Bird Hall of the British Museum (Natural History). The interiors were rather more dusty in the fall of 1988 than the Museum corridors.

c. Matilda Hayes (1776–1827) was not the eldest daughter, but rather a middle child in the Hayes family (Jackson 1985, p. 283).

d. Volume I, published 1809–11, is not engraved in stipple (minute dots), but in parallel lines that imitate the filaments of actual feathers. These plates were printed in color, as were those of Levaillant's books. Six to eight colors of inks were applied to each plate, and the first edition of Volume I is considered one of the finest examples of color printing in a bird book.

e. Please refer to note d.

f. J. W. Ludlow's pigeons appear in R. Fulton and L. Wright, *The Illustrated Book of Pigeons*, 1876; his poultry appears in L. Wright, *The Illustrated Book of Poultry*, 1873. See Bibliography.

g. A superb example of Lear as ornithological draughtsman is his *Illustrations of the Family of Psittacidae, or Parrots* (1830–32), our plate 30. Lear was also the artist on stone for two illustrations to the works of John Gould that are among our plates: "Ramphastos culmenatus" appears on the dust jacket as well as serving for plate 32; the "Eagle Owl" is shown on plate 35.

PLATE CXXXVI

Meadow Lark. STURNUS LUDOVICIANUS, Linn. Male 1. Females 2. Gerardia flava.

Drawn from Nature by J.J.Audubon F.R.S.F.L.S.

Engraved, Printed & Coloured by R.Havell, London, 1827.

THE BIBLIOGRAPHY

by Handasyde Buchanan and James Fisher

THOUGH ONE OF THE COMPILERS of this bibliography is a bookseller and the other an ornithologist, we have found no difficulty in agreeing. First, we set ourselves the task of compiling a list of all *books* (but not all publications, for we have excluded series-periodicals) published between the years 1700 and 1900, inclusive. Secondly, we have made a subjective choice of some particular books to mark with one or more asterisks to denote that they are really fine; very fine books indeed, get two asterisks; and the finest of all, three. Neither of us has been in a moment's doubt about these 'awards'. We could not, *a priori*, take notice of the absolute merits of the text, since our outlook had to be aesthetic rather than scientific. Bannermans' *Birds of Tropical West Africa* (1930–51) is, purely ornithologically, of far greater importance than Levaillant's *Oiseaux d'Afrique*, as is Witherby's *Handbook of British Birds* (1938–41) than Gould's *Birds of Great Britain*; yet as examples of book production the latter are in a different class from their successors. The economics of publishing and bookselling have now entirely changed from those that obtained in the Age of Patronage, and a standard—indeed the only standard—that was possible in the eighteenth and early nineteenth centuries, when books were subscribed before publication to wealthy clients, who possessed *the money, the taste* and *the leisure* to enjoy them is not, at least by the first and last of those requirements, feasible today.

An age which could employ Capability Brown and Repton, and which could support aviaries such as those at Osterley Park and Knowsley, could also employ or sustain artists such as the Hayes family or Edward Lear and help them to produce fine books.

A 'Fine Book' is, in our meaning, one which is finely produced. Well printed on hand-made paper, preferably finely bound, it should be enjoyable to look at and to handle. The pictures must not only be well drawn but reproduced as near perfectly as possible. And if the pictures are of birds, or flowers, the nearer these can be to life size the more agreeable they will be; hence the large book—such as the masterpiece of Audubon—will (everything else being equal) always beat the small book. If we agree to this standard, the ascent of the coloured bird books is much the same as the evolution of flower books or other colour-plate books. It shows a general high level, slowly rising with the copper-plate engravings of the eighteenth century. Its peak was in the first thirty years of the nineteenth century with the French books, stipple-engraved or acquatinted, and partially printed, partially hand-painted, in colours; in this period, of course, the ordinary copper-plate books kept on. The peak had just been passed with the early hand-coloured lithograph books, in which the reproductions are still magnificent

---

PLATE 23

John James Audubon's The Birds of America *(London 1827–38)*
brought bird behavior to life for armchair naturalists.
Audubon positions these Meadowlarks to show the protective plumage of their grassy backs,
and the yellow shirt and black cravat of their breasts.
This bower scene benefits from Audubon's observation of birds in nature.

Iceland or Jer Falcon.
FALCO ISLANDICUS, *Lath.*

but the general style of the book is lower (book-lovers should compare a Gould with a Levaillant title-page or look at any page of the text). The final decline came at the end of the nineteenth century into chromolithography by which magnificent drawings—for instance those in Bowdler Sharpe—are reproduced much more cheaply and much less well, while the overall level of book production is distinctly less good. Bensley, in 1796, laid out the title-page of Miller's *Natural History (Cimelia Physica)*, while Manetti's *Storia Naturale degli Uccelli* and Nozeman's *Nederlandsche Vogelen* similarly have wonderful title-pages. Their successors seem to have given up bothering about such details.

The quality of the paper on which these various books were produced follows the same course; and bindings—though not perhaps so relevant to us—were, of course far finer in the eighteenth and early nineteenth centuries.

To collectors, or dealers, the rarity of a book must count for very much, quite irrespective of its other merits. Frisch's *Vorstellung der Vögel in Teutschland* is not only an attractive book but it is very, very seldom seen. And there is no doubt whatever that this makes it much more exciting, when we do see it, or possess it.

We hope it is fair to suggest that the standard, both typographical and reproductive, of the colour-plate book is now once more nearly capable of reaching the heights of the period 1766–1840; and that it is only the economic factor which prevents our reaching a high standard more generally and more often. But hand-colouring can rarely be excelled by printing.

A short justification of our bibliographical notes must be given. An early printed book needs very careful collation in that the pages are often unnumbered and its completeness can only be checked by counting the gatherings (or groups of leaves formed when the printed sheet is folded), each of which usually has a signature in the lower margin of the first leaf; this is a task not always easy.

A first edition possesses 'points': that is to say one edition of a book may have two or more title-pages, one of which appears in the first issue and one in the second; or it may have advertisement sheets of different dates bound in at the back; the text may vary; or even, as with the *Forsyte Saga*, a genealogical tree may pull out to the left or to the right! The presence or absence of half titles in a Jane Austen first edition is of considerable importance. Some colour-plate books such as the *Microcosm of London*, and Thornton's *Temple of Flora*, contain, in different copies, plates in varying states: extra work may have been done on the plates later or titles of plates may have been changed.

But with the exception of the great double-elephant Audubon we do not think that these special considerations apply seriously to any Fine Bird Books. As long as the book is complete, with title page, full consecutive text and a full set of coloured plates, and in fine condition, then it is as good as the next copy, save that variations of binding are of course important.

PLATE 24

John James Audubon silhouetted white birds against dark skies
to great effect in The Birds of America *(London 1827–38).*
Printmaker Robert Havell recreated the effect with aquatint etching
for this plummeting Gyrfalcon. Audubon's great skill allowed him to capture this instant
in the bird's descent as no artist had previously done.

In compiling this bibliography we soon realised that we were treading in the footsteps of devoted ornithologists and bibliophiles whose knowledge was far greater, and scholarship keener, than we could ever attain. We owe practically all to them. But it is true to say that no bibliography specially devoted to all Fine Bird Books with coloured plates has ever previously been compiled. In the nineteenth century, when such bibliographies were still possible, came the general zoological book-lists and collations of Carus and Engelmann, to whom we all owe so much, and the marvellous historical notes of Newton (1884, 1896), a bibliography in themselves. In the twentieth century we have only specialist bibliographies—but what models of excellence! The indefatigable Mullens and Swann (1917) wrote a bibliography of British ornithology that is more than a bibliography, for it goes into painstaking and useful biographical detail. In 1926 a library catalogue that, in our opinion, has never been excelled, was published: J. T. Zimmer's wonderful *Catalogue of the Edward E. Ayer Ornithological Library*. This two-part work of over seven hundred pages goes into immense collative detail, over the dating of text and plates; Zimmer is a notable systematist, and the proper naming of birds depends in many cases on the firm establishing of the actual date of publication of a description. Zimmer's researches on dates, conducted to aid the scientific ornithologist, are also of the utmost importance to collectors. In 1931 came another great library catalogue from across the Atlantic, Casey Wood's *Introduction to the Literature of Vertebrate Zoology*, with its accurate and comprehensive entries, and its useful and witty comments on the thousands of books listed. A little book purely on ornithological illustration (though not intended as a *catalogue raisonnée*) is the *Schöne Vogelbücher* of Nissen (1936) which we have found very useful; and Jean Anker's catalogue (1938) of the books containing plates (black-and-white as well as coloured) of birds and their eggs in the University Library at Copenhagen, is an admirable (and beautiful) work to which we have continually referred. In acknowledging the use of these and other works in the compilation of this Bibliography we would like to show our appreciation of the patent bibliophily of these bibliographers. It takes a book-lover to make a scholarly compilation and collation.

We would also like to thank Miss Scheffer of the Royal Zoological Society's Museum in Amsterdam for her notes on Barbara Regina Dietzsch; Mr. Lionel Robinson for his kind help on Audubon's *Birds of America*; and Major the Hon. H. R. Broughton for much encouragement.

SIZES

One of the most difficult problems which faces a bibliographer is to give an adequate, but not confusing, size of a book. The terms used to express size indicate the number of times which each sheet of paper used has been folded. Thus a folio is folded once producing two leaves (four pages); a quarto twice, producing four leaves; an octavo four times, producing eight leaves; and so on through 12mo, 16mo, 24mo, and 32mo.

The *American Century Dictionary* lists 30 different variations in the sizes 8vo and above. This tends to confusion, and more especially with old books which have in most cases been rebound, since the exact size (e.g., 30¾ × 21¼ ins.) could only be given if all copies were in their original uncut state.

Mr. John Carter says in his *A B C of Book Collecting* (Hart-Davis 1952) 'the object, after all, is to give a reasonably clear idea of the size of the book' and 'large folio, small folio, large quarto, small quarto are terms in constant use'. We are, therefore, following along these lines in describing the sizes, and further since with Bird books it is the size and not the precise number of times which the sheet is folded that is of interest, in a few cases we list what is technically perhaps an outsize octavo as a small folio, or a very small quarto as an octavo. This seems to us a common-sense practice, which is followed by the majority of booksellers as well as the great book auctioneers such as Sotheby's. For octavos alone we are using four specific terms, royal 8vo (aprox. 10 × 6¼ ins.), demy 8vo (approx. 8¾ × 5⅝ ins.), crown 8vo (approx. 7½ × 5 ins.) and foolscap (or post) 8vo (approx. 6¾ × 4¼ ins.).

Throughout the Bibliography, asterisks indicate that a plate number is repeated once (*), or twice (**), as in the entry for Vieillot (1805–*c.* 1809). In the subsequent entry for Vieillot (1807–*c.* 1809) the plate collation features the numeral suffix "bis" to indicate repeated plate numbers. Authors resorted to these bibliographic conventions when supplementing their publication with additional plates. Such plates often feature species variations made known to the author during the course of publication.

Pl. 14.

The Nebuleux shewing its finery!

Engraved & Published, by R. Havell, 77, Oxford Street.

THE BIBLIOGRAPHY

ADAM, VICTOR, see de BUFFON 1749 (1839)

ADAMS, HENRY B. see H. G. ADAMS, 1874

ADAMS, HENRY GARDINER
> FAVOURITE SONG BIRDS; CONTAINING A POPULAR
> DESCRIPTION OF THE FEATHERED SONGSTERS OF
> BRITAIN; WITH AN ACCOUNT OF THEIR HABITS,
> HAUNTS, AND CHARACTERISTIC TRAITS.
> INTERSPERSED WITH CHOICE PASSAGES FROM THE
> POETS AND QUOTATIONS FROM EMINENT
> NATURALISTS
> 16mo.
> London 1851.
> 12 coloured lithographs by Edward Gilks.

ADAMS, HENRY GARDINER
> NESTS AND EGGS OF FAMILIAR BIRDS DESCRIBED
> AND ILLUSTRATED; WITH AN ACCOUNT OF THE
> HAUNTS AND HABITS OF THE FEATHERED
> ARCHITECTS, AND THEIR TIMES AND MODES OF
> BUILDING
> Crown 8vo.
> London 1854.
> 8 coloured lithographs of eggs.
> New edition 1871, with 16 coloured lithographs.

ADAMS, HENRY GARDINER and CHARLES
WILKINS WEBBER
> HUMMING BIRDS
> Crown 8vo.
> London 1856.
> 8 coloured lithographs.

ADAMS, HENRY GARDINER and HENRY B.
> THE SMALLER BRITISH BIRDS
> Royal 8vo.
> London 1874.
> 32 coloured lithographs.
> Another edition 1894.

ADAMSON, CHARLES MURRAY
> SOME MORE ILLUSTRATIONS OF WILD BIRDS,
> SHOWING THEIR NATURAL HABITS
> Royal 8vo (oblong).
> London 1887.
> 24 coloured plates.
> Only 200 copies printed.

ALBIN, ELEAZAR
> A NATURAL HISTORY OF BIRDS WITH 306 COPPER
> PLATES, CURIOUSLY ENGRAVEN FROM THE LIFE. AND
> EXACTLY COLOUR'D BY THE AUTHOR, ELEAZAR
> ALBIN. TO WHICH ARE ADDED, NOTES AND
> OBSERVATIONS BY W. DERHAM
> 3 vols. 4to.
> London 1731–1738.
> 306 hand-coloured engravings by Eleazar and Eliz-
> abeth Albin
> (Vol. 1. 101; Vol. 2. 104; Vol. 3. 101).
> Volume 3 issued as a supplement but the book is
> imperfect without it.
> Second edition 1738–1740.
> French edition 1750.
> The earliest coloured book on British Birds.

ALBIN, ELEAZAR
> A NATURAL HISTORY OF ENGLISH SONG-BIRDS, AND
> SUCH OF THE FOREIGN AS ARE USUALLY BROUGHT
> OVER AND ESTEEM'D FOR THEIR SINGING. TO
> WHICH ARE ADDED, FIGURES OF THE COCK, HEN
> AND EGG OF EACH SPECIES, EXACTLY COPIED FROM
> NATURE, BY ELEAZAR ALBIN, AND CURIOUSLY
> ENGRAVEN ON COPPER. ALSO A PARTICULAR
> ACCOUNT HOW TO ORDER THE CANARY-BIRDS IN
> BREEDING; LIKEWISE THEIR DISEASES AND CURE
> 12mo.
> London 1737.
> 23 hand-coloured engravings.
> New editions 1741, 1759, 1779.
> Anonymous pirated editions 1754, reprinted 1776 and
> another edition 1791.

ALPHÉRAKY, SERGIUS
> UTKĪ ROSĪĪ (DUCKS OF RUSSIA)
> Small folio.

PLATE 25
The aquatint etching "The Nebuleux" illustrates
Robert Havell's A Collection of the Birds of Paradise *(London c. 1835).*
Havell published this book even as he etched the 435 prints of Audubon's The Birds of America.
The figures are reduced from prints illustrating
Levaillant's Histoire naturelle des oiseaux de paradis *(plate 18).*

St Petersburg 1900.
16 coloured lithographs.

ANDERSON, JOHN
ANATOMICAL AND ZOÖLOGICAL RESEARCHES:
COMPRISING AN ACCOUNT OF THE ZOÖLOGICAL
RESULTS OF THE TWO EXPEDITIONS TO WESTERN
YUNNAN IN 1868 AND 1875; AND A MONOGRAPH OF
THE TWO CETACEAN GENERA, PLATANISTA AND
ORCELLA
2 vols. Royal 8vo.
London 1878 (1879).
51 hand-coloured lithographs, 10 of birds by John
Gerrard Keulemans.

ANONYMOUS
COLLECTION D'OISEAUX INDIGENES ET EXOTIQUES
ODER SAMMLUNG IN- UND AUSLÄNDER VÖGEL
Folio.
Nuremberg 1786.
18 hand-coloured engravings.

ANONYMOUS
A NATURAL HISTORY OF BIRDS, CONTAINING A
VARIETY OF FACTS SELECTED FROM SEVERAL
WRITERS
3 vols. 12mo.
London 1786–1787.
113 hand-coloured engravings.

ANONYMOUS
ORNITHOLOGIE ABREGEE DE LA FRANCE,
CONTENANT LES FIGURES, ET LA NOMENCLATURE
EN UN GRAND NOMBRE DE LANGUES DE 134
ESPECES D'OISEAUX
4to.
Neuwied 1794.
134 hand-coloured engravings.

ANONYMOUS
THE NATURAL HISTORY OF BIRDS, FROM THE WORKS
OF THE BEST AUTHORS, ANTIENT AND MODERN
2 vols. 8vo.
Bungay 1815.
152 hand-coloured engravings.
Also London edition 1815.

ANONYMOUS
A TREATISE ON BRITISH SONG BIRDS
8vo.
London 1823.
15 hand-coloured engravings.

ANONYMOUS
THE ATLAS OF NATURE, BEING A GRAPHIC DISPLAY
OF THE MOST INTERESTING SUBJECTS IN THE THREE

KINGDOMS OF NATURE FOR STUDY AND REFERENCE
Folio.
London 1823.
83 engravings, mostly coloured, of which 13 coloured
plates are of birds.

ANONYMOUS
THE POETRY OF BIRDS SELECTED FROM VARIOUS
AUTHORS BY A LADY
8vo.
London (Ackermann) 1833.
22 coloured lithographs.

ANONYMOUS
BRITISH BIRDS
12mo.
London 1840.
24 coloured plates.

ANONYMOUS
AFBILDNINGER TIL FUGLENES NATURHISTORIE MED
OPLYSENDE TEXT. HEMPEL
Folio.
Odense, Denmark 1863.
30 coloured plates.
A translation of *Naturgeschichte der Vögel in Bildern* 1841
(cited by Anker, 1938, p. 93).

ANONYMOUS
DIE NESTER UND EIER DER VÖGEL; MIT 304
GRÖSSTENTHEILS NACH DER NATUR ENTWORSENEN
UND GENAU KOLORIRTEN ABBILDUNGEN. NEUE
AUSGABE
Sq. folio.
Stuttgart 1866.
8 coloured plates of eggs and nests.

ANONYMOUS
DIE NATURGESCHICHTE IN GETREUEN
ABBILDUNGEN UND MIT AUSFÜHRLICHER
BESCHREIBUNG DER-SELBEN. VÖGEL
4to.
Halberstadt n.d.
183 coloured plates.

ANONYMOUS
LES OISEAUX, DESCRIPTION DES PRINCIPALES
ESPECES DES OISEAUX D'EUROPE; DESSINS ET
GRAVURES DE PAUQUET FRERES
4to.
Paris n.d.
8 coloured plates by the Pauquets.

APLIN, OLIVER VERNON, see BUTLER 1896

APOSTOLIDOS, NIKOLAOS CHRISTO
THE ANIMAL KINGDOM (in modern Greek)
4to.
Athens 1885.
90 coloured plates, of which many of birds.

ARNOLD, FRIEDRICH
DIE VÖGEL EUROPAS. IHRE NATURGESCHICHTE UND
LEBENS WEISE IN FREIHEIT UND GEFANGENSCHAFT.
NEBST ANLEITUNG ZUR AUFZUCHT,
EINGEWÖHNUNG, PFLEGE, SAMT DEN FANG- UND
JAGDMETHODEN
4to.
Stuttgart 1897.
48 coloured plates.

ATKINSON, JOHN CHRISTOPHER
BRITISH BIRDS' EGGS AND NESTS, POPULARLY
DESCRIBED
Foolscap 8vo.
London 1861 (reissued 1862, 1866, 1870, 1886 and 1892;
revised edition 1898, 1904).
12 coloured lithographs by William Stephen Cole-
man.

d'AUBUSSON, LOUIS MAGAUD
LES OISEAUX DE LA FRANCE PREMIERE
MONOGRAPHIE; CORVIDES. HISTOIRE NATURELLE
GENERALE ET PARTICULIERE DES PASSEREAUX
DEODACTYLES CULTRIROSTRES OBSERVES EN
FRANCE
Folio.
Paris 1883.
20 plates, of which 18 coloured.

**AUDEBERT, JEAN BAPTISTE & VIEILLOT, LOUIS
JEAN PIERRE
OISEAUX DORES OU A REFLETS METALLIQUES
2 vols. Large folio and large 4to.
Paris. AN XI (1802).
190 engravings by Audebert, printed in colours, including gold, by a method invented by Audebert.
Vol. I. Histoire naturelle et générale des Colibris,
Oiseauxmouches, Jacamars et Promerops.
85 plates numbered 1–70, 1–6, 1–9.
Vol. II. Histoire naturelle et générale des Grimpereaux
et des Oiseaux de Paradis.
105 plates numbered 1–88, 26 bis. 1–16.
In the quarto edition the letterpress under the plates is
printed in black, in the folio edition in gold.
12 copies were issued with the complete text printed in
gold.
One copy was printed in gold on vellum.
Audebert died in the middle of publication—the book
was originally published in 30 parts—and the work
was continued by Vieillot, whom see also under his
own name.

Italian edition *Storia naturale generale dei colibri* etc.
2 vols. Folio Milan 1830–1840.

AUDOUIN, JEAN VICTOR, see de SAVIGNY 1810.

AUDUBON, JOHN JAMES LAFOREST
THE BIRDS OF AMERICA FROM ORIGINAL DRAWINGS
MADE DURING A RESIDENCE OF TWENTY FIVE
YEARS IN THE UNITED STATES
4 vols. Double elephant folio.
London, published by the Author, 1827–1838.
Originally published in 87 parts each with 5 plates.
There are thus 435 plates. These are engraved in aqua-
tint, and coloured by hand. Plate 64 is drawn by Lucy
Audubon, all the rest by J. J. Audubon.
The first plate was engraved by W. H. Lizars of Edinburgh in 1826 and the first version of the first five
plates published in July 1827 as Part I. But Audubon
had difficulties with delivery and was not satisfied
with Lizars's workmanship and transferred the busi-
ness, after Lizars had engraved Plates I–X (and perhaps, though not provedly, one or two more) to
Robert Havell and Robert Havell Junior of London,
trading as Robert Havell and son. Some customers
who opened their subscriptions after the beginning of
the series were supplied with versions of at least eight
of the original ten plates revised by the Havells.
There appear to have been at least three states of Plate
I. In the first the title is given as:—'Great American
Cock, Male, Vulgo (Wild Turkey) *Meleagris Gallopavo*', with the engraver's name Lizars: in the second
state the title is the same but 'Retouched by R. Havell,
Jr.' is added after Lizars. In the third state the words
'Great American Cock' are omitted.
The Havell-revised states of the first ten plates were
probably all published in 1829 (certainly this is so of
Plates II and VII). There appears to have been enough
stock of satisfactory copies of Plates VIII and IX engraved by Lizars, and we know of no copies of these
plates revised by the Havells, apart from slight alterations to the inscriptions.
The remaining ninety plates in Volume One were
engraved by the Havells, in most (and all the later)
cases by Havell Jr., Havell Sr. printing and colouring.
All the work from Volume Two onwards was done by
Havell Jr.; after Havell Sr.'s death in 1832 Havell Jr.
simply signed himself 'R. Havell', which has led to
confusion.
Dates of publication of the plates are as follows (those
marked with an asterisk are putative but unprovable
on present evidence).

VOLUME ONE (1827–30).

Part 1:	Plate I	Lizars July 1827, Havell 1829.*
	Plate II	Lizars July 1827, Havell 1829.
	Plates III–V	Lizars July 1827, Havell 1829.*
Part 2:	Plate VI	Lizars 1827, Havell 1829.*
	Plate VII	Lizars 1827, Havell 1829.

	Plates VIII–IX	Lizars 1827.	
	Plate X	Lizars 1827,	Havell 1829.*
Parts 3–5	Plates XI–XXV	1827 (all henceforth Havell).	
Parts 6–10	Plates XXVI–L	1828.	
Parts 11–15	Plates LI–LXXV	1829.	
Parts 16–20	Plates LXXVI–C	1830.	

VOLUME TWO (1831–34).

Parts 21–23	Plates CI–CXV	1831.
Parts 24–25	Plates CXVI–CXXV	1831.*
Parts 26	Plates CXXVI–CXXX	1832.*
Parts 27–31	Plates CXXXI–CLV	1832.
Parts 32–37	Plates CLVI–CLXXXV	1833.
Parts 38–40	Plates CLXXXVI–CC	1834.

VOLUME THREE (1834–35).

Parts 41–47	Plates CCI–CCXXXV	1834.
Parts 48–57	Plates CCXXXVI–CCLXXXV	1835.
Part 58	Plate CCLXXXVI	1835 though dated 1836.
	Plate CCLXXXVII	1835.
	Plate CCLXXXVIII	1835 though dated 1836.
	Plates CCLXXXIX–CCXC	1835.
Parts 59–60	Plates CCXCI–CCC	1835 though dated 1836.

VOLUME FOUR (1836–38, though 1835–38 on title page).

Parts 61–70	Plates CCCI–CCCL	1836.
Parts 71–80	Plates CCCLI–CCCC	1837.
Parts 81–86	Plates CCCCI–CCCCXXX	1838.
Part 87	Plates CCCCXXXI–CCCCXXXV	20 June 1838.

The plates are inconsistently (and in a few cases, wrongly) numbered in Arabic and Roman numerals: we know of sets numbered (a) I–X, 11–435; (b) I–LIII, 54, LV–C, 101–435; (c) I–X, 11–14, XV, 16–55, LVI–CCCCXXXV.

The Birds of America is an Atlas of Plates, and was published quite separately from and independently of any text, with the object of avoiding the expense of furnishing free copies to the copyright libraries of Britain, which, had the publication been a Book within the law of copyright, would have been compulsory. The corresponding text is a publication entitled *Ornithological Biography* . . . in five volumes (1831–39) of which the fifth concerns species not figured in the great double-elephant folio atlas. As this is not a Fine Bird Book in our definition we are fortunately excused the complex task of explaining its various editions and printings which, notwithstanding the lucid collation of Witmer Stone (1906) have given rise, in the words of Casey Wood, to 'a good deal of doubt and confusion . . . in the mind of the collector'.

The 435 engravings in *The Birds of America* contain 1,065 life sized figures of 489 supposedly distinct species. A few of these cannot be identified with existing known species.

It is unlikely that as many as two hundred complete sets were bound up, or that more than three hundred impressions were taken of any plate (even the earliest).

Yet the present total value of the published work of Audubon probably exceeds one million pounds sterling.

AUDUBON, JOHN JAMES LAFOREST, see BAIRD 1860, BONAPARTE 1825

BÄDEKER, FRIEDRICH WILHELM JUSTUS, CHRISTIAN LUDWIG BREHM and CARL WILHELM GOTTFRIED PÄSSLER
DIE EIER DER EUROPÄISCHEN VÖGEL NACH DER NATUR GEMALT
2 vols. in 1. Folio.
Leipzig and Iserlohn 1855–63.
80 hand-coloured lithographs by Bädeker.
Supplement (no plates) 1867.

BAILLY, JEAN BAPTISTE
ORNITHOLOGIE DE LA SAVOIE.
4 vols. 8vo.
Paris 1853–54.
110 coloured lithographs.

BAIRD, SPENCER FULLERTON, JOHN CASSIN and GEORGE NEWBOLD LAWRENCE
REPORTS OF EXPLORATION AND SURVEYS, . . . FOR A RAILROAD FROM THE MISSISSIPPI RIVER TO THE PACIFIC OCEAN . . . VOLUME IX . . . PART II . . . BIRDS (CATALOGUE OF NORTH AMERICAN BIRDS, CHIEFLY IN THE MUSEUM OF THE SMITHSONIAN INSTITUTION)
4to.
Washington 1858.
7 hand-coloured lithographs (38 plates in all).
Reprint 1858 with other title. Second edition much altered, 8vo. 1859. 1860 edition as (enlarged) *Birds of North America*, which see.

BAIRD, SPENCER FULLERTON, ADOLPHUS L. HEERMAN and C.B.R. KENNERLY
REPORTS OF EXPLORATIONS AND SURVEYS, . . . FOR A RAILROAD FROM THE MISSISSIPPI RIVER TO THE PACIFIC OCEAN . . . VOLUME X . . . REPORT(S) ON BIRDS COLLECTED ON THE SURVEY
4to.
Washington 1859.
25 hand-coloured lithographs.
For full collation of these *Pacific Railroad Surveys* (which also include Cooper and Suckley 1860 and Newberry 1857) see Zimmer (1926, pp. 646–48) and Anker (1938, pp. 113–14, 171).

BAIRD, SPENCER FULLERTON
REPORT ON THE UNITED STATES AND MEXICAN BOUNDARY SURVEY . . . VOLUME II . . . PART II . . .

BIRDS OF THE BOUNDARY . . . WITH NOTES BY THE
NATURALISTS OF THE SURVEY
4to.
Washington 1859.
25 hand-coloured lithographs (used also in *Birds of
North America* 1860, below).

BAIRD, SPENCER FULLERTON, JOHN CASSIN and
GEORGE NEWBOLD LAWRENCE
THE BIRDS OF NORTH AMERICA; THE DESCRIPTIONS
OF SPECIES BASED CHIEFLY ON THE COLLECTIONS IN
THE MUSEUMS OF THE SMITHSONIAN INSTITUTE
2 vols. 4to.
Philadelphia 1860.
100 hand-coloured lithographs of 'Birds not given in
Audubon', some of which from *Birds of the Boundary*
1859, others from *Pacific Railroad Survey*, above.
Plates numbered I–XXXVIII (*Birds of North America*).
I–XXIV (*United States and Mexican Boundary*).
LXIII–C (*Birds of North America*).
Second edition Salem 1870.

BAIRD, SPENCER FULLERTON, THOMAS MAYO
BREWER, ROBERT RIDGWAY, ELLIOTT COUES
and THEODORE NICHOLAS GILL
A HISTORY OF NORTH AMERICAN BIRDS
5 vols. Demy 8vo.
Boston 1874–75 and 1884.
Part I: Land Birds, 3 vols., first ed. (1874) with 64
plates and 573 woodcuts, all uncoloured; second
(1875) with 64 chromolithographs, 39 hand-coloured
and 437 uncoloured woodcuts.
Part II: Water Birds, 2 vols. (1884) and 493 woodcuts,
of which a varying number are found hand-coloured
(*e.g.* 0, 336, 457 in sets we know of).

BALDAMUS, AUGUST CARL EDOUARD
DAS LEBEN DER EUROPÄISCHEN KUCKUCKE. NEBST
BEITRÄGEN ZUR LEBENSKUNDE DER ÜBRIGEN
PARASITISCHEN KUCKUCKE UND STÄRLINGE
Royal 8vo.
Berlin 1892.
8 chromolithographs (of eggs) by W. A. Meyn.

BALDAMUS, AUGUST CARL EDOUARD, see
NAUMANN 1795 (1860)

BALL, HENRY LIDGBIRD, see PHILLIP 1789

BANNISTER, HENRY M., see DALL 1867

BARBOZA du BOCAGE, JOSE VICENTE
ORNITHOLOGIE D'ANGOLA OUVRAGE PUBLIE SOUS
LES AUSPICES DU MINISTERE DE LA MARINE ET DE
COLONIES
Royal 8vo.

Lisbon 1877–1881.
10 coloured lithographs by John Gerrard Keulemans.
(Plates I, III, IV, IX 1877; rest 1881).

BARKER, EDMOND, see EDWARDS 1758

BARKER-WEBB, PHILIP, SABIN BERTHELOT and
ALFRED MOQUIN-TANDON
HISTOIRE NATURELLE DES ILES CANARIES.
ORNITHOLOGIE CANARIENNE . . .
Large 4to.
Paris 1841.
4 coloured plates by Edouard Traviès.

BARTHELEMY-LAPOMMERAYE, CHRISTOPH
JEROME, see JAUBERT 1859

BARTLETT, EDWARD
A MONOGRAPH OF THE WEAVER-BIRDS AND
ARBOREAL AND TERRESTRIAL FINCHES
4to. 5 parts.
Maidstone 1888–89.
31 coloured lithographs.

BASCHIERI, ANTONIO, see GAZZADI 1843

BECHSTEIN, JOHANN MATTHÄUS
NATURGESCHICHTE DER STUBENVÖGEL ODER
ANLEITUNG ZUR KENNTNISS UND WARTUNG DER
JENIGEN VÖGEL, WELCHE MAN IN DER STUBE
HALTEN KANN
Foolscap 8vo.
Gotha 1795–1797.
Illuminated title and 4 hand-coloured engravings.
Other editions 1812, 1840, 1853 (English, incorporat-
ing Robert Sweet's *British Warblers*, which see), *c.* 1860
(English), 1870, 1879 (English), 1881 (English), 1900
(English), rising to 30 coloured plates.

BECHSTEIN, JOHANN MATTHÄUS
GEMEINNÜTZIGE NATURGESCHICHTE
DEUTSCHLANDS NACH ALLEN DREY REICHEN. EIN
HANDBUCH ZUR DEUTLICHERN UND
VOLLSTÄNDIGERN SELBST-BELEHRUNG BESONDERS
FÜR FORSTMÄNNER, JUGENDLEHRER UND
OEKONOMEN
4 vols. Crown 8vo, of which Vols. II–IV are *Gemein-
nützige Naturgeschichte der Vögel Deutschlands*.
Leipzig 1801–1809 (Vols. II–IV 1805–1809).
Vols. II–IV have 91 plates by Johann Stephan Capieux
and Haussen, of which 70 are coloured.
First edition 1789–1795 (no coloured plates).

BECHSTEIN, JOHANN MATTHÄUS
ORNITHOLOGISCHES TASCHENBUCH VON UND FÜR
DEUTSCHLAND ODER KURZE BESCHREIBUNG ALLER

Roseate Spoonbill.

VÖGEL DEUTSCHLANDS FÜR LIEBHABER DIESES
THEILS DER NATURGESCHICHTE
3 vols. 12 mo.
Leipzig 1802–1812.
39 hand-coloured and 7 uncoloured engravings.
Second edition 1811–1812.

BECHSTEIN, JOHANN MATTHÄUS, see LATHAM
1781 (1793), LEVAILLANT 1796 (1797)

BEECHEY, FREDERICK WILLIAM and NICHOLAS
AYLWARD VIGORS
THE ZOOLOGY OF CAPTAIN BEECHEY'S VOYAGE;
COMPILED FROM THE COLLECTIONS AND NOTES
MADE BY CAPTAIN BEECHEY, THE OFFICERS AND
NATURALIST OF THE EXPEDITION, DURING A
VOYAGE TO THE PACIFIC AND BEHRING'S STRAITS
PERFORMED IN HIS MAJESTY'S SHIP 'BLOSSOM',
UNDER THE COMMAND OF CAPTAIN F. W. BEECHEY,
R.N., F.R.S., ETC., ETC. IN THE YEARS
1825–26–27–28
4to.
London 1839.
44 hand-coloured lithographs by George Bret-
tingham Sowerby, and Edward Lear, of which 12 of
birds by Lear.

BEETON, SAMUEL ORCHART
BOOK OF BIRDS, SHOWING HOW TO REAR AND
MANAGE THEM IN SICKNESS AND IN HEALTH
8vo.
London n.d. (c. 1860).
5 coloured lithographs.

BEKKER, C. W. and BEKKER, Jr. see BORKHAUSEN
1800

BENDIRE, CHARLES EMIL
LIFE HISTORIES OF NORTH AMERICAN BIRDS, FROM
THE PARROTS TO THE GRACKLES, WITH SPECIAL
REFERENCE TO THEIR BREEDING HABITS AND EGGS
2 vols. 8vo. (size of large 4to).
Washington 1892, 1895.
19 chromolithographs of eggs from drawings by John
Livzey Ridgway.

BERNARD, PIERRE, JEAN JOSEPH LOUIS
COUAILHAC, FRANÇOIS LOUIS PAUL GERVAIS
and JEAN EMMANUEL MARIE LeMAOUT

LE JARDIN DES PLANTES. . . .
2 vols. 4to.
Paris 1842–1843.
In first vol. 16 plates of birds, of which 9 hand-coloured lithographs afterwards used in LeMaout 1853,
which see.

BERTHELOT, SABIN, see WEBB 1841

BESEKE, JOHANN MELCHIOR GOTTLIEB
BEYTRAG ZUR NATURGESCHICHTE DER VÖGEL
KURLANDS MIT GEMALTEN KUPFERN
Foolscap 8vo.
Mitau 1792.
6 hand-coloured engravings by C. Müller and W.
Waitz.
Second edition, Berlin 1821.

BETTONI, EUGENIO
STORIA NATURALE DEGLI UCELLI CHE NIDIFICANO
IN LOMBARDIA ETC.
2 vols. in 3. Large and double elephant folio.
Milan 1865–1871.
126 chromolithographs by Oscar Dressler.
Rare (only 100 copies issued).

BEXON, l'Abbé GABRIEL LEOPOLD CHARLES
AIME, see de BUFFON 1749, 1770

BIANCHI, VALENTIN L'VOVICH, see PLESKE 1889

BILLBERG, GUSTAV JOHANN, see PALMSTRUCH
1806

BLAAUW, FRANS ERNST
A MONOGRAPH OF THE CRANES
Large folio.
London 1897 (170 copies printed).
22 coloured lithographs by John Gerrard Keulemans
and Heinrich Leutemann.

de BLAINVILLE, HENRI MARIE DUCROTAY, see
VAILLANT 1841

BLAKSTON, W. A., WALTER SWAYSLAND and
AUGUST F. WIENER
THE ILLUSTRATED BOOK OF CANARIES AND CAGE-
BIRDS, BRITISH AND FOREIGN
4to.

PLATE 26
*John James Audubon painted his figures life-size
for* The Birds of America *(London 1827–38). Printmaker Robert Havell used paper
measuring 29½″ × 39½″ to equal Audubon's originals, from Chickadees to Whooping Cranes.
The long-legged, long-necked Roseate Spoonbill
thus stretches comfortably across its swampy home in characteristic feeding posture.*

London 1877–1880.

55 coloured lithographs.

New ed. 1890, 56 chromolithographs.

Foreign Cage-birds offprinted by Wiener, n.d., 18 coloured plates.

BLANCHARD, EMILE, see de SOUANCE 1857

de la BLANCHERE, PIERRE RENE HENRI MOULIN du COUDRAY

LES OISEAUX GIBIERS, CHASSE-MOERS-ACCLIMATION

Large 4to.

Paris 1876.

45 chromolithographs by Benjamin Fawcett.

Scarce.

BLANFORD, WILLIAM THOMAS

OBSERVATIONS ON THE GEOLOGY AND ZOOLOGY OF ABYSSINIA, MADE DURING THE PROGRESS OF THE BRITISH EXPEDITION TO THAT COUNTRY IN 1867–68

8vo.

London 1870.

6 coloured lithographs of birds by John Gerrard Keulemans.

BLANFORD, WILLIAM THOMAS

EASTERN PERSIA. AN ACCOUNT OF THE JOURNEYS OF THE PERSIAN BOUNDARY COMMISSION 1870–71–72. VOL. II. THE ZOOLOGY AND GEOLOGY

8vo.

London 1876.

10 hand-coloured lithographs by John Gerrard Keulemans.

BLASIUS, JOHANN HEINRICH, see NAUMANN 1795 (1860)

BLUMENBACH, JOHANN FRIEDRICH

ABBILDUNGEN NATURHISTORISCHER GEGENSTÄNDE

Demy 8vo.

Göttingen 1796–1810.

100 engravings, 19 of birds; 11 coloured, 9 of birds.

BLYTH, EDWARD and WILLIAM BERNHARD TEGETMEIER

THE NATURAL HISTORY OF THE CRANES

4to.

London 1881.

2 coloured lithographs.

BLYTH, EDWARD, see CUVIER 1817 (1840)

BOITARD, PIERRE

HISTOIRE NATURELLE DES OISEAUX DE PROIE D'EUROPE

4to.

Paris 1824.

15 hand-coloured engravings.

BOITARD, PIERRE

HISTOIRE NATURELLE DES OISEAUX D'EUROPE AVEC LA FIGURE DE CHAQUE ESPECE ET VARIETE, DESSINEE ET COLORIEE D'APRES NATURE

4to.

Paris 1825–1826.

18 hand-coloured engravings.

BOITARD, PIERRE and CORBIE

LES PIGEONS DE VOLIERE ET DE COLOMBIER

8vo.

Paris 1824.

25 hand-coloured engravings by Boitard.

*BOLTON, JAMES

HARMONIA RURALIS; OR, AN ESSAY TOWARDS A NATURAL HISTORY OF BRITISH SONG BIRDS: ETC.

2 vols. (usually bound together). 4to.

Stannary, nr. Halifax, published by the author.

1794–1796.

80 hand-coloured engravings (40 in each vol.) by Bolton.

Numbered.

Later editions.

1823.

1824.

1830 London: pub. W. Simpkin & R. Marshall.

1845 London: pub. Henry G. Bohn.

Plate 40, i.e., the last plate in Vol. I, is used as the frontispiece and is unnumbered.

**BONAPARTE, PRINCE CHARLES LUCIEN JULES LAURENT

AMERICAN ORNITHOLOGY; OR THE NATURAL HISTORY OF BIRDS INHABITING THE UNITED STATES, NOT GIVEN BY WILSON

4 vols. Folio.

Philadelphia 1825–1833.

27 hand-coloured engravings, from drawings by Titian Ramsay Peale, A. Rider and (plate 10) Audubon and A. Rider. This book was designed as a supplement to Alexander Wilson's *American Ornithology* (which see, in particular for later issues when both books were published together). It is not nowadays considered from a collector's viewpoint as complete in itself, i.e., without Wilson. It was originally intended to be issued in 3 vols. 1825–28, but is imperfect without the final volume, 1833.

*BONAPARTE, PRINCE CHARLES LUCIEN JULES LAURENT

ICONOGRAPHIA DELLA FAUNA ITALICA PER LE QUATTRO CLASSI DEGLI ANIMALI VERTEBRATI

3 vols. Folio.

Rome 1832–1841.

182 hand-coloured lithographs, 24 of which are of birds, by Petrus Quattrocchi and Carolus Ruspi.

BONAPARTE, PRINCE CHARLES LUCIEN JULES
LAURENT and HERMANN SCHLEGEL
MONOGRAPHIE DES LOXIENS
4to.
Leyden and Düsseldorf 1850.
54 hand-coloured lithographs by Schlegel and
Friedrich Wilhelm Justus Bädeker.

**BONAPARTE, PRINCE CHARLES LUCIEN JULES
LAURENT
ICONOGRAPHIE DES PIGEONS NON FIGURES PAR
MME. KNIP DANS LES DEUX VOLUMES DE MM.
TEMMINCK ET FLORENT PREVOST
Large folio.
Paris 1857–1858.
55 coloured plates, drawn by Paul Louis Oudart, F.
Willy and E. Blanchard and lithographed by Lemer-
cier.
A supplement to Knip and others 1809 (which see).

BONAPARTE, PRINCE CHARLES LUCIEN JULES
LAURENT, see AUDUBON, T. BROWN 1831, KNIP
1808, de SOUANCE 1857, WILSON 1808

BOOTH, EDWARD THOMAS
ROUGH NOTES ON THE BIRDS OBSERVED DURING 25
YEARS' SHOOTING AND COLLECTING IN THE BRITISH
ISLES
3 vols. Large folio.
London 1881–87.
114 hand-coloured lithographs by Edward Neale.
Plates dated by J. T. Zimmer (1926, pp. 80–81).

**BORKHAUSEN, MORITZ BALTHASAR, J. W.
LICHTHAMMER, C. W. BEKKER, GEORG
LEMBCKE and BEKKER Jun. (dem Jüngeren)
TEUTSCHE ORNITHOLOGIE ODER
NATURGESCHICHTE ALLER VÖGEL TEUTSCHLANDS
IN NATURGETREUEN ABBILDUNGEN UND
BESCHREIBUNGEN
Folio.
Darmstadt 1800–1817.
132 hand-coloured engravings drawn and engraved by
H. Curtmann, Johann Conrad Susemihl, E. F. Licht-
hammer, Johann Theodor Susemihl (brother of J. C.),
and Erwin Eduard Susemihl (son of J. C.). Published
in 22 parts of 6 plates each, of which 21 appeared in
1800–11; no. 22 (1817) is very rare, and the title-page
rarer. Often bound in two volumes.
A second edition 1837–1841.

BORRER, WILLIAM
THE BIRDS OF SUSSEX
Post 8vo.
London 1891.
6 chromolithographs by John Gerrard Keulemans.

BOUCHARD, MADDALENA
RECUEIL DE CENT-TRENTE-TROIS OISEAUX DES PLUS
BELLES ESPECES, . . .
Large folio.
Rome 1771–1775.
87 hand-coloured engravings by Bouchard. No text.

de BOUGAINVILLE, Baron LOUIS ANTOINE and
RENE PRIMEVERE LESSON
JOURNAL DE LA NAVIGATION AUTOUR DU GLOBE DE
LA FREGATE LA THETIS ET DE LA CORVETTE
L'ESPERANCE PENDANT LES ANNEES 1824, 1825 ET
1826 ETC.
3 vols. 4to and large folio.
Paris 1837.
13 coloured plates, 3 hand-coloured of birds, by P.
Bessa.

*BOURJOT SAINT-HILAIRE, ALEXANDRE
HISTOIRE NATURELLE DES PERROQUETS, . . .
LAISSES INEDITES PAR LEVAILLANT OU RECEMMENT
DECOUVERTES.
Large folio and large 4to.
Paris and Strasburg 1837–1838 [1835–1839].
111 hand-coloured lithographs by M. Werner.
Many of the plates in this book are lifted straight from
Lear's *Parrots* 1832, or from Temminck's big work—a
supplement to de Buffon—which appeared 1820–
1838. See also de Souancé 1857–58.

BOUTEILLE, HIPPOLYTE and M. de LABATIE
ORNITHOLOGIE DU DAUPHINÉ . . .
2 vols. Royal 8vo.
Grenoble 1843–1844.
72 coloured plates by M. V. Cassien.

BRANDT, JOHANN FREDERICK
DESCRIPTIONES ET ICONES ANIMALIUM
ROSSICORUM NOVORUM VEL MINUS RITE
COGNITORUM . . . AVES . . .
4to.
St Petersburg 1836.
6 hand-coloured lithographs from drawings by
Zagorsky and Wilhelm Georg Pape.

BRANDT, JOHANN FREDERICK
SPICILEGIA ORNITHOLOGICA EXOTICA
4to.
St Petersburg 1839.
4 coloured plates by Pape.

BRANDT, JOHANN FREDERICK
FULIGULAM (LAMPRONETTAM) FISCHERI NOVAM
AVIUM ROSSICARUM SPECIEM PRAEMISSIS
OBSERVATIONIBUS AD FULIGULARUM GENERIS
SECTIONUM ET SUBGENERUM QUORUNDAM
CHARACTERES ET AFFINITATES SPECTANTIBUS

Couroucou *temnure*.

Prêtre.

DESCRIPSIT
4to.
St Petersburg 1847.
1 coloured plate by F. Prüss.

BREE, CHARLES ROBERT
A HISTORY OF THE BIRDS OF EUROPE, NOT
OBSERVED IN THE BRITISH ISLES
4 vols. 4to (size of royal 8vo).
London 1859–1863. Though title pages vary, since the
book appears to have been completed in 1867.
238 wood engravings by Benjamin Fawcett printed in
colour.
Second edition 1875–1876. 253 coloured plates in 5
vols.

BREE, CHARLES ROBERT, see DesMURS 1886

BREHM, ALFRED EDMUND
DAS LEBEN DER VÖGEL DARGESTELLT FÜR HAUS
UND FAMILIE
8vo.
Glogau 1861.
21 tinted and 3 coloured plates.
Later editions 1867, 1878, 1890–93 (10 vols.), some
enlarged and several translations (English 1871–74,
1895; Danish 1871, 1876).

BREHM, ALFRED EDMUND
ILLUSTRIRTES THIERLEBEN. ALLGEMEINE KUNDE DES
TIERREICHS. . . .
6 vols. 8vo.
Hildburghausen 1863–1869.
37 coloured plates of birds by Robert Kretschmer and
E. Schmidt.
Many subsequent editions, 3 vols. popular, 8vo.
1868–70; second 10 vols. 8vo. 1876–80 (woodcuts);
third 10 vols. 8vo. 1890–93 of which *Die Vögel* 3 vols.
1891–92 with 29 chromolithographic plates after
Gustav Mützel, Kretschmer, Anton Göring, Ludwig
Beckmann and Christian Johann Kröner.

BREHM, ALFRED EDMUND and THOMAS RYMER
JONES
CASSELL'S BOOK OF BIRDS
4 vols. in 2. Demy 8vo.
London, Paris and New York, 1869–1873.
40 coloured lithographs.
Mostly translated from Brehm's *Illustrirtes Thierleben*,
above, Vols. 3 and 4.

BREHM, ALFRED EDMUND and FRIEDRICH
HERMANN OTTO FINSCH
GEFANGENE VÖGEL. EIN HAND- UND LEHRBUCH
FÜR LIEBHABER UND PFLEGER EINHEIMISCHER UND
FREMDLÄNDISCHER KÄFIGVÖGEL
2 vols. Royal 8vo.
Leipzig and Heidelberg 1870–1876.
1 coloured plate.

BREHM, CHRISTIAN LUDWIG
LEHRBUCH DER NATURGESCHICHTE ALLER
EUROPÄISCHEN VÖGEL
Foolscap 8vo.
Jena 1823–1824.
1 coloured plate.

BREHM, CHRISTIAN LUDWIG
HANDBUCH DER NATURGESCHICHTE ALLER VÖGEL
DEUTSCHLANDS, . . .
Crown 8vo.
Ilmenau 1831.
47 hand-coloured engravings by Friedrich Wilhelm
Justus Bädeker and Th. Götz.

BREHM, CHRISTIAN LUDWIG
HANDBUCH FÜR DEN LIEBENHABER DER STUBEN-,
HAUS- UND ALLER DER ZÄHMUNG WERTHEN
VÖGEL, ETC.
Demy 8vo.
Ilmenau 1832.
8 coloured plates by Götz and Bädeker.

BREHM, CHRISTIAN LUDWIG
MONOGRAPHIE DER PAPAGEIEN; ODER,
VOLLSTÄNDIGE NATURGESCHICHTE ALLER BIS JETZT
BEKANNTEN PAPAGEIEN MIT GETREUEN UND
AUSGEMALTEN ABBILDUNGEN, . . .
Folio.
Jena and Paris 1842–1855.
70 hand-coloured engravings.

BREHM, CHRISTIAN LUDWIG, see BÄDEKER
1855–63, THIENEMANN 1825

BRENCHLEY, JULIUS LUCIUS and GEORGE
ROBERT GRAY
JOTTINGS DURING THE CRUISE OF H.M.S. CURAÇOA
AMONG THE SOUTH SEA ISLANDS IN 1865
Royal 8vo.
London 1873.
39 coloured lithographs, of which 10 of birds by
Joseph Smit.

PLATE 27
Dutch ornithologist Coenraad Temminck collaborated with
Meiffren Laugier de Chartrouse for Nouveau recueil de planches coloriées d'oiseaux *(Paris 1820–39).*
"Couroucou" is one of its 600 bright color-printed and hand-colored engravings.
Jean Prêtre, a painter of vélins at the Muséum d'histoire naturelle,
contributed this illustration.

BREWER, THOMAS MAYO
NORTH AMERICAN OÖLOGY; BEING AN ACCOUNT
OF THE HABITS AND GEOGRAPHICAL DISTRIBUTION
OF THE BIRDS OF NORTH AMERICA DURING THEIR
BREEDING SEASON; WITH FIGURES AND
DESCRIPTIONS OF THEIR EGGS
Large 4to.
Washington 1857.
74 coloured lithographs by Otto Knirsch.
Reprinted plain in 1859.

BREWER THOMAS MAYO, see BAIRD 1874–75, 1884,
WILSON 1808 (1840)

BRITISH MUSEUM, CATALOGUE OF THE BIRDS
IN THE, see under SHARPE

BRODRICK, WILLIAM, see F. H. SALVIN 1855

BROINOWSKI, GRACIUS J.
THE BIRDS OF AUSTRALIA, . . .
6 vols. 4to.
Melbourne, etc. 1887–1891.
300 chromolithographs by Broinowski.

BROOKSHAW, GEORGE
SIX BIRDS, ACCURATELY DRAWN AND COLOURED
AFTER NATURE, WITH FULL INSTRUCTION FOR THE
YOUNG ARTIST; INTENDED AS A COMPANION TO
THE TREATISE ON FLOWER PAINTING
Folio.
London 1817.
6 coloured lithographs.

BROWN, PETER and THOMAS PENNANT
NEW ILLUSTRATIONS OF ZOOLOGY, CONTAINING
FIFTY COLOURED PLATES OF NEW, CURIOUS, AND
NON-DESCRIPT BIRDS, WITH A FEW QUADRUPEDS,
REPTILES AND INSECTS. TOGETHER WITH A SHORT
AND SCIENTIFIC DESCRIPTION OF THE SAME
4to.
London 1776
50 hand-coloured engravings by Brown, of which 42
are of birds.
Text in French and English. The book is a supplement
to George Edward's *Natural History of Birds*. It was
published by Gilbert White's brother Benjamin.

BROWN, Captain THOMAS
ILLUSTRATIONS OF THE AMERICAN ORNITHOLOGY
OF ALEXANDER WILSON AND CHARLES LUCIAN [*sic*]
BONAPARTE
Very large folio.
Edinburgh 1831–1835.
124 hand-coloured engravings, 16 of which were also
separately published in 1834 under the title *Illustrations
of the Game Birds of North America Chiefly the size of
Nature*. Edinburgh (very rare).
For collation see W. Faxon (1903, 1919).

BROWN, Captain THOMAS
ILLUSTRATIONS OF THE GENERA OF BIRDS,
EMBRACING THEIR GENERIC CHARACTERS; WITH
SKETCHES OF THEIR HABITS
Folio.
London 1845–1846.
56 coloured plates.

BROWN, THOMAS, see LAUDER 1833

BROWNE, ALEXANDER MONTAGU
THE VERTEBRATE ANIMALS OF LEICESTERSHIRE AND
RUTLAND
4to.
Birmingham 1889.
2 chromolithographs of birds.

BUC'HOZ, PIERRE JOSEPH
PREMIERE (& SECONDE) CENTURIE DES PLANCHES
ENLUMINEES ET NON-ENLUMINEES REPRESENTANT
AU NATUREL CE QUI SE TROUVE DE PLUS
INTERESSANT ET DE PLUS CURIEUX PARMI LES
ANIMAUX, LES VEGETAUX ET LES MINERAUX
2 vols. Large folio.
Paris (1775) 1781.
200 hand-coloured engravings, 26 of birds, by Des-
moulins.
The plates are usually found in two states, plain and
coloured.
A magnificent book, but birds are a sideline in it.
German edition: *Abbildungen der Vögel* etc. Nurem-
berg 1785.
40 hand-coloured engravings.

de BUFFON. Comte GEORGES-LOUIS LECLERC,
LOUIS JEAN MARIE DAUBENTON, PHILIB.
GUENEAU de MONTBEILLARD, l'Abbé GABRIEL
LEOPOLD CHARLES AIME BEXON and Comte
BERNARD GERMAIN ETIENNE de la VILLE
LACEPEDE
HISTOIRE NATURELLE GENERALE, . . . AVEC LA
DESCRIPTION DU CABINET DU ROI
44 vols. 4to.
Paris 1749–1804.
The nine volumes of birds (23–31) were published in
1770–1783.
New editions, German Leipzig 1750–82, 11 vols. 4to
of which birds three (9–11); French Paris 1752–1805, 71
vols. 12mo, of which birds 18 vols. (47–64). Many
other editions, for example:
Amsterdam 1766–99, 36 vols. in 19, 4to, of which
birds 9 vols. (16–24).
Berlin 1772–1809, 35 vols. 8vo. 1,575 Hand-coloured
engravings.
Deux-Ponts (Zweibrücken) 1785–91, 54 vols.
Foolscap 8vo, of which birds 1785–87, 18 vols. at least
109 coloured engravings.

Edinburgh 1791, 8vo (singing birds only).

Perth 1791, 2 vols. in 1, 8vo (abridged translation).

London 1792 (abridged translation).

London 1792–93 (birds only), 9 vols. 8vo. transl. William Smellie.

Paris 1793, 15 vols. 8vo (in English).

Paris 1799–1803, 80 vols. 18 mo, of which birds 16 vols., ed. R. R. de Castel.

Paris (1799) 1800–1805 (1808), 127 vols. 8vo of which birds 28 vols. (37–64) containing 256 hand-coloured engravings by François Nicolas Martinet. There was a papier velin edition of this with plates plain and coloured. Perhaps the best-known edition of Buffon, ed. Charles Nicolas Sigisbert Sonnini de Manoncour and Jules Joseph Virey and known as the 'Sonnini Edition'.

Paris 1807–11, 16 vols. 8vo (in English).

Alnwick 1814, 4 vols. 16 mo (abridged translation, contains some other matter).

Paris 1817–19, 17 vols. Post 8vo, of which birds 4 vols. (9–12) containing 126 coloured plates by Jean Gabriel Prêtre, ed. Comte Bernard Germain Étienne de la Ville Lacépède and known as the 'Lacépède Edition'.

Paris 1824–31 (1832), 26 vols. Post 8vo, of which birds 11 vols. (30–40; the numbering is from a collection including other addenda Suites à Buffon), containing 244 fine coloured plates by Paul Louis Oudart, ed. M. Lamouroux and known as the 'Lamouroux Edition'.

Brussels 1828–33. 20 vols. 8vo, a reset reprint of the above.

Paris 1825–28, 34 vols. 8vo, of which birds 10 vols. (20–28 and atlas), containing 118 coloured plates by Vauthier, ed. Baron Georges Léopold Chrétien Frédéric Dagobert Cuvier and Achille Richard and known as the 'Richard Edition'.

Paris 1839, 6 vols. Royal 8vo, of which birds 2 vols. (5, 6).

Paris 1839 (birds only) 8vo, (as Description des Oiseaux, suivie d'un Exposé de l'Art de les preparer et les conserver), two frontispieces and 38 hand-coloured lithographs by Victor Adam, ed. Joseph Achille Comte.

London 1841 (birds only), 8vo, the 38 hand-coloured lithographs by Victor Adam, ed. Joseph Achille Comte and transl. Benjamin Clarke.

Paris 1851–53, 5 vols. Large 8vo, of which birds 2 vols. (4, 5) with 37 hand-retouched colour engravings by Edouard Traviès and ed. Achille Richard (see 1825).

Paris 1852, 8vo, 150 hand-coloured plates by Victor Adam, ed. Joseph Achille Comte and Alcide Charles Victor Dessalines D'Orbigny (rare).

Brussels 1852, 9 vols. Royal 8vo, of which birds 2 vols. (8, 9).

Paris 1853–57, 12 vols. 4to, with coloured frontispieces and 150 hand-coloured steel plates engraved by Edouard Traviès and Henri Gobin, of which birds 4 vols. (5–8), ed. Marie Jean Pierre Flourens. One of the rarest and finest editions.

The 1,008 hand-coloured engravings for the first edition of this work, 973 of which are of birds, are by François Nicolas Martinet, and were published quite separately in two forms cited under E. L. Daubenton, which see, and below under Buffon, Montbeillard, Bexon and Daubenton. They were insufficient (see Zimmer 1926, p. 105) to provide a set for each copy and a new set of 262 uncoloured plates was made for the bird volumes; these used in some later editions of the bird volumes, e.g. London 1792–93, ed. William Smellie.

***de BUFFON, Comte GEORGES-LOUIS LECLERC, PHILIB. GUENEAU de MONTBEILLARD, l'Abbé GABRIEL LEOPOLD CHARLES AIME BEXON and EDME LOUIS DAUBENTON

> HISTOIRE NATURELLE DES OISEAUX
> 10 vols. in 20 (plates in separate volumes). Small folio, and 'grand-papier' folio edition.
> Paris 1770–1786.
> An edited version of the nine bird volumes of the Hist. nat. générale, above, with the 1,008 Planches enluminées drawn by François Nicholas Martinet from E. L. Daubenton's work (which see) including the 35 non-ornithological plates. This edition was certainly the most ambitious and comprehensive bird book which had appeared at the time of its publication, and ranks still as one of the most important of all bird books from the Collector's point of view.

de BUFFON, Comte GEORGES-LOUIS LECLERC, see BOURJOT SAINT-HILAIRE 1837, E. L. DAUBENTON 1765, DesMURS 1849

BUHLE, CHRISTIAN ADAM ADOLPH

> DIE NATURGESCHICHTE IN GETREUEN ABBILDUNGEN UND MIT AUSFÜHRLICHER BESCHREIBUNG DERSELBEN . . . VÖGEL
> 4to. (size of royal 8vo).
> Leipzig 1832–1835 (bird section of general work 1829–41).
> Published in 27 parts, 183 plates, sometimes coloured, not all, and often only partly.

BUHLE, CHRISTIAN ADAM ADOLPH

> NATURGESCHICHTE DER DOMESTICIRTEN VÖGEL IN ÖKONOMISCHER UND TECHNISCHER HINSICHT. EIN HAND- UND HÜLFSBUCH FÜR JEDERMANN BESONDERS FÜR STADT- UND LANDWIRTHE
> 6 vols. 8vo.
> Halle 1842–1845.
> 6 hand-coloured lithographic frontispieces from drawings by Johann Friedrich Naumann.

BUHLE, CHRISTIAN ADAM ADOLPH, see J. F. NAUMANN 1818

PLATE XLI

Ruffed Grouse. TETRAO UMBELLUS. Linn. Male 1, 2 Female 3.

BULLER, Sir WALTER LAWRY

A HISTORY OF THE BIRDS OF NEW ZEALAND

Large 4to.

London 1872–1873.

35 hand-coloured lithographs and 1 uncoloured by John Gerrard Keulemans.

2nd edition 1887–88, 2 vols. Imp. 4to, 50 plates (48 coloured) by Keulemans.

(A supplement was published in 1905–06 with 12 coloured plates by Keulemans).

BULLER, Sir WALTER LAWRY and FREDERICK WOLLASTON HUTTON

MANUAL OF THE BIRDS OF NEW ZEALAND

8vo.

Wellington 1882.

39 coloured plates, all but four photolithographs of plates by John Gerrard Keulemans in Buller 1872–73, above.

BURBACH, OTTO, see LENZ 1891

BURMEISTER, CARL HERMANN CONRAD

ZOOLOGISCHER HAND-ATLAS . . . VÖGEL

4to.

Berlin 1859–1860 (the general work 1858–61).

8 hand-coloured copperplates by Christoph Gottfried Andreas Giebel.

BURROUGHS, JOHN, see DOUBLEDAY 1898

de BUS de GISIGNIES, BERNARD LEONARD

ESQUISSES ORNITHOLOGIQUES; DESCRIPTION ET FIGURES D'OISEAUX NOUVEAUX OU PEU CONNUS

4to.

Brussels 1845–1848.

37 hand-coloured lithographs by G. Severeyns and J. Dekeghel.

BUTLER, ARTHUR GARDINER

BRITISH BIRDS' EGGS: A HANDBOOK OF BRITISH OÖLOGY

Post 8vo.

London 1886.

38 chromolithographs of eggs.

BUTLER, ARTHUR GARDINER

FOREIGN BIRDS FOR CAGE AND AVIARY

2 vols. 4to.

London 1890.

Coloured frontispiece.

BUTLER, ARTHUR GARDINER

FOREIGN FINCHES IN CAPTIVITY

2 vols. Folio.

London 1894.

60 hand-coloured lithographs by Frederick William Frohawk.

Second edition Hull and London 1899, large folio, in which the plates are reproduced by chromolithography.

BUTLER, ARTHUR GARDINER, OLIVER VERNON APLIN, JOHN CORDEAUX, HENRY OGG FORBES, Mrs ANNA FORBES, HUGH ALEXANDER MacPHERSON, MURRAY ALEXANDER MATHEW, HENRY HORROCKS SLATER, and WILLIAM BERNARD TEGETMEIER

BRITISH BIRDS WITH THEIR NESTS AND EGGS

6 vols. Large 4to.

London 1896–1898.

24 coloured lithographs of eggs and 318 uncoloured plates of birds by Frederick William Frohawk.

CABANIS, JEAN LOUIS, see von der DECKEN 1869, von TSCHUDI 1844

CAPEN, ELWIN A.

OÖLOGY OF NEW ENGLAND: A DESCRIPTION OF THE EGGS, NESTS, AND BREEDING HABITS OF THE BIRDS KNOWN TO BREED IN NEW ENGLAND, WITH COLORED ILLUSTRATIONS OF THEIR EGGS

Folio.

Boston 1886.

25 coloured plates of eggs.

CARPENTER, WILLIAM BENJAMIN, see CUVIER 1817 (1849, 1863)

CASSIN, JOHN

ILLUSTRATIONS OF THE BIRDS OF CALIFORNIA, TEXAS, OREGON, BRITISH AND RUSSIAN AMERICA

4to.

Philadelphia 1853–1856 (reissued in 1862 and 1865).

50 hand-coloured lithographs by George G. White.

CASSIN, JOHN

NARRATIVE OF THE EXPEDITION OF AN AMERICAN SQUADRON TO THE CHINA SEAS AND JAPAN . . . 1852–54, UNDER THE COMMAND OF COMMODORE M. C. PERRY . . . VOL. II . . . [PART] BIRDS

4to.

Washington 1856.

6 hand-coloured lithographs by William E. Hitchcock.

———

PLATE 28

"Ruffed Grouse" illustrated John James Audubon's
The Birds of America (London 1827–38). His birds are dynamic protagonists
flying, feeding, and courting in their natural surroundings.
This tableau shows two males lunging for wild grapes,
while a female stays out from underfoot.

CASSIN, JOHN, see BAIRD 1858, 1860, WILKES 1858

**CASTEELS, PETER
ICONES AVIUM
Folio.
London 1730.
12 hand-coloured engravings drawn by Casteels.
A companion volume to Robert Furber's *Twelve Months of Flowers*, and *Twelve Months of Fruit*, also drawn by Casteels. Very rare.

de CASTEL, R. R., see de BUFFON 1749 (1799)

de CASTELNAU, Comte FRANCIS L. de LAPORTE and MARC ATHANESE PARFAIT OEILLET DesMURS
EXPEDITION DANS LES PARTIES CENTRALES DE L'AMERIQUE DU SUD, DE RIO DE JANEIRO A LIMA, ET DE LIMA AU PARA; EXECUTEE PAR ORDRE DU GOUVERNEMENT FRANÇAIS PENDANT LE ANNEES 1843 A 1847, ETC . . . ANIMAUX NOUVEAUX OU RARES RECUEILLIS PENDANT L'EXPEDITION . . . OISEAUX
4to.
Paris 1856.
20 coloured lithographs.

CATESBY, MARK
THE NATURAL HISTORY OF CAROLINA, FLORIDA, AND THE BAHAMA ISLANDS: CONTAINING FIGURES OF BIRDS, BEASTS, FISHES, SERPENTS, INSECTS AND PLANTS: PARTICULARLY THE FOREST-TREES, SHRUBS, AND OTHER PLANTS, NOT HITHERTO DESCRIBED, OR VERY INCORRECTLY FIGURED BY AUTHORS. TOGETHER WITH THEIR DESCRIPTIONS IN ENGLISH AND FRENCH. TO WHICH ARE ADDED, OBSERVATIONS ON THE AIR, SOIL, AND WATERS: WITH REMARKS UPON AGRICULTURE, GRAIN, PULSE, ROOTS, ETC. TO THE WHOLE IS PREFIXED A NEW AND CORRECT MAP OF THE COUNTRIES TREATED OF
2 vols. Large folio.
London 1731–1743.
220 hand-coloured engravings by Catesby (109 of which are birds).
The earliest coloured book on American Birds.
New edition, revised by George Edwards 1748–1756, and a further edition 1771 both have the same number of plates.
Latin-German eds. Nuremberg 1750, 1777.

CATESBY, MARK see EDWARDS 1743 (1749 etc.)

CATLOW, MARIA E.
SCRIPTURE NATURAL HISTORY; CONTAINING A FAMILIAR HISTORY OF THE ANIMALS MENTIONED IN THE BIBLE

16mo.
London 1865.
6 coloured plates of birds.

CHAPMAN, FRANK MICHLER
HANDBOOK OF BIRDS OF EASTERN NORTH AMERICA WITH KEYS TO THE SPECIES AND DESCRIPTIONS OF THEIR PLUMAGES, NESTS, AND EGGS, THEIR DISTRIBUTION AND MIGRATIONS AND A BRIEF ACCOUNT OF THEIR HAUNTS AND HABITS WITH INTRODUCTORY CHAPTERS ON THE STUDY OF ORNITHOLOGY, HOW TO IDENTIFY BIRDS AND HOW TO COLLECT AND PRESERVE BIRDS THEIR NESTS, AND EGGS
Crown 8vo.
New York 1895.
2 coloured plates.
Many subsequent editions with increased number of colour plates.

CHAPMAN, FRANK MICHLER
BIRD-LIFE; A GUIDE TO THE STUDY OF OUR COMMON BIRDS
8vo.
New York 1897.
74 coloured plates by Ernest Seton Thompson.
New edition 1898.

CHENU, JEAN CHARLES, MARC ATHANESE PARFAIT OEILLET DesMURS and JULES VERREAUX [VERRAUX]
LEÇONS ELEMENTAIRES SUR L'HISTOIRE NATURELLE DES OISEAUX
2 vols. 8vo.
Paris 1862.
340 hand-coloured plates by Antoine Germain Bévalet from Gould, Audubon, etc.

CHENU, JEAN CHARLES, see DesMURS 1886

de CHERVILLE, GASPARD
LES OISEAUX DE CHASSE
Small 4to.
Paris n.d. (c. 1885).
34 coloured lithographs, 4 of eggs, by E. de Liphart.

de CHERVILLE, GASPARD
LES OISEAUX CHANTEURS
8vo.
Paris 1891.
12 coloured lithographs after Millot.

CLARKE, BENJAMIN, see de BUFFON 1749 (1841)

*COLLINS, CHARLES
ICONES AVIUM CUM NOMINIBUS ANGLICIS [TWELVE ENGRAVINGS OF BRITISH BIRDS].

Large oblong folio.
London 1736.
12 hand-coloured engravings.
Hardly a book and very rare.

COMTE, JOSEPH ACHILLE, see de BUFFON 1749
(1839, 1841, 1852)

COOPER, JAMES GRAHAM and GEORGE
SUCKLEY
THE NATURAL HISTORY OF WASHINGTON
TERRITORY,. . . . PARTS OF THE FINAL REPORTS ON
THE SURVEY OF THE NORTHERN PACIFIC RAILROAD
ROUTE, . . . PART III . . . ZOOLOGICAL REPORT . . .
NO. 3. REPORT UPON THE BIRDS COLLECTED ON
THE SURVEY
4to.
New York 1859.
10 plates, of which 8 hand-coloured lithographs. New
edition Washington 1860 (8 coloured plates only), as
*Reports of explorations and surveys, . . . for a railroad from
the Mississippi River to the Pacific Ocean. . . . Volume
XII. Book II. Part III. . . . Zoological Report . . . No. 3.
Report upon the birds collected on the survey.* See also
Baird.

COOPER, JAMES GRAHAM, see BAIRD 1859

COOPER, SUSAN FENIMORE
RURAL HOURS. BY A LADY. WITH ILLUSTRATIONS
8vo.
New York 1850.
20 coloured plates, of which 15 of birds.
Several subsequent editions.

CORBIE, see BOITARD 1824

CORDEAUX, JOHN, see BUTLER 1896

CORY, CHARLES BARNEY
BIRDS OF THE BAHAMA ISLANDS; CONTAINING
MANY BIRDS NEW TO THE ISLANDS, AND A NUMBER
OF UNDESCRIBED WINTER PLUMAGES OF NORTH
AMERICAN SPECIES
4to.
Boston 1880.
8 hand-coloured plates.
2nd edition 1890.

CORY, CHARLES BARNEY
THE BEAUTIFUL AND CURIOUS BIRDS OF THE
WORLD
8vo and double-elephant folio atlas.
Boston 1880–1883.
20 hand-coloured lithographs, of which 8 by Joseph
Smit.

CORY, CHARLES BARNEY
THE BIRDS OF HAITI AND SAN DOMINGO
4to.
Boston 1884–1885.
22 hand-coloured lithographs.

COSTA, ORONZIO-GABRIELLE
FAUNA DEL REGNO DI NAPOLI OSSIA
ENUMERAZIONE DI TUTTI GLI ANIMALI CHE
ABITANO LE DIVERSE DI QUESTO REGNO E LE
ACQUE CHE LE BAGNANO CONTENENTE LA
DESCRIZIONE DE NUOVI O POCO ESATTAMENTE
CONOSCIUTI CON FIGURE RICAVATE DA ORIGINALI
VIVENTI E DIPINTE AL NATURALE . . . UCCELLI
4to.
Naples 1857.
15 coloured plates by Salv. Calyó.

COTTON, JOHN
THE RESIDENT SONG BIRDS OF GREAT BRITAIN
2 vols. 8vo.
London 1835.
33 hand-coloured engravings.
2nd edition 1838.

COTTON, JOHN, ed. ROBERT TYAS
BEAUTIFUL BIRDS, THEIR NATURAL HISTORY
3 vols. 12mo.
London 1854–1856 (two publishers).
36 coloured lithographs by James Andrews.

COUAILHAC, JEAN JOSEPH LOUIS, see BERNARD
1842

COUES, ELLIOT, see BAIRD 1874

COUPER, WILLIAM, see SAMUELS 1883

la COUPRIERE, M.
MANUEL DE L'AMATEUR DES OISEAUX DE CHAMBRE
Post 8vo.
Paris 1832.
Coloured vignette title page and 4 coloured plates.

de COURCELLES, ANTOINETTE PAULINE
JACQUELINE RIFER, see KNIP

CRETZSCHMAR, PHILIPP JAKOB, see RÜPPEL 1826

CUNNINGHAM, ROBERT OLIVER
NOTES ON THE NATURAL HISTORY OF THE STRAIT
OF MAGELLAN AND WEST COAST OF PATAGONIA
MADE DURING THE VOYAGE OF H.M.S. 'NASSAU' IN
THE YEARS 1866–67–68–69
Post 8vo.
Edinburgh 1871.
21 plates, of which 5 coloured; 3 of birds.

PLATE CCVI.

Summer or Wood Duck.

ANAS SPONSA.

1, 2. Males 3, 4. Females.

Platanus occidentalis — Button-wood Tree.

Drawn from Nature by J.J.Audubon. FR.S. F.L.S.

Engraved, Printed, & Coloured, by R. Havell, 1834.

CUVIER, Baron GEORGES LEOPOLD CHRETIEN FREDERIC DAGOBERT and PIERRE ANDRE LATREILLE

LE REGNE ANIMAL DISTRIBUE D'APRES SON ORGANISATION, POUR SERVIR DE BASE A L'HISTOIRE NATURELLE DES ANIMAUX ET D'INTRODUCTION A L'ANATOMIE COMPAREE

4 vols. 8vo.

Paris 1817.

Two uncoloured plates of birds.

Some of the many later editions contain a considerable number of coloured bird plates. We may mention:
Stuttgart and Tübingen 1821–25, 4 vols. Crown 8vo (birds in Vols. 1 and 4), transl. and ed. Heinrich Rudolph Schinz.
London 1827–35, 16 vols. Demy 4to of which birds 3 vols. (6–8) containing 138 coloured plates, transl. and ed. Edward Griffith, with Edward Pidgeon, John Edward Gray and William Swainson. A classified index and synopsis to this was published in 1844.
Paris 1829–30, 5 vols. Demy 8vo, of which birds in Vols. 1 and 5 with two plates by Laurillard.
Paris 1829–38, 50 parts, 4to (large paper) and 8vo, containing 450 engravings printed in colour and re-touched by hand, of which 70 of birds, an *Iconographie* ed. Félix Edouard Guérin-Méneville.
Zürich and Leipzig 1830–36 (birds only), 2 vols. Folio (as *Naturgeschichte und Abbildungen der Vögel-Gattungen; nach der Natur*), 144 hand-coloured lithographs by K. Joseph Brodtmann, translated, edited and added to by Heinrich Rudolf Schinz (rare).
Leipzig 1831–43, 6 vols. 8vo, of which birds in Vol. I, transl. and ed. Friedrich Siegfried Voigt.
New York 1831, 4 vols., 8vo, transl. and ed. Henry M. M'Murtrie.
London 1834, the New York 1831 version.
Bruxelles 1836, 3 vols. 8vo.
Paris 1836–49, 22 vols. 4to, of which birds 2 vols. (supplemented by D'Orbigny's *Galerie ornithologique ou Collection d'Oiseaux d'Europe*) ed. by Alcide Dessalines D'Orbigny (whom see), with 102 plates, 95 of which are printed in colour and touched up by hand by Verner, Alcide Dessalines D'Orbigny and Edouard Traviès. The 'Disciples Edition' ('par une réunion de [dix] disciples de Cuvier').
Edinburgh 1840, in *Edinb. J. Nat. Hist.* 2: Folio, ed. William MacGillivray.
London 1840, 8vo, the birds ed. Edward Blyth, of which 66 wood engravings.
Berlin 1846, 8vo, only one vol. publ. ed. Aug. Vollr.

Streubel.
Zürich 1846–53 (birds only), 2 vols. Crown folio and royal 4to, as *Naturgeschichte der Vögel*, an improved ed. of Zürich 1830–36, above, with 125 coloured plates, ed etc. Heinrich Rudolf Schinz 'The earlier plates are passably good but the less said of the later ones the better.' Zimmer (1926, p. 552).
From London there were further editions by two different publishers in 1849, one in 1851 (with 28 coloured plates) and another in 1863; all ed. and added to by William Benjamin Carpenter and John Obadiah Westwood.

CUVIER, Baron G. L. C. F. D., see de BUFFON 1749 (1825)

DALL, WILLIAM HEALEY and HENRY M. BANNISTER

LIST OF THE BIRDS OF ALASKA, WITH BIOGRAPHICAL NOTES

4to.

Chicago 1867–1869 (*Trans. Chicago Acad. Sci.* 1: 267–324).

8 coloured plates by Edwin Sheppard.

Rare. Less than 25 copies with title survived in 1870.

DALLAS, WILLIAM S. ed. JOHN RICHARDSON

THE MUSEUM OF NATURAL HISTORY; . . . BIRDS

4to.

London c. 1868.

Part of Vol. I (pp. 229–432) of a two-volume general work, first published Glasgow 1859–62. Present edition has 31 bird plates, of which 7 coloured.

DALMAN, JOHAN WILHELM, see PALMSTRUCH 1806

van DAM, D. C. see POLLEN 1867

DARWIN, CHARLES, JOHN GOULD, THOMAS CAMPBELL EYTON and GEORGE ROBERT GRAY

THE ZOOLOGY OF THE VOYAGE OF H.M.S. BEAGLE, UNDER THE COMMAND OF CAPTAIN FITZROY, R.N., DURING THE YEARS 1832 TO 1836. . . . PART III. BIRDS

4to. (5 parts in 3 vols.)

London 1838–1841.

50 hand-coloured lithographs from sketches by John Gould: lithographed by E. Gould.

The whole of Darwin's report consisted of 5 parts, and was originally issued in numbers of which 3, 6, 9, 11 and 15 contained the ornithological section.

PLATE 29

The Wood Duck's colorful plumage is drawn with great detail in John James Audubon's The Birds of America *(London 1827–38).*
The duck's aerial nest is sited in the hollow branch of a sycamore tree.
The wealth of information conveyed in this image bears comparison with Manetti's earlier print, our plate 7.

***DAUBENTON, EDME LOUIS
[PLANCHES ENLUMINEES D'HISTOIRE NATURELLE].
Large and small folio.
Paris 1765–1781 (perhaps to 1783).
1,008 very fine hand-coloured engravings (973 of birds) drawn and engraved by François Nicolas Martinet, published without title-page in 42 parts as the illustrations to the first edition of the *Hist. nat. générale* of de Buffon and others, which see; and later combined with the bird volumes of that work as the *Hist. nat. Oiseaux* of de Buffon and others, which see. Admirable analysis of the complex relationships of these works in J. T. Zimmer (1926, pp. 104–06). Interesting early analysis and re-naming of plates by P. Boddaert (1783, 1874).

DAUBENTON, EDME LOUIS, see de BUFFON 1770

DAUBENTON, LOUIS JEAN MARIE, see de BUFFON 1749

DAUDIN, FRANÇOIS MARIE
TRAITE ELEMENTAIRE ET COMPLET D'ORNITHOLOGIE OU HISTOIRE NATURELLE DES OISEAUX
2 vols. 4to.
Paris An VIII (1800).
29 hand-coloured engravings by Jacques Barraband. Scarce.

DAVID, ARMAND and EMILE OUSTALET
LES OISEAUX DE LA CHINE
2 vols. 8vo text, and royal 8vo plates.
Paris 1877.
124 hand-coloured lithographs by Arnoul.

DAVIES, HUGH, see LATHAM 1795, PENNANT 1769

von der DECKEN, Baron CARL CLAUS, JEAN LOUIS CABANIS, FRIEDRICH HERMANN OTTO FINSCH and GUSTAV HARTLAUB
REISEN IN OST-AFRIKA IN DEN JAHREN 1859–1865. HERAUSGEGEBEN IM AUFTRAGE DER MUTTER DES REISENDEN, FÜRSTIN ADELHEID VON PLESS. WISSENSCHAFTLICHER THEIL. VOLS. III & IV. VÖGEL
Royal 8vo.
Leipzig and Heidelberg 1869–1870.
29 chromolithographs by Finsch.

DeKAY, JAMES ELLSWORTH
THE NATURAL HISTORY OF THE STATE OF NEW YORK—THE ZOOLOGY OF NEW-YORK, OR THE NEW-YORK FAUNA; . . . PART II. BIRDS
1 vol. in 2, 4to.
Albany 1844.
141 hand-coloured lithographs from drawings by John William Hill.

DERHAM, WILLIAM, see ALBIN 1731–38

*DESCOURTILZ, JEAN THEODORE
OISEAUX BRILLANS DU BRESIL
Folio.
Paris 1834.
60 hand-coloured lithographs designed by Descourtilz.

**DESCOURTILZ, JEAN THEODORE
ORNITHOLOGIE BRESILIENNE OU HISTOIRE DES OISEAUX DU BRESIL, REMARQUABLES PAR LEUR PLUMAGE, LEUR CHANT OU LEURS HABITUDES
Very large folio.
Rio de Janeiro 1854–1856.
48 hand-coloured lithographs designed by Descourtilz.
Issued in 4 parts. English edition with the same illustrations, printed by Waterlow and Sons and published under the title *Brasilian Ornithology* appeared in 1856.

**DESMAREST, ANSELME-GAËTAN
HISTOIRE NATURELLE DES TANGARES, DES MANAKINS ET DES TODIERS
Large folio.
Paris AN XIII 1805(–1807).
72 plates printed in colour from drawings by Antoinette Pauline Jacqueline Rifer de Courcelles (Madame Knip, whom see).
Originally issued in 12 parts.

*DesMURS, MARC ATHANESE PARFAIT OEILLET
ICONOGRAPHIE ORNITHOLOGIQUE NOUVEAU RECUEIL GENERAL DE PLANCHES PEINTES D'OISEAUX, POUR SERVIR DE SUITE ET DE COMPLEMENT AUX PLANCHES ENLUMINEES DE BUFFON, . . . ET AUX PLANCHES COLORIEES DE MM. TEMMINCK ET LAUGIER DE CHARTROUSE, ETC.
Folio.
Paris 1849 (originally issued in parts 1845–1849).
72 coloured lithographs, 24 by Alphonse Prévost, 48 by Paul Louis Oudart. A supplement to Temminck 1820–39 and Buffon 1770–83, which see.

DesMURS, MARC ATHANESE PARFAIT OEILLET, JEAN CHARLES CHENU and JULES VERREAUX (VERRAUX)
MUSEE ORNITHOLOGIQUE ILLUSTRE; DESCRIPTION DES OISEAUX D'EUROPE, DE LEURS ŒUFS ET DE LEURS NIDS
4 vols. in 5. 4to.
Paris 1886.
345 coloured lithographs, mostly taken from Francis Orpen Morris 1866, 1870, and Charles Robert Bree 1859, which see.

DesMURS, MARC ATHANESE PARFAIT OEILLET,
see de CASTELNAU 1856, CHENU 1862, GAY 1844, de
PETIT-THOUARS 1846

DIETZ, H. see PRÜTZ 1887

**DIETZSCH, BARBARA REGINA, ADAM LUDWIG
WIRSING and BENEDICT CHRISTIAN VOGEL
    SAMMLUNG MEISTENS DEUTSCHER VÖGEL
    2 vols. Folio.
    Nuremberg 1772 (–76).
    50 hand-coloured engravings.
    A rare book with very fine coloured title pages. In the
    Royal Zoological Society's Museum at Amsterdam
    there is a copy of this book with 100 plates in 4 vol-
    umes. The text, however, is only for the first 50 plates.
    No other such copy is known and it is likely that this is
    unique. The plates are drawn by J. M. Seligmann,
    Barbara Regina Dietzsch and others. All engravings
    by Adam Ludwig Wirsing.
    A copy with 50 plates, must, from a collectors point of
    view be considered complete.

DIGGLES, SILVESTER
    COMPANION TO GOULD'S HANDBOOK; OR,
    SYNOPSIS OF THE BIRDS OF AUSTRALIA
    2 vols. Large folio.
    Brisbane 1866–1870.
    126 coloured lithographs by H. G. Eaton.
    First published in parts. 2nd ed. 1877 with 3 plates
    omitted.

DILLWYN, LEWIS LLEWELLYN see JAMES MOTLEY
1855

DIXON, CHARLES
    THE NESTS AND EGGS OF BRITISH BIRDS, WHEN AND
    WHERE TO FIND THEM
    8vo.
    London 1894.
    12 coloured lithographs of eggs.

DIXON, CHARLES
    THE NESTS AND EGGS OF NON-INDIGENOUS BRITISH
    BIRDS OR SUCH SPECIES THAT DO NOT BREED
    WITHIN THE BRITISH ARCHIPELAGO
    8vo.
    London 1894.
    Coloured frontispiece of eggs.

DIXON, CHARLES
    THE GAME BIRDS AND WILD FOWL OF THE BRITISH
    ISLANDS
    Large 8vo (also 4to and folio).
    London 1895.
    13 coloured plates
    Earlier edition (no plates) 1893; later edition Sheffield
    1900.
    41 coloured plates by Charles Whymper.

DIXON, CHARLES, see SEEBOHM 1882

*DONOVAN, EDWARD
    THE NATURAL HISTORY OF BRITISH BIRDS; OR A
    SELECTION OF THE MOST RARE, BEAUTIFUL, AND
    INTERESTING BIRDS WHICH INHABIT THIS COUNTRY:
    ETC.
    10 vols. in 5. 4to.
    London 1794–1819.
    244 hand-coloured engravings.
    Re-issue of Vols. 1–5, 1799.
    Re-issue of Vols. 1–10, 1815–1820.

DONOVAN, EDWARD
    NATURAL HISTORY OF THE NESTS AND EGGS OF
    BRITISH BIRDS
    Vol. I (all issued) Post 8vo.
    London 1826.
    17 hand-coloured engravings.

DONOVAN, EDWARD
    THE NATURALIST'S REPOSITORY, OR MISCELLANY OF
    EXOTIC NATURAL HISTORY, EXHIBITING RARE AND
    BEAUTIFUL SPECIMENS OF FOREIGN BIRDS, INSECTS,
    SHELLS, QUADRUPEDS, FISHES, AND MARINE
    PRODUCTIONS; ETC.
    5 vols. 4to (size of 8vo).
    London 1822–1826.
    180 hand-coloured engravings, 28 of them showing
    birds.
    Reissue 1834.

D'ORBIGNY, ALCIDE CHARLES VICTOR
DESSALINES (ed.)
    DICTIONNAIRE UNIVERSEL D'HISTOIRE NATURELLE
    16 vols. Royal 8vo.
    Paris 1837.
    288 coloured plates, many of birds.
    Many other editions, e.g., 1849, 13 vols., 300 coloured
    plates.

D'ORBIGNY, ALCIDE CHARLES VICTOR
DESSALINES, see de BUFFON 1749 (1852)

D'ORBIGNY, ALCIDE DESSALINES
    VOYAGE DANS L'AMERIQUE MERIDIONALE . . .
    EXECUTE . . . 1826–33 . . . VOL. IV. PART III . . .
    OISEAUX . . . VOL. IX. ATLAS ZOOLOGIQUE
    Large 4to.
    Paris 1835–1847.
    67 colour-printed engravings in Atlas (1847) by Lang-
    lois and Folliau.

D'ORBIGNY, ALCIDE DESSALINES
    GALERIE ORNITHOLOGIQUE OU COLLECTION
    D'OISEAUX D'EUROPE
    4to.

Paris 1836–1839.
106 coloured plates by Edouard Traviès, Thiolat and J. Delarue, as cited by Nissen (1936, p. 44). Appears to be a supplement or companion to D'Orbigny's contemporaneous edition (the 'Disciples Edition') of Cuvier's *Règne animal*, which see.

D'ORBIGNY, ALCIDE DESSALINES, see CUVIER 1817 (1836), de la SAGRA 1839

DOUBLEDAY, Mrs NELLIE and JOHN BURROUGHS
BIRD NEIGHBOURS
8vo.
London 1898.
52 coloured plates.

D'OYLY, Sir C., see C. W. SMITH 1829

DRAPIEZ, AUGUST JOS.
ICONOGRAPHIE DES OISEAUX OU COLLECTION DE FIGURES REPRESENTANT LES OISEAUX QUI PEUVENT SERVIR DE TYPES POUR CHAQUE FAMILLE
32mo.
Paris 1829.
48 coloured plates.

DRESSER, HENRY EELES, RICHARD BOWDLER SHARPE, and ARTHUR HAY Viscount WALDEN
A HISTORY OF THE BIRDS OF EUROPE, INCLUDING ALL THE SPECIES INHABITING THE WESTERN PALÆARCTIC REGION
9 vols. including Supplement. Large 4to.
London 1871–1896.
720 hand-coloured lithographs, by John Gerrard Keulemans, Joseph Wolf, Edward Neale, Archibald Thorburn and others.
Originally published in 93 parts.

DRESSER, HENRY EELES
A MONOGRAPH OF THE MEROPIDÆ, OR FAMILY OF THE BEE-EATERS
Large 4to.
London 1884–1886.
34 hand-coloured lithographs by Keulemans.

DRESSER, HENRY EELES
A MONOGRAPH OF THE CORACIIDÆ, OR FAMILY OF THE ROLLERS
Large 4to.
Farnborough, Kent 1893.
27 hand-coloured lithographs by Keulemans.

DUBOIS, ALPHONSE JOSEPHE CHARLES
FAUNE ILLUSTREE DES VERTEBRES DE LA BELGIQUE: OISEAUX

2 vols. 4to.
Brussels 1876–1894.
400 coloured lithographs.

DUBOIS, ALPHONSE JOSEPHE CHARLES
SYNOPSIS AVIUM. NOUVEAU MANUEL D'ORNITHOLOGIE
2 vols. 4to.
Brussels 1899–1904.
Issued in 17 parts; 16 coloured plates by Dubois.

DUBOIS, ALPHONSE JOSEPHE CHARLES, see C. F. DUBOIS 1861

DUBOIS, CHARLES FREDERIC
ORNITHOLOGISCHE GALLERIE ODER ABBILDUNGEN ALLER BEKANNTEN VÖGEL
4to (published in 22 parts).
Aix and Leipzig 1836–1839.
132 hand-coloured lithographs designed by Dubois.

DUBOIS, CHARLES FREDERIC
NATURGESCHICHTE DER VÖGEL EUROPAS
4to (1 part only).
Aix 1835.
8 hand-coloured lithographs designed by Dubois.

DUBOIS, CHARLES FREDERIC
PLANCHES COLORIEES DES OISEAUX DE LA BELGIQUE ET DE LEURS ŒUFS
3 vols. Royal 8vo.
Brussels and Leipzig 1854–1860.
429 hand-coloured lithographs designed by Dubois.

DUBOIS, CHARLES FREDERIC and ALPHONSE JOSEPHE CHARLES
LES OISEAUX DE L'EUROPE ET DE LEURS ŒUFS
2 vols. Royal 8vo.
Brussels 1861–1872.
200 hand-coloured lithographs designed by father and son.

DUMONT D'URVILLE, JULES SEBASTIEN CESAR, JEAN RENE CONSTANT QUOY and JEAN PAUL GAIMARD
VOYAGE DE DECOUVERTES DE L'ASTROLABE EXECUTE PAR ORDRE DU ROI, PENDANT LES ANNEES 1826–1827–1828–1829 . . .
4 vols. 8vo text and large folio atlas.
Paris 1830–1835.
Birds in Vol. 1, in which 31 coloured plates by Jean Gabriel Prêtre, Alphonse Prévost and Paul Louis Oudart.

DUMONT D'URVILLE, JULES SEBASTIEN CESAR, J. B. HOMBRON, C. HONORE JACQUINOT and JACQUES PUCHERAN

VOYAGE AU POLE SUD ET DANS L'OCEANIE SUR LES CORVETTES L'ASTROLABE ET LA ZELEE; EXECUTE PAR ORDRE DU ROI PENDANT LES ANNEES 1837–1838–1839–1840. . .
7 vols. in 6. 8vo and large folio.
Paris 1842–1854.
Birds in Vol. 3 and Atlas; 36 coloured plates by Oudart, Johann Carl Werner and Prévost.

DUPERREY, LOUIS ISIDORE, RENE PRIMEVERE LESSON and PROSPER GARNOT
VOYAGE AUTOUR DU MONDE, EXECUTE PAR ORDRE DU ROI, SUR LA CORVETTE DE SA MAJESTE, LA COQUILLE, PENDANT LES ANNEES 1822, 1823, 1824 ET 1825, . . . ZOOLOGIE
2 vols. and atlas in 5. Folio.
Paris 1826–1830.
44 coloured plates of birds by Prêtre and Prévost.

DURAND, DAVID, see EDWARDS 1743 (1745)

D'URBAN, WILLIAM STEWART MITCHELL and MURRAY ALEXANDER MATHEW
THE BIRDS OF DEVON
Post 8vo.
London 1892.
4 chromolithographs by John Gerrard Keulemans.
Second edition 1895.

DUTTON, F. G., see GREENE 1883

EATON, JOHN MATTHEWS and JOHN MOORE
A TREATISE ON THE ART OF BREEDING AND MANAGING TAME, DOMESTICATED, FOREIGN, AND FANCY PIGEONS, ETC.
Post 8vo.
London 1858.
18 hand-coloured engravings by D. Wolstenholme.

**EDWARDS, GEORGE
A NATURAL HISTORY OF UNCOMMON BIRDS, AND OF SOME OTHER RARE AND UNDESCRIBED ANIMALS, QUADRUPEDS, REPTILES, FISHES, INSECTS, ETC., EXHIBITED IN TWO HUNDRED AND TEN COPPER-PLATES, FROM DESIGNS COPIED IMMEDIATELY FROM NATURE, AND CURIOUSLY COLOURED AFTER LIFE. WITH A FULL AND ACCURATE DESCRIPTION OF EACH FIGURE. TO WHICH IS ADDED, A BRIEF AND GENERAL IDEA OF DRAWING AND PAINTING IN WATER-COLOURS; WITH INSTRUCTIONS FOR ETCHING ON COPPER WITH AQUA FORTIS: LIKEWISE SOME THOUGHTS ON THE PASSAGE OF BIRDS; AND ADDITIONS TO MANY OF THE SUBJECTS DESCRIBED IN THIS WORK
4 parts in 2 vols. Small folio (4to size).
London 1743–1751.
and

GLEANINGS OF NATURAL HISTORY, EXHIBITING FIGURES OF QUADRUPEDS, BIRDS, INSECTS, PLANTS, ETC. MOST OF WHICH HAVE NOT, TILL NOW, BEEN EITHER FIGURED OR DESCRIBED, ETC.
3 parts in 3 vols. Small folio (4to size).
London 1758–1764.

Text in English and French, the French transl. by J. du Plessis and Edmond Barker.

Though, in a sense, two books, these are now considered as one and either must rank as imperfect without the other. The first part contains 210 hand-coloured engravings (190 of birds) from drawings by Edwards; the second 152 (128 of birds). The numbers of the plates run from 1–362 throughout.

At its date of issue the *Natural History and Gleanings* was one of the most important of all Bird Books, both as a Fine Bird Book and a work of Ornithology. It is still high on each list.

Various subsequent editions are worthy of note:
London 1745–51, *Natural History*, 4 parts in 2 vols. in 4, crown folio (in French) transl. David Durand; some plates.

London *c.* 1745–51, *Natural History*, first ed. partly reset; same plates.

**Nuremberg 1749–76 *N.H. and G.*, with Mark Catesby's *Nat. Hist. Carolina, etc.* (which see), transl. and ed. by Georg Leonhard Huth and the plates re-engraved by Johann Michael Seligmann, extra figures being added, as *Sammlung verschiedenen ausländischer und seltener Vögel*, in 9 parts, royal folio, 473 hand-coloured engravings, of which 425 of birds.

London 1758–64, *Gleanings*, first ed., partly re-grouped; same plates.

**Nuremberg 1768–76, French ed. of Nuremberg 1749–76, above, as *Recueil de divers Oiseaux étrangers et peu communs*, 422 hand-coloured engravings.

London 1770, 8vo. *Essays upon Natural History*, based upon the *Gleanings* with an index to the plates (rare).

**Amsterdam 1772–81, Dutch ed. of Nuremberg 1749–76, above, transl. from German into Dutch by Martinus Houttuyn, as *Verzameling van uitlandsche en zeldzaame Vogelen, etc.*, 5 vols. in 4, large folio, with Seligmann's 473 hand-colored engravings, of which 425 of birds.

London 1802–05, *N.H. and G.* in large-paper folio edition, limited to 25 copies (Mullens & Swann 1917, p. 196).

London 1805–06, *N.H. and G.*, usual 7 parts in 4 vols. Folio; same plates (but many reversed), text reset; the ordinary 'Posthumous Edition'.

MACROCERCUS ARARAUNA.

Blue & Yellow Maccaw.

⅔ Nat: Size.

EDWARDS, GEORGE, see P. BROWN 1776,
CATESBY 1731

EHRENBERG, CHRISTIAN GOTTFRIED and
FRIEDRICH WILHELM HEMPRICH
SYMBOLAE PHYSICAE SEU ICONES ET
DESCRIPTIONES CORPORUM NATURALIUM
NOVORUM AUT MINUS COGNITORUM, QUAE EX
ITINERIBUS PER LIBYAM AEGYPTUM NUBIAM
DONGOLAM SYRIAM ARABIAM ET HABESSINIAM
PUBLICO INSTITUTIS . . . [F. W. H. ET C. G. E.
1820–25] . . . REDIERUNT . . . AVIUM DECAS I
Large folio.
Berlin 1828–1833.
10 coloured plates by Müller.

**ELLIOT, DANIEL GIRAUD
A MONOGRAPH OF THE PITTIDÆ, OR FAMILY OF ANT
THRUSHES
Large folio.
New York 1861–1863.
32 hand-coloured lithographs by Elliot and Paul Louis
Oudart, originally published in 6 parts.
Reprint 1867; Second edition 1893–1895, 51 coloured
lithographs.

**ELLIOT, DANIEL GIRAUD
A MONOGRAPH OF THE TETRAONINÆ, or family of
the grouse
Double elephant folio.
New York (1864–)1865.
27 hand-coloured lithographs by Elliot, Joseph Wolf
and William S. Morgan.
Originally published in five parts.

ELLIOT, DANIEL GIRAUD
THE NEW AND HERETOFORE UNFIGURED SPECIES OF
THE BIRDS OF NORTH AMERICA
2 vols. Double elephant folio.
New York (1866–)1869.
72 hand-coloured lithographs from drawings by
Elliot, Joseph Wolf and Edwin Sheppard.
Originally published in 15 parts.

**ELLIOT, DANIEL GIRAUD
A MONOGRAPH OF THE PHASIANIDÆ OR FAMILY OF
THE PHEASANTS
2 vols. Double elephant folio.
New York (1870–)1872.

81 lithographs of which 79 are hand-coloured from
drawings by Joseph Wolf and Joseph Smit,
lithographed by Smit and John Gerrard Keulemans,
numbered: Vol. I, I–XXXII, XXIX bis: Vol. II,
I–XLVII, XIII bis. Originally published in 6 parts.

**ELLIOT, DANIEL GIRAUD
A MONOGRAPH OF THE PARADISEIDÆ OR BIRDS OF
PARADISE
Double elephant folio.
London 1873.
37 plates, of which 36 are hand-coloured lithographs
from drawings by Wolf and Smit.
Originally published in 7 parts.

**ELLIOT, DANIEL GIRAUD
A MONOGRAPH OF THE BUCEROTIDÆ, OR FAMILY
OF THE HORNBILLS
Folio.
London 1877–1882.
60 plates, of which 57 are hand-coloured lithographs
by John Gerrard Keulemans.
Originally published in 10 parts.

ESCHSCHOLZ, FRIEDRICH and MARTIN
HEINRICH RATHKE
ZOOLOGISCHER ATLAS, ENTHALTEND ABBILDUNGEN
UND BESCHREIBUNGEN NEUER THIERARTEN,
WÄHREND DES FLOTTCAPITAINS VON KOTZEBUE
ZWEITER REISE UM DIE WELT, AUF DER RUSSISCH-
KAISERLICHEN KRIEGSSCHLUPP PREDPRIAETIË IN
DEN JAHREN 1823–1825.
Small folio.
Berlin 1829–1833.
3 coloured plates of birds by Eschscholz or E. Bom-
mer.

EVANS, ARTHUR HUMBLE, see S. B. WILSON 1890

EYDOUX, JOSEPH FORTUNE THEODORE, see
LAPLACE 1836, VAILLANT 1841

EYTON, THOMAS CAMPBELL
A MONOGRAPH OF THE ANATIDÆ OR DUCK TRIBE
4to.
London 1838.
6 hand-coloured lithographs from drawings by Edward Lear, John Gould and George Scharf.

EYTON, THOMAS CAMPBELL, see DARWIN 1838

PLATE 30
Edward Lear began his career as an artist-naturalist by drawing
the forty-two lithographs of Illustrations of the Family of Psittacidae, or Parrots *(London 1830–32).*
His lithographs are noted for their freshness of line
and for the whimsical individuality of each parrot,
such as this Blue and Yellow Macaw.

FERGUSON, G.
FERGUSON'S ILLUSTRATED SERIES OF RARE AND
PRIZE POULTRY, INCLUDING COMPREHENSIVE ESSAYS
UPON ALL CLASSES OF DOMESTIC FOWL
Demy 8vo.
London 1854.
22 hand-coloured lithographs by C. J. Culliford, all
but one of birds.

FINSCH, FRIEDRICH HERMANN OTTO and
GUSTAV HARTLAUB
BEITRAG ZUR FAUNA CENTRALPOLYNESIENS.
ORNITHOLOGIE DER VITI-, SAMOA- UND TONGA-
INSELN
Royal 8vo.
Halle 1867.
14 hand-coloured lithographs by Finsch.

FINSCH, FRIEDRICH HERMANN OTTO
DIE PAPAGEIEN, MONOGRAPHISCH BEARBEITET
2 vols. in 3. 8vo.
Leyden 1867–1868.
5 hand-coloured lithographs by Finsch.

FINSCH, FRIEDRICH HERMANN OTTO, see A. E.
BREHM 1870, von der DECKEN 1869, von HEUGLIN
1869, THOMSON 1881

FISHER, ALBERT KENRICK
THE HAWKS AND OWLS OF THE UNITED STATES IN
THEIR RELATION TO AGRICULTURE
8vo.
Washington *Bull U.S. Div. Orn. Mammal.* No. 3 1893.
26 coloured plates by John Livzey and Robert Ridgway.

FITZINGER, LEOPOLD JOSEF FRANZ JOHANN
WISSENSCHAFTLICH-POPULÄRE NATURGESCHICHTE
DER VÖGEL
8vo. and atlas of plates folio.
Vienna and Leipzig 1862–1864.
164 chromolithographs.

FLETCHER, JAMES COOLEY, see KIDDER 1857

FLOURENS, J. P., see de BUFFON 1749 (1853)

FORBES, Mrs ANNA, see BUTLER 1896

FORBES, HENRY OGG, see BUTLER 1896

FORBES, JAMES
ORIENTAL MEMOIRS: SELECTED AND ABRIDGED
FROM A SERIES OF FAMILIAR LETTERS WRITTEN
DURING SEVENTEEN YEARS RESIDENCE IN INDIA:
INCLUDING OBSERVATIONS ON PARTS OF AFRICA

AND SOUTH AMERICA, AND A NARRATIVE OF
OCCURRENCES IN FOUR INDIAN VOYAGES
4 vols. 4to.
London 1813.
93 engravings, of which many are hand-coloured
plates of birds.
Second edition (2 vols. and atlas, 85 plates) 1834–35.

FORBES, WILLIAM ALEXANDER
IN MEMORIAM. THE COLLECTED SCIENTIFIC PAPERS
OF THE LATE WILLIAM ALEXANDER FORBES, ETC.
Royal 8vo.
London 1885.
9 coloured plates of birds.

FORBES, WILLIAM ALEXANDER, see THOMSON
1881

FORSTER, JOHANN REINHOLD
INDISCHE ZOOLOGIE, . . .
Folio.
Halle 1781.
15 hand-coloured engravings after Pieter Cornelis de
Bevere, being the 12 (of which 11 birds) of Pennant's
Indian Zoology 1769, which see, plus 3 given to Forster
by Pennant. Relationship between this work and that
of Latham and Davies discussed by Zimmer (1926, pp.
374–75)
New edition 1795.

FORSTER, JOHANN REINHOLD, see LATHAM
1795, PENNANT 1769

FRASER, LOUIS
ZOOLOGICAL TYPICA, OR FIGURES OF NEW AND
RARE MAMMALS AND BIRDS, DESCRIBED IN THE
PROCEEDINGS, OR EXHIBITED IN COLLECTIONS OF
THE ZOOLOGICAL SOCIETY OF LONDON
Folio.
London (1845) 1846–1848 (1849).
70 lithographs coloured by hand of which 42 are of
birds, by H. N. Turner Jr. and Charles Couzens.

von FRAUENFELD, GEORG Ritter
NEU AUFGEFUNDENE ABBILDUNG DER DRONTE. . . .
Large folio.
Vienna 1868.
2 chromolithographs of the Dodo after Jacob
Hoefnagel.

FRAUENHOLZ, JOHANN FRIEDRICH, see
JOHANN WOLF 1799, 1839

de FREYCINET, LOUIS CLAUDE DESAULSES,
JEAN RENE CONSTANT QUOY and JEAN PAUL
GAIMARD

VOYAGE AUTOUR DU MONDE, ENTERPRIS PAR
ORDRE DU ROI, . . . EXECUTE SUR LES CORVETTES
DE S.M. L'URANIE ET LA PHYSICIENNE, PENDANT
LES ANNEES 1817, 1818, 1819 ET 1820; ETC. . . .
ZOOLOGIE
2 vols. 4to text and large folio atlas.
Paris 1824–1826.
71 coloured plates (out of 96) of which 27 birds by Paul
Louis Oudart and Jean Gabriel Prêtre, printed in col-
ours and retouched by hand.

FRIČ [FRITSCH], ANTONÍN JAN
NATURGESCHICHTE DER VÖGEL EUROPA'S [and in
Czech]
8vo. Folio atlas of plates.
Prague 1853–1870.
61 chromolithographs.
The volume of plates also published London 1877.
New edition Prague 1898.

FRIDERICH, C. G.
NATURGESCHICHTE ALLER DEUTSCHEN ZIMMER-,
HAUS-UND JAGDVÖGEL, NEBST EINEM ANHANGE
ÜBER DIE AUSLANDISCHEN VÖGEL, WELCHE IN
DEUTSCHLAND IM HANDEL VORKOMMEN
8vo.
Stuttgart 1849.
Several coloured plates.
Several subsequent editions with increasing number
of plates, e.g., 1876 (20), 1883 (60), 1905 (410 figs. on
57).

***FRISCH, JOHANN LEONHARD and JODOCUS
LEOPOLD, and Baron FRIEDRICH AUGUST ZORN
von PLOBSHEIM
VORSTELLUNG DER VÖGEL IN TEUTSCHLAND UND
BEYLÄUFFIG AUCH EINIGER FREMDEN, MIT IHREN
EIGENSCHAFTEN BESCHRIEBEN. . . . UND NACH
IHREN NATÜRLICHEN FARBEN
1 vol. in 2. Folio.
Berlin 1733–1763.
Frontispiece uncoloured and 255 hand-coloured en-
gravings (252 of birds, 3 of bats) by Ferdinand
Helfreich Frisch, Philipp Jacob Frisch and Johann
Christoph Frisch.
Issued in 14 parts and a supplement. Plates numbered
1–241: 31, 114B, and 212 are 'bis' plates and the plates in
the supplement are numbered 28, 31, 33, 106, 107, 109,
152, 157, 165, 185A, 185B.
Re-issued in 1764 and in 1817.
One of the most enjoyable of all bird books but rare.

von FÜHRER, LUDWIG, see REISER 1896

FULTON, ROBERT and LEWIS WRIGHT, ed.
THE ILLUSTRATED BOOK OF PIGEONS WITH
STANDARDS FOR JUDGING.
4to.

London and New York 1876
50 chromolithographs after J. W. Ludlow
Several subsequent editions

FUNKE, KARL PHILIPP
KUPFER-SAMMLUNG BESONDERS ZU FUNKE NATUR-
GESCHICHTE UND TECHNOLOGIE ABER AUCH ZU
JEDEM ANDERN LEHRBUCHE DER
NATURGESCHICHTE BRAUCHBAR. . . .
3 vols. 8vo.
Brunswick 1790–1792.
No plates first ed., but 24 in colours by fifth (1805–06)
of which five of birds, after Nicolas Maréchal.

FURBER, ROBERT, see CASTEELS 1730

FÜRBRINGER, MAX
UNTERSUCHUNGEN ZUR MORPHOLOGIE UND
SYSTEMATIK DER VÖGEL ZUGLEICH EIN BEITRAG
ZUR ANATOMIE DER STÜTZ- UND
BEWEGUNGSORGANE
2 vols. Large 4to.
Amsterdam 1888.
31 coloured plates (anatomical) by Fürbringer.

FÜRST, HERMANN
DEUTSCHLANDS NÜTZLICHE UND SCHÄDLICHE
VÖGEL
2 vols. Folio.
Berlin 1893–1894.
32 chromolithographs by A. Weczerzick.

GADOW, HANS, see SHARPE 1874, S. B. WILSON
1890

GAIMARD, JEAN PAUL, see DUMONT D'URVILLE
1830, de FREYCINET 1824

GARNOT, PROSPER, see DUPERREY 1826

GARROD, ALFRED HENRY, see THOMSON 1881

GAY, CLAUDIO and MARC ATHANESE PARFAIT
OEILLET DesMURS
HISTORIA FISICA Y POLITICA DE CHILE SEGUN
DOCUMENTOS ADQUIRIDOS EN ESTA REPUBLICA
DURANTE DOCE AÑOS DE RESIDENCIA EN ELLA Y
PUBLICADA BAJO LOS AUSPICIOS DEL SUPREMO
GOBIERNO . . . ZOOLOGIA
8 vols. Demy 8vo and Small folio.
Paris 1844–1854?
Of the 25 vols. of the whole work, 8 are zoological, of
which 2 (vols 1 and 8 of Zool. Ser.) contain birds, of
which there are 13 coloured plates by Johann-Carl
Werner, Alphonse Prévost, Paul Louis Oudart and
Gay.

Toucan Ariel.

Theod.Descourtil.del.   lith de Callier.

GAZZADI, DOMENICO and ANTONIO BASCHIERI
ZOOLOGIA MORALE ESPOSTA IN CENTOVENTI
DISCORSI IN VERSI O IN PROSA
2 vols. Folio.
Florence 1843–1846.
119 coloured plates, many of birds.

GEBAUER, CHRISTIAN AUGUST
VOLKS NATURGESCHICHTE ODER GEMEINFASSLICHE
BESCHREIBUNG DER MERKWÜRDIGSTEN,
NÜTZLICHSTEN UND SCHÄDLICHSTEN THIERE,
PFLANZEN UND MINERALIEN . . . VÖGEL
8vo.
Stuttgart 1837–1838.
6 coloured lithographs of birds, 40 coloured plates in
all; and 40 in 2nd. ed. 1841; 48 in 3rd. ed. 1844; 48 in 4th
ed. 1857; 45 in 5th ed. 1864–66; 34 in 6th ed. 1869–70;
48 in 7th ed. 1875 (collected by Anker, 1938, p. 126).

GENTRY, THOMAS GEORGE
NESTS AND EGGS OF BIRDS OF THE UNITED STATES
Small folio.
Philadelphia 1880–1882.
Published in 25 parts, with illuminated title-page and
54 coloured plates of birds, nests and eggs by Edwin
Sheppard.

GEOFFROY SAINT-HILAIRE, ISIDORE and VICTOR
JACQUEMONT
DESCRIPTION DES COLLECTIONS DE VICTOR
JACQUEMONT. MAMMIFERES ET OISEAUX
Large 4to.
Paris 1842–1843.
7 coloured plates by Johann-Carl Werner and Al-
phonse Prévost, of which 2 of birds.

GERINI, GIOVANNI, see MANETTI 1767

GERVAIS, FRANÇOIS LOUIS PAUL, see BERNARD
1842, LAPLACE 1836

GIGLIOLI, ENRICO HILLYER
ICONOGRAFIA DELL' AVIFAUNA ITALICA OVVERO
TAVOLE ILLUSTRANTI LE SPECIE DI UCCELLI CHE
TROVANSI IN ITALIA
2 vols. Folio.
Prato 1879–1906.
400 coloured lithographs by Alberto Manzella.

GILL, THEODORE NICHOLAS, see BAIRD 1874

GODMAN, FREDERICK DuCANE, see O. SALVIN
1879

GOLDSMITH, OLIVER
A HISTORY OF THE EARTH AND ANIMATED NATURE
TO WHICH IS SUBJOINED AN APPENDIX BY THOMAS
BROWN
12 vols. 12 mo.
Glasgow 1832 (and 1838).
4 coloured title pages and 74 coloured plates by R.
Scott, many of birds.
First ed. was 1774. An earlier colour-plate edition
London 1819 (1 vol. 4to. 73 col. pl.)

GOLDSMITH, OLIVER
GOLDSMITH'S HISTORY OF BRITISH AND FOREIGN
BIRDS
12mo.
London 1838.
46 coloured plates. Rare.

de GOMBAUD, OGIER
HISTOIRE NATURELLE DES OISEAUX DE CAYENNE
2 vols. Large folio.
Cayenne 1803–1808.
168 coloured plates.
No text. This collection was drawn and published by
the author while serving a sentence of deportation.
Very rare.

GORDON, WILLIAM JOHN
OUR COUNTRY'S BIRDS AND HOW TO KNOW THEM.
A GUIDE TO ALL THE BIRDS OF GREAT BRITAIN
Demy 8vo.
London 1892.
22 coloured lithographs.

GOSSE, PHILIP HENRY
POPULAR BRITISH ORNITHOLOGY
Small 4to.
London 1849.
20 coloured lithographs.
Second edition 1853.

GOSSE, PHILIP HENRY
ILLUSTRATIONS OF THE BIRDS OF JAMAICA
Folio.
London 1849.
52 coloured lithographs.
Very rare.

PLATE 31
*Jean Theodore Descourtilz pioneered the study of
Amazonian natural history. He illustrated* Oiseaux brillans du Brésil *(Paris 1834),
a book known in only a handful of copies.
Its lithographs are distinguished by dynamic and original compositions and bright coloring,
exemplified by "Toucan Ariel."*

RAMPHASTOS CULMENATUS.
Culmenated Toucan.

GÖTZ, GEORG FRIEDRICH
NATURGESCHICHTE EINIGER VÖGEL, . . .
8vo.
Hanau 1782.
6 hand coloured copperplate engravings by Joh. Jakob Müller.

*GOULD, JOHN and NICHOLAS AYLWARD VIGORS
A CENTURY OF BIRDS FROM THE HIMALAYA MOUNTAINS
Large folio.
London (1831–)1832.
80 hand-coloured lithographs, printed by C. Hull-mandel from sketches by Gould drawn on stone by Mrs E. Gould. The backgrounds of the plates are sometimes coloured, sometimes not.

***GOULD, JOHN
THE BIRDS OF EUROPE
5 vols. Large folio.
London (1832–)1837
448 hand-coloured lithographs printed by C. Hull-mandel. Some of these plates were drawn and lithographed by Edward Lear. The rest by Mrs Gould from sketches by Gould. Published originally in 22 parts. There are actually 449 different drawings but 447 and 448 are on one plate.

***GOULD, JOHN and RICHARD OWEN
A MONOGRAPH OF THE RAMPHASTIDÆ, OR FAMILY OF TOUCANS
Large Folio.
London 1833–1835.
33 hand-coloured lithographs printed by C. Hull-mandel: drawn and lithographed by J. and E. Gould, and by Edward Lear.
Also 1 uncoloured plate.
Originally published in 3 parts.
New edition in 1852–54 with 52 coloured lithographs; of which those not figured in the first edition, drawn and lithographed by Gould and H. C. Richter, were re-published in 1855 as a Supplement to that edition, with an extra plate (making 20 in all) from Part I of Icones Avium 1837.
A German edition, Nuremberg 1841–47 has 38 coloured plates.

***GOULD, JOHN
A MONOGRAPH OF THE TROGONIDÆ, OR FAMILY OF TROGONS

Large folio.
London 1836–1838.
36 hand-coloured lithographs printed by C. Hull-mandel: drawn and lithographed by J. and E. Gould.
Originally issued in 3 parts.
A revised edition with 47 new coloured plates were issued in 1858–75 (4 parts). The dating, etc., of the plates in this is given by Waterhouse (1885, pp. 58–59).

*GOULD, JOHN
THE BIRDS OF AUSTRALIA, AND THE ADJACENT ISLANDS
Large folio.
London 1837–1838.
20 hand-coloured lithographs (issued in 2 parts) by J. and E. Gould, of which 9 were reprinted in the full 1840–48 edition of the Birds of Australia.
This work, begun before Gould's visit to Australia and discarded incomplete on his departure, is the rarest of his books.

GOULD, JOHN
A SYNOPSIS OF THE BIRDS OF AUSTRALIA, AND THE ADJACENT ISLANDS
Large 8vo. (4to. size).
London 1837–1838.
73 hand-coloured lithographs (issued in 4 parts) by J. and E. Gould.

GOULD, JOHN
ICONES AVIUM, OR FIGURES AND DESCRIPTIONS OF NEW AND INTERESTING SPECIES OF BIRDS FROM VARIOUS PARTS OF THE GLOBE
Large folio.
London 1837–1838.
18 hand-coloured lithographs printed by C. Hull-mandel.
Drawn and lithographed by J. and E. Gould.
2 parts, only, with 10 and 8 plates respectively, appeared.

*GOULD, JOHN
THE BIRDS OF AUSTRALIA
8 vols. Large folio.
London 1840–1869.
Published in 36 parts (vols. 1–7, 1840–48, 600 plates), plus 54-part supplement (vol. 8, 1851–69).
681 hand-coloured lithographs printed by Hull-mandel and Walter or C. Hullmandel from drawings by J. and E. Gould or J. Gould and H. C. Richter and lithographed by the artists.

PLATE 32
This Culmenated Toucan from
A Monograph of the Ramphastidae, or Family of Toucans *(London 1833–35)*
shows the distinctive drawn line of lithographic artist Edward Lear.
John Gould and Richard Owen collaborated on the text
to this jewel among the many bird books produced by Gould.

For dates, etc., of parts see Waterhouse (1885, pp. 28–44).

The absence of the Supplement does not mean that the original 7 volumes need be considered incomplete, in a collector's sense.

GOULD, JOHN
A MONOGRAPH OF THE ODONTOPHORINÆ OR PARTRIDGES OF AMERICA
Large folio.
London 1844–1850.
Originally published in 3 parts.
32 hand-coloured lithographs: printed by C. Hullmandel, drawn by J. Gould and H. C. Richter. For dates, etc., of plates see Waterhouse (1885, pp. 56–57).

***GOULD, JOHN and RICHARD BOWDLER SHARPE
A MONOGRAPH OF THE TROCHILIDÆ, OR FAMILY OF HUMMING-BIRDS
6 vols. Large folio.
London 1849–1887.
Originally published in 25 parts (Vols. 1–5, 1849–61, 360 plates), plus 5-part supplement (Vol. 6, 1880–87).
418 hand-coloured lithographs printed by Hullmandel and Walter (some by Walter and Cohn) from drawings by J. Gould, H. C. Richter and William Hart, lithographed by the artists. Gould died after publication of the second part of the Supplement in 1881, and Sharpe completed it. For dates, etc., of plates see Waterhouse (1885, pp. 45–55).
The absence of the Supplement does not mean that the original 5 volumes need by considered incomplete, in a collector's sense.

***GOULD, JOHN and RICHARD BOWDLER SHARPE
THE BIRDS OF ASIA
7 vols. Large folio.
London 1850–1883.
Originally issued in 35 parts, the last 3 after Gould's death by Sharpe.
530 lithographs coloured by hand, printed by Hullmandel and Walter, Walter, or Walter and Cohn from drawings by J. Gould, H. C. Richter and Joseph Wolf, assisted in the lithography by Hart. For dates etc, of plates see Waterhouse (1885, pp. 15–27).

***GOULD, JOHN
THE BIRDS OF GREAT BRITAIN
5 vols. Large folio.
London 1862–1873.
Originally issued in 25 parts.
367 lithographs coloured by hand, printed by Walter from drawings by Gould, Joseph Wolf, H. C. Richter and Hart, mostly lithographed by Richter and Hart. For dates, etc. of plates see Waterhouse (1885, pp. 6–14).

***GOULD, JOHN and RICHARD BOWDLER SHARPE
THE BIRDS OF NEW GUINEA AND THE ADJACENT PAPUAN ISLANDS, INCLUDING MANY NEW SPECIES RECENTLY DISCOVERED IN AUSTRALIA
Completed after Gould's death by Sharpe.
5 vols. Large folio.
London 1875–1888.
Originally issued in 25 parts.
320 hand-coloured lithographs printed by Walter or Mintern Bros. Drawn and lithographed by Gould and Hart.
Some of these plates used in Sharpe 1891–98, which see.

GOULD, JOHN and RICHARD BOWDLER SHARPE
MONOGRAPH OF THE PITTIDÆ
Large folio.
London 1880.
Sharpe (1893, p. xxiii) states that only one part was published. The 10 hand-coloured lithographs are mostly taken from the *Birds of Asia, Birds of Australia,* and *Birds of New Guinea.*
The book was cut short by Gould's death.

GOULD, JOHN, see DARWIN 1838, HINDS 1843

GRANDIDIER, ALFRED and ALPHONSE MILNE-EDWARDS
HISTOIRE PHYSIQUE, NATURELLE ET POLITIQUE DE MADAGASCAR. . . . HISTOIRE NATURELLE DES OISEAUX
4 vols. Large 4to.
Paris 1876–1885.
437 coloured lithographs by John Gerrard Keulemans, J. Hüet and Faguet.

GRANDIDIER, ALFRED, see MILNE-EDWARDS 1866

GRÄSSNER, FÜRCHTEGOTT
DIE VÖGEL DEUTSCHLANDS UND IHRE EIER
Large 4to.
Halle 1860.
10 coloured plates of eggs by Johann Friedrich Naumann, whom see (1818–28).

*GRAVES, GEORGE
BRITISH ORNITHOLOGY. WITH AN ACCURATELY COLOURED REPRESENTATION OF EVERY KNOWN SPECIES OF BRITISH BIRDS
3 vols. 8vo.
London 1811–1821.
144 hand-coloured engravings by Graves.
2nd edition 1821.

GRAVES, GEORGE
OVARIUM BRITANNICUM; BEING A CORRECT

DELINEATION OF THE EGGS OF SUCH BIRDS AS ARE
NATIVES OF, OR DOMESTICATED IN GREAT BRITAIN
8vo.
London 1816.
15 hand-coloured engravings by Graves.

GRAY, GEORGE ROBERT
THE GENERA OF BIRDS: COMPRISING THEIR GENERIC
CHARACTERS, A NOTICE OF THE HABITS OF EACH
GENUS, AND AN EXTENSIVE LIST OF SPECIES
REFERRED TO THEIR SEVERAL GENERA
3 vols. Large 4to.
London 1844–1849.
Issued in 50 parts: 185 coloured plates.

GRAY, GEORGE ROBERT
A FASCICULUS OF THE BIRDS OF CHINA
Small folio.
London 1871.
12 coloured plates by William Swainson.

GRAY, GEORGE ROBERT, see BRENCHLEY 1873,
DARWIN 1838, RICHARDSON 1844

GRAY, JOHN EDWARD and THOMAS HARDWICKE
ILLUSTRATIONS OF INDIAN ZOOLOGY
2 vols. in 1. Large folio.
London 1830–1835.
202 hand-coloured lithographs (90 of birds) 76 by
T. W. Lewin, Farquhar, Benjamin Waterhouse
Hawkins and various 'English and Native Artists'
(Kinnear, 1925).

GRAY, JOHN EDWARD
GLEANINGS FROM THE MENAGERIE AND AVIARY AT
KNOWSLEY HALL
Large folio.
Knowsley 1846–1850.
Published in 2 parts: 79 plates in all, mostly in colour;
the only illustrations of birds are 9 hand coloured
lithographs, all in part 1, from drawings by Edward
Lear, who at that time was Curator to Lord Derby at
Knowsley.
Rare.

GRAY, JOHN EDWARD, see CUVIER 1817 (1827),
RICHARDSON 1844

GREEN, JOSEPH F.
OCEAN BIRDS
Folio.
London 1887.
10 coloured plates.

GREENE, WILLIAM THOMAS and F. G. DUTTON
PARROTS IN CAPTIVITY

3 vols. Royal 8vo.
London 1883–1887 (1888).
81 coloured lithographs after A. F. Lydon.

GRIEVE, SYMINGTON
THE GREAT AUK, OR GAREFOWL (ALCA IMPENNIS,
LINN.) ITS HISTORY, ARCHÆOLOGY, AND REMAINS
4to.
London and Edinburgh 1885.
2 chromolithographs of eggs.

GRIFFITH, EDWARD, see CUVIER 1817 (1827)

GUERIN-MENEVILLE, FELIX EDOUARD, see
CUVIER, 1817 (1829), SEBA 1734 (1827)

GÜNTHER, FRIEDRICH CHRISTIAN, see WIRSING
1767

HAACKE, JOHANN WILHELM
DIE SCHÖPFING DER TIERWELT . . .
4to.
Leipzig 1893.
6 coloured plates of birds after Friedrich Wilhelm Karl
Kuhnert.

HAGELBERG, W.
ZOOLOGISCHER HAND-ATLAS. NATURGETREUE
DARSTELLUNG DES THIERREICHS IN SEINEN
HAUPTFORMEN. B. VÖGEL. AVES
Royal 8vo.
Berlin 1879–1881.
24 plates on which are mounted 285 embossed chro-
molithographic cards, the size of large stamps
(1 × 1¼ in.) bearing portraits of birds.

*HAHN, CARL WILHELM and HEINRICH CARL
KÜSTER
DIE VÖGEL AUS ASIEN, AFRICA, AMERICA UND
NEUHOLLAND, IN ABBILDUNGEN NACH DER NATUR
MIT BESCHREIBUNGEN
4to.
Nuremberg 1818–1850.
Issued in 20 parts, the first 19 in 1818–36.
120 hand-coloured engravings.
Part-revised edition 1823–50.

HAHN, CARL WILHELM
NATURGETREUE ABBILDUNGEN ZUR ALLGEMEINEN
NATURGESCHICHTE DER THIERE BAYERNS
8vo.
Nuremberg 1826–1828.
100 hand-coloured engravings.

HAHN, CARL WILHELM and HEINRICH CARL
KÜSTER
ORNITHOLOGISCHER ATLAS ODER NATURGETREUE
ABBILDUNG UND BESCHREIBUNG DER

PHAROMACRUS MOCINNO.

J.Gould & W. Hart del. et lith.

Walter, Imp.

AUSSEREUROPÄISCHEN VÖGEL
Post 8vo.
Nuremberg 1834–1841.
Published in 17 part, the last 11 by Küster.
136 hand-coloured plates.

HAHN, CARL WILHELM, see von REIDER 1830

d'HAMONVILLE, JEAN CHARLES LOUIS TARDIF
ATLAS DE POCHE DES OISEAUX DE FRANCE,
BELGIQUE ET SUISSE UTILES OU NUISIBLES . . .
2 vols. Small 8vo.
Paris 1898.
144 chromolithographs after G. Denise.

HANCOCK, JOHN
A FASCICULUS OF 8 DRAWINGS ON STONE OF
GROUPS OF BIRDS: THE WHOLE BEING
REPRESENTATIVE OF SPECIMENS STUFFED AND
CONTRIBUTED BY THE AUTHOR TO THE GREAT
EXHIBITION OF 1851
Large folio.
Newcastle-upon-Tyne 1853.
8 lithographs in 2 states, plain and coloured (mostly of
falcons and eagles).

HARDWICKE, THOMAS, see J. E. GRAY 1830

HARGITT, EDWARD, see SHARPE 1874

HARTERT, ERNST, see SHARPE, 1874

HARTING, JAMES EDMUND and LEO PAUL
SAMUEL ROBERT
GLIMPSES OF BIRD LIFE PORTRAYED WITH PEN AND
PENCIL
Folio.
London 1880.
20 coloured plates by Robert, whom see.

HARTLAUB, GUSTAV, see von der DECKEN 1869,
FINSCH 1867

***HAVELL, ROBERT
A COLLECTION OF FIGURES OF BIRDS OF PARADISE
Folio.
London n.d. (c. 1835).
Engraved title page, hand-coloured and 22 hand-col-
oured engravings.
Very rare.

HAVELL, ROBERT
A SELECTION OF BRITISH BIRDS FROM DRAWINGS BY
C. L. E. PERROTT, HON. CORRESPONDING MEMBER
OF THE WORCESTER NATURAL HISTORY SOCIETY.
ENGRAVED BY ROBERT HAVELL, ENGRAVER, ETC. OF
THE BIRDS OF AMERICA. PUBLISHED BY ROBERT
HAVELL
Large folio.
London n.d. (c. 1835).
Part 1 only: all published.
5 very fine hand-coloured engravings.
Extremely rare. This interesting fragment is not men-
tioned in any previous bibliography.

*HAYES, CHARLES
THE PORTRAITS OF BRITISH BIRDS, INCLUDING
DOMESTIC POULTRY AND WATER-FOWL
4to.
London 1808–1816.
120 hand-coloured engravings by Hayes.

**HAYES, WILLIAM
A NATURAL HISTORY OF BRITISH BIRDS, ETC., WITH
THEIR PORTRAITS, ACCURATELY DRAWN, AND
BEAUTIFULLY COLOURED FROM NATURE
Large folio.
London (1771–)1775.
40 hand-coloured engravings, many of which are
often found signed in ink, by Hayes and Gabriel
Smith.
Zimmer (1926, p. 294) notes a miscellaneous collec-
tion of plates of this and the works cited below, re-
vised, with no text or title, 1771–c. 1779.

**HAYES, WILLIAM
PORTRAITS OF RARE AND CURIOUS BIRDS, WITH
THEIR DESCRIPTIONS. ACCURATELY DRAWN AND
BEAUTIFULLY COLOURED FROM SPECIES IN THE
MENAGERIE OF CHILD, THE BANKER, AT OSTERLEY
PARK, NEAR LONDON
2 vols. (almost invariably bound in one). 4to.
London 1794–1799.
101 hand-coloured engravings (etchings) from draw-
ings by Hayes and other members of his family.

HAYES, WILLIAM
FIGURES OF RARE AND CURIOUS BIRDS,
ACCURATELY DRAWN FROM LIVING SPECIMENS AND
FAITHFULLY COLOURED
4to.
London 1822.
4 hand-coloured engravings.

PLATE 33
John Gould followed his successful monograph on toucans
with another book about colorful exotics, A Monograph of the Trogonidae, or Family of Trogons (London 1836–38).
This Quetzal Trogon illustrates the second edition of the work (1858–75),
all of whose plates were new drawings.

werner del.

Lith. de Benard et Frey.

KACATOËS A HUPPE BLANCHE.

HEERMAN, ADOLPHUS L., see BAIRD 1859

HEMPRICH, FRIEDRICH WILHELM
SYMBOLAE PHYSICAE SEU ICONES ET
DESCRIPTIONES AVIUM QUAE EX ITINERE PER
AFRICAM BOREALEM ET ASIAM OCCIDENTALEM
NOVAE AUT ILLUSTRATAE REDIERUNT
Folio.
Berlin 1829.
10 hand-coloured lithographs designed by Wilhelm
Müller.

HEMPRICH, FRIEDRICH WILHELM, see
EHRENBERG 1828

HENDERSON, GEORGE and ALLAN OCTAVIAN
HUME
LAHORE TO YARKAND, INCIDENTS OF THE ROUTE
AND NATURAL HISTORY OF THE COUNTRIES
TRAVERSED BY THE EXPEDITION OF 1870, UNDER
T. D. FORSYTH, ESQ., C.B.
Royal 8vo.
London 1873.
32 coloured lithographs of birds by John Gerrard Keu-
lemans

HENNICKE, CARL RICHARD, see NAUMANN 1795
(1896).

HENSHAW, HENRY WEATHERBEE, see WHEELER
1875

HERKLOTS, JANUS ADRIAN, see SCHLEGEL 1854

HESSELBERG, ABRAHAM
ZWÖLF VÖGEL GEZEICHNET
4to.
Uttweil a. Bodensee 1859.
12 coloured lithographs.

von HEUGLIN, MARTIN THEODOR and
FRIEDRICH HERMAN OTTO FINSCH
ORNITHOLOGIE NORDOST-AFRIKA'S, DER
NILQUELLEN UND KÜSTEN-GEBIETE DES ROTHEN
MEERES UND DES NÖRDLICHEN SOMAL-LANDES
2 vols. Royal 8vo.
Cassel 1869–1875.
Published in 57 parts; 51 chromolithographs after von
Heuglin.

von HEUGLIN, MARTIN THEODOR
REISE IN NORDOST-AFRIKA. SCHILDERUNGEN AUS
DEM GEBIETE DER BENI AMER UND HABAB NEBST
ZOOLOGISCHEN SKIZZEN UND EINEM FÜHRER FÜR
JAGDREISENDE
2 vols. in 1. Post 8vo.
Brunswick 1877.
2 coloured plates of birds.

HEWITSON, WILLIAM CHAPMAN
BRITISH OOLOGY; BEING ILLUSTRATIONS OF THE
EGGS OF BRITISH BIRDS, WITH FIGURES OF EACH
SPECIES, AS FAR AS PRACTICABLE, DRAWN AND
COLOURED FROM NATURE: ACCOMPANIED BY
DESCRIPTIONS OF THE MATERIALS AND SITUATION
OF THEIR NESTS, NUMBERS OF EGGS, ETC.
3 vols. 8vo.
Newcastle and London (1831–1838).
155 hand-coloured engravings of eggs.
A supplement with 14 more coloured plates published
1842.
New edition as *Coloured Illustrations of The Eggs of
British Birds*, 2 vols. Post 8vo. 138 coloured plates
1842–46; and another 1853–56 with 149 coloured
plates.

HILL, JOHN
AN HISTORY OF ANIMALS, ETC.
Folio.
London 1752.
28 hand-coloured engravings, including 8 of birds
(17–24).

HINDS, RICHARD BRINSLEY and JOHN GOULD
THE ZOOLOGY OF THE VOYAGE OF H.M.S. SULPHUR,
UNDER THE COMMAND OF CAPTAIN SIR EDWARD
BELCHER, . . . DURING THE YEARS 1836–42 . . .
BIRDS
Large 4to.
London 1843–1844.
Published in 2 parts; 8 coloured lithographs of birds
by Gould.

HOFFMANN, RALPH, see LANSING 1898

HOLDEN, GEORGE HENRY
CANARIES AND CAGE BIRDS
4to.
New York 1883.
7 coloured plates.

PLATE 34
Alexandre Bourjot Saint-Hilaire's Histoire naturelle des perroquets
*(Paris and Strasbourg 1835–39) continues Levaillant's work by picturing newly discovered species.
The author commends taxidermist Florent Prévost,
zoologist at the Muséum d'histoire naturelle, for posing the mounted cockatoo
Werner drew for this dramatic lithograph.*

HOLUB, EMIL and AUGUST von PELZELN
BEITRÄGE ZUR ORNITHOLOGIE SÜDAFRIKAS. MIT
BESONDERER BERÜCKSICHTIGUNG DER VON DR
HOLUB AUF SEINEN SÜDAFRIKANISCHEN REISEN
GESAMMELTEN UND IM PAVILLON DES AMATEURS
ZU WIEN AUSGESTELLTEN ARTEN
Royal 8vo.
Vienna 1882.
3 coloured plates by J. Sommer.

HOMBRON, J. B., see DUMONT D'URVILLE 1842

HORSFIELD, THOMAS
ZOOLOGICAL RESEARCHES IN JAVA, AND THE
NEIGHBOURING ISLANDS
4to.
London 1821–1824.
72 lithographs by Auguste Pelletier and after John
Curtis, of which 64 coloured, many of birds.

HOUTTUYN, MARTINUS, see EDWARDS 1743
(1772), NOZEMAN 1770

HÜBNER, JAKOB
SAMMLUNG AUSERLESENER VÖGEL UND
SCHMETTERLINGE
8vo.
Augsburg 1793.
100 hand-coloured engravings.

HUDSON, WILLIAM HENRY
BRITISH BIRDS
8vo.
London 1895.
8 coloured plates.

HUDSON, WILLIAM HENRY
BIRDS IN LONDON
8vo.
London 1898.
15 coloured plates.

HUDSON, WILLIAM HENRY, see P. L. SCLATER
1888

HUME, ALLAN OCTAVIAN and CHARLES HENRY
TILSON MARSHALL
THE GAME BIRDS OF INDIA, BURMAH, AND CEYLON
3 vols. Small 4to.
Calcutta 1879–1881.
148 hand-coloured lithographs by C. Davenport,
William Foster, M. Herbert, Edward Neale, A. W.
Strutt and Stanley Wilson.
Second edition 1890.

HUME, ALLAN OCTAVIAN, see HENDERSON 1873

HUNT, JOHN
BRITISH ORNITHOLOGY; CONTAINING PORTRAITS OF
ALL THE BRITISH BIRDS, INCLUDING THOSE OF
FOREIGN ORIGIN, WHICH HAVE BECOME
DOMESTICATED; DRAWN, ENGRAVED AND
COLOURED AFTER NATURE
3 vols. Post 8vo.
Norwich 1815–1822.
191 hand-coloured engravings by Hunt.

HUTTON, FREDERICK WOLLASTON, see BULLER
1882

INGERSOLL, ERNEST
NESTS AND EGGS OF AMERICAN BIRDS
4to.
Salem 1879–c. 1882 (probably never completed).
10 coloured plates

INGERSOLL, ERNEST, see POPE 1877

IRBY, LEONARD HOWARD LLOYD
THE ORNITHOLOGY OF THE STRAITS OF GIBRALTAR
Post 8vo.
London 1895.
The 2nd edition of a book first published with no plates
in 1875; 8 coloured plates by Archibald Thorburn.

JACQUEMONT, VICTOR, see GEOFFROY SAINT-
HILAIRE 1842

von JACQUIN, JOSEPH FRANZ EDLEN
BEYTRÄGE ZUR GESCHICHTE DER VÖGEL
4to.
Vienna 1784.
19 hand-coloured engravings by his father Nicolaus
Joseph von Jacquin.

JACQUINOT, C. HONORE, see DUMONT
D'URVILLE 1842

JÄGERSKIÖLD, AXEL LEONARD KRISTER
EDVARD, see KOLTHOFF 1895

JAMESON, ROBERT, see WILSON 1808 (1831)

JANSEN, KNUD, see WALLENGREN 1896

JARDINE, Sir WILLIAM, PRIDEAUX JOHN SELBY
and others
ILLUSTRATIONS OF ORNITHOLOGY
4 vols. 4to.
Edinburgh 1826–1843.
207 hand-coloured engravings by Jardine, Selby, John
Gould, Edward Lear, R. Mitford, A. F. Rolfe, James
Stewart and J. Thompson.
An excellent analysis of this complex publication in
Zimmer (1926, pp. 322–24).

JARDINE, Sir WILLIAM, PRIDEAUX JOHN SELBY
and WILLIAM SWAINSON
THE NATURALIST'S LIBRARY
40 vols. Foolscap 8vo.
Volumes XIV–XXVII alone deal with birds.
Edinburgh 1833–1843.
The section on birds is sub-headed Ornithology and
the volumes are numbered, in addition to the above,
I–XIV in their own sub-heading.
Vols. I and II Humming-Birds 1833.
64 coloured plates.
Vol. III Gallinaceous Birds 1834.
30 coloured plates, some copied from Gould and Au-
dubon, by James Stewart.
Vol. IV Game birds 1834.
30 coloured plates.
Vol. V Pigeons by Selby 1835.
30 coloured plates by Edward Lear and Jean Gabriel
Prêtre.
Vol. VI Parrots by Selby 1836.
30 coloured plates by Lear.
Vols. VII–VIII Birds of Western Africa by Swainson
1837.
64 coloured plates by Swainson.
Vols. IX, XI, XII, XIV British Birds 1838–1843.
129 coloured plates by Stewart.
Vol. X Flycatchers, by Swainson 1838.
31 coloured plates by Swainson.
Vol. XIII Sunbirds 1843.
30 coloured plates by Stewart.
All without author's name as by Jardine.
The *Naturalist's Library* was reprinted in 1844,
1845–46, 1848, 1852–55 and 1864; there was a special
edition of the *Humming-Birds* in 1840. Full analysis by
Zimmer (1926, pp. 324–32).

JARDINE, Sir WILLIAM (editor)
CONTRIBUTIONS TO ORNITHOLOGY
5 vols. 8vo and 4to.
Edinburgh 1848–1853.
103 hand-coloured lithographs.
Rare.

JARDINE, Sir WILLIAM, see SELBY 1821 etc.,
WILSON 1808 (1832)

JASPER, THEODORE, see J. H. STUDER 1874

JAUBERT, JEAN BAPTISTE MARIE and CHRISTOPH
JEROME BARTHELEMY-LAPOMMERAYE
RICHESSES ORNITHOLOGIQUES DU MIDI DE LA
FRANCE, OU DESCRIPTION METHODIQUE DE TOUS
LES OISEAUX OBSERVES EN PROVENCE ET DANS LES
DEPARTEMENTS CIRCON VOISINS
Large 4to.
Marseilles 1859(–1862).
21 hand-coloured lithographs by J. Susini.

JENNINGS, C.
THE EGGS OF BRITISH BIRDS, DISPLAYED IN A SERIES
OF ENGRAVINGS, COPIED AND COLOURED FROM
NATURE
8vo.
London 1853.
6 coloured plates.

JERDON, THOMAS CLAVERHILL
ILLUSTRATIONS OF INDIAN ORNITHOLOGY,
CONTAINING FIFTY FIGURES OF NEW, UNFIGURED
AND INTERESTING SPECIES OF BIRDS, CHIEFLY FROM
THE SOUTH OF INDIA
4to (also 8vo).
Madras 1843–1847.
Published in 4 parts: 50 coloured plates 'by native East
Indian artists'.

JERRARD, PAUL
THE HUMMING BIRD KEEPSAKE
Small folio.
London n.d. (*c.* 1850)
12 coloured lithographs.

JOHNSON, G. W., see WINGFIELD 1853

JONES, HOWARD E. and S. H. McMULLIN
ILLUSTRATIONS OF THE NESTS AND EGGS OF BIRDS
OF OHIO
1 vol. in 3. Folio.
Circleville, Ohio 1879–1886.
68 coloured lithographs by Genevieve E. Jones, Eliza
J. Schulze, Virginia E. Jones and Nellie D. Jacob.

JONES, THOMAS RYMER, see A. E. BREHM 1869

JONSTON, JOHANNES
HISTORIÆ NATURALIS DE QUADRUPEDIBUS, . . . DE
INSECTIS, . . . DE SERPENTIBUS ET DRACONIBUS,
. . . DE AVIBUS . . . CUM ÆNIS FIGURIS
6 books in 1 vol. Small folio.
Frankfurt-am-Main 1650–*c.* 1652.
6 illuminated titles, and 245 hand-coloured engravings, of which 62 (Book 6) are of 'birds', including
those fabulous and monstrous, probably by Matthæus (Jr) and Kaspar Merian.
Other editions Amsterdam 1657–*c.* 1665 and Frankfurt-am-Main 1657–68 with same plates (sometimes
reversed). All these mentioned here because the source
of several eighteenth-century editions, of which we
can cite:

JONSTON, JOHANNES
IOANNIS IONSTONI THEATRVM VNIVERSALE DE
AVIBUS TABVLIS DVABVS ET SEXAGINTA AB ILLO
CELEBERRIMO MATHIA MERIANO AERI INCISIS
ORNATVM EX SCRIPTORIBVS TAM ANTIQVIX, QVAM

EAGLE OWL.
Bubo maximus (Sibbald)

Drawn on Stone by E. Lear.   Printed by C. Hullmandel.

RECENTORIBVS, THEOPHRASTO. . . . PISONE ET
ALIIS MAXIMA CVRA CONLECTVM ET OB RARITATEM
DENVO INPRIMENDVM SUSCEPIT
4to.
Heilbronn 1756.
The 2nd volume of the three volumes of an edition of
1755–69: 62 coloured engravings as in seventeenth-
century eds.

*JONSTON, JOHANNES
COLLECTION DES OISEAUX PLUS RARES, TRADUITE
DU LATIN DE JONSTON—DE LAQUELLE ON A FAIT
PRECEDER L'HISTOIRE PARTICULIERE DES OISEAUX
DE LA MENAGERIE DU ROI PEINT D'APRES NATURE
PAR LE CELEBRE ROBERT (NICOLAS ROBERT). POUR
SERVIR DE SUITE A L'HISTOIRE DES INSECTES ET
PLANTES DE MADEMOISELLE DE MERIAN
Large folio.
Paris 1772(–1774).
85 fine hand-coloured engravings after Nicolas
Robert.
A very rare book.

KEARTON, RICHARD
BIRDS' NESTS, EGGS, AND EGG-COLLECTING
8vo.
London 1890.
16 coloured plates.

KEARTON, RICHARD, see SWAYSLAND 1883

KEELER, CHARLES AUGUSTUS
EVOLUTION OF THE COLORS OF NORTH AMERICAN
LAND BIRDS
8vo.
San Francisco 1893.
18 coloured lithographic plates by Keeler.

KENNEDY, ALEXANDER WILLIAM MAXWELL
CLARK
THE BIRDS OF BERKSHIRE AND BUCKINGHAMSHIRE:
A CONTRIBUTION TO THE NATURAL HISTORY OF
THE TWO COUNTIES
Crown 8vo.
Eton and London 1868.
4 hand-coloured photographs.

KENNERLY, C.B.R., see BAIRD 1859

KEULEMANS, JOHN GERRARD
ONZE VOGELS IN HUIS EN TUIN, BESCHREVEN EN
AFGEBEELD
3 vols. Small folio.
Leyden 1869–1876.
200 hand-coloured lithographs by Keulemans.

KEULEMANS, JOHN GERRARD
A NATURAL HISTORY OF CAGE BIRDS
8vo.
London 1871.
24 coloured lithographs by Keulemans.

KIDDER, DANIEL PARISH and JAMES COOLEY
FLETCHER
BRAZIL AND THE BRAZILIANS, PORTRAYED IN
HISTORICAL AND DESCRIPTIVE SKETCHES
8vo.
Philadelphia 1857.
2 coloured plates of birds.

KINBERG, JOHAN GUSTAF HJALMAR, see
SUNDEVALL 1856

KING, W. ROSS
THE SPORTSMAN AND NATURALIST IN CANADA, OR
NOTES ON THE NATURAL HISTORY OF THE GAME,
GAME BIRDS AND FISH OF THAT COUNTRY
Royal 8vo.
London 1866.
3 coloured plates of birds by W. L. Walton.

von KITTLITZ, FRIEDRICH HEINRICH
ÜBER DIE VÖGEL INSELGRUPPE VON BONIN-SIMA
8vo.
St Petersburg 1830.
5 hand-coloured engravings by von Kittlitz.

von KITTLITZ, FRIEDRICH HEINRICH
ÜBER EINIGE VÖGEL VON CHILI
4to.
St Petersburg 1830–1834.
17 hand-coloured engravings by von Kittlitz.

von KITTLITZ, FRIEDRICH HEINRICH
ÜBER EINIGE NOCH UNBESCHRIEBENE VÖGEL VON
DER INSEL LUZON, DEN CAROLINEN UND DEN
MARIANEN
4to.
St Petersburg 1831.
14 hand-coloured engravings by von Kittlitz.
Above 3 publ. in *Mem. Acad. Sci. St. Petersb.* 1 and 2.

PLATE 35
*Edward Lear drew "Bubo Maximus" before he created the fictional suitor
of* The Owl and the Pussy-Cat *(1871). Clearly, he had a gift for drawing owls.
It is one of the many hand-colored lithographs by Lear
that illustrate John Gould's* The Birds of Europe *(London 1832–37).*

Dessiné par M. WOLF.

Publié chez A. ARNZ et Comp. à LEIDE.

LE GROËNLANDAIS, FAUCON BLANC MUÉ.

von KITTLITZ, FRIEDRICH HEINRICH
> KUPFERTAFELN ZUR NATURGESCHICHTE DER VÖGEL
> Demy 8vo.
> Frankfurt-am-Main 1832–1833.
> 36 hand-coloured copper-plates.

KJÆRBOLLING, NIELS
> DANMARKS FUGLE (ORNITHOLOGIA DANICA:
> ICONES ORNITHOLOGIÆ SCANDINAVICÆ)
> Crown 8vo and small folio atlas.
> Copenhagen 1851–1856.
> 104 hand-coloured plates by Kjærbolling, some en-
> gravings and some lithographs. Two volumes (61
> plates) publ. 1851–52 as *Danmarks Fugle*; first suppl.
> (35 pl.) 1854 as *Ornithologia Danica*; second suppl. (8
> pl.) 1856 as *De i det ovrige Scandinavien: . . . forekom-
> mende Fuglearter.*
> New edition 1858–1865 and again 1872–1879, the lat-
> ter ed. Jonas Collin with 106 coloured plates, the two
> new ones by Carl Christian Larsen Cordts, publ. sep-
> arately in 1879 as *To nye Tavler til Dr Kjærbolling's
> Skandinaviens Fugle.*

KLEIN, JAKOB THEODOR
> OVA AVIUM PLURIMARUM AD NATURALEM
> MAGNITUDINEM DELINEATA ET GENUINIS
> COLORIBUS PICTA
> 4to.
> Leipzig 1766.
> 21 hand-coloured engravings of 145 eggs by Klein.

**KNIP, Madame ANTOINETTE PAULINE
JACQUELINE RIFER (née de COURCELLES),
COENRAAD JACOB TEMMINCK and FLORENT
PREVOST
> LES PIGEONS, PAR MADAME KNIP, NEE PAULINE DE
> COURCELLES, PREMIER PEINTRE D'HISTOIRE
> NATURELLE DE S.M. L'IMPERATRICE REINE MARIE-
> LOUISE
> 2 vols. Large folio.
> Paris. Vol. I, 1809–1811 and altered reprint 1838, Vol.
> II, 1838–*c.* 1843.
> 147 coloured plates from paintings by Knip. Vol. I, 87
> coloured plates engraved by Jean César Macret,
> printed in colour and finished by hand. Superbly
> painted and reproduced these are among the finest of
> all bird plates. The numbers of the plates are unusually
> difficult to follow running I–XI, I–XXXII, XXXI
> (33), XXXIV–LIX, I–XVI and one unnumbered (25
> bis). Text of this volume by Temminck.

Vol. II: 60 coloured plates a few engraved by François
Jacques Dequevauviller or Guyard, the rest
lithographs. Numbering normal save that plate VI is
wrongly numbered XI. Text by Prévost.
Both volumes originally issued in 15 parts. The first
volume of this book was originally to be called 'Histoire naturelle générale des Pigeons', but Knip altered
this at the 9th part, when she 'took over' the publication of the book from Temminck and re-issued a new
title page. 12 copies received by Temminck for himself, bore the original title.
Prince Bonaparte's *Pigeons* 1857–58 (which see) is a
supplement to these volumes, but unlike his *American
Ornithology*, ranks as a completely separate work.
A good explanation of the plates by Zimmer (1926,
pp. 356–57) and of the theft of the work by Knip from
Temminck by Coues (1878, pp. 794–96).

KNIP, A. PAULINE J. R., see BONAPARTE 1857,
DESMAREST 1805

KNOBEL, EDWARD
> FIELD KEY TO THE LAND BIRDS
> Crown 8vo.
> Boston 1899.
> 9 coloured plates by Knobel.

KOEHLER, FR. EUGEN
> SCHÄDLICHE VOGELARTEN
> 8vo.
> Gera-Untermhaus 1896.
> 25 coloured plates.

KOEHLER, FR. EUGEN
> NÜTZLICHE VOGELARTEN UND IHRE EIER
> 8vo.
> Gera-Untermhaus 1898.
> 24 coloured plates.
> Later editions.

KOLTHOFF, GUSTAF ISAK and AXEL LEONARD
KRISTER EDVARD JÄGERSKIÖLD
> NORDENS FÄGLAR
> Folio.
> Stockholm 1895–1902.
> 69 coloured plates by L. L. Ljunggren, all publ. by
> 1898.

PLATE 36
*The aristocratic history of falconry stimulated Hermann Schlegel
and A. H. de Wülverhorst to produce* Traité de fauconnerie *(Leiden and Düsseldorf 1844–53).
The text is a comprehensive history and bibliography,
with an ornithology of the hawks.
This Greenland Falcon modeling leather hood accoutrement
is one of the beautiful lithographs by Joseph Wolf.*

KÖRNER, M. P.
SKANDINAVISKA FOGLAR, TECKNADE EFTER
NATUREN, . . .
4to.
Lund 1839–1846.
62 hand-coloured lithographs by Körner.
2nd edition 1859.
Scarce.

KÜHL, HEINRICH
CONSPECTUS PSITTACORUM . . .
4to.
Bonn 1820.
3 coloured plates by Huard and Alphonse Prévost.

KÜSTER, HEINRICH CARL, see HAHN 1818, 1834

de LABATIE, see BOUTEILLE 1843

LACEPEDE, Comte BERNARD GERMAIN
ETIENNE de la VILLE, see de BUFFON 1749 (1817, 1828)

LACROIX, ADRIEN
CATALOGUE RAISONNE DES OISEAUX OBSERVES
DANS LES PYRENEES FRANÇAISES ET LES REGIONS
LIMITROPHES . . .
8vo.
Toulouse and Paris 1873–1875.
8 coloured plates by Lacroix.

LAISHLEY, RICHARD
A POPULAR HISTORY OF BRITISH BIRDS' EGGS
Crown 8vo.
London 1858.
20 coloured plates of eggs.

LAMOUROUX, M., see de BUFFON 1749 (1824)

LANDBECK, CHRISTIAN LUDWIG
SYSTEMATISCHE AUFZAHLUNG DER VÖGEL
WÜRTEMBERGS, MIT ANGABE IHRER
AUFENTHALTSÖRTER UND IHRER STRICHZEIT. . . .
Post 8vo.
Stuttgart and Tübingen 1834.
This will probably be found to contain plates, though
as extras. The author's own copy (Zimmer, 1926, p.
368) contains '13 plates, two of which are original
drawings, 2 apparently unpublished lithographs, 8
lithographs prepared for publication as pl. I–V, VIII,
IX and XI of the author's *Naturgeschichte und Ab-
bildungen sämmtlicher Vögel Europa's* (which never appeared) and 1 etching of uncertain origin'.

LANIER, SIDNEY
BOB; THE STORY OF OUR MOCKING-BIRD
8vo.
New York 1899.
16 coloured plates.

LANSING, Mrs JENNY H. and RALPH HOFFMANN
BIRD WORLD; A BIRD BOOK FOR CHILDREN
8vo.
Boston 1898.
8 coloured plates.

LAPLACE, CYRILLE PIERRE THEODORE, JOSEPH
FORTUNE THEODORE EYDOUX and FRANÇOIS
LOUIS PAUL GERVAIS
VOYAGE AUTOUR DU MONDE PAR LES MERS DE
L'INDE ET DE CHINE EXECUTE SUR LA CORVETTE DE
L'ETAT LA FAVORITE PENDENT LES ANNEES 1830,
1831 ET TO 1832 . . . ZOOLOGIE
8vo.
Paris 1836–1839.
The fifth of a five-volume report (1833–39), first pub-
lished in parts, and as a whole with slight alterations in
1839. 30 coloured plates of birds by Edouard Traviès,
Jean Gabriel Prêtre and Alphonse Prévost.

*LATHAM, JOHN
A GENERAL SYNOPSIS OF BIRDS
3 vols. in 6. 4to.
London 1781–1785.
1st supplement 1787; 2nd supplement 1802 (probably
1801).
All plates by Latham.
Vols. I–III, 106 hand-coloured engravings and 6 illuminated titles. 1st supplement 13 hand-coloured engravings and an illuminated title, 2nd supplement 23
hand-coloured engravings and an illuminated title.
New edition Winchester 1821–1828 as *A General History of Birds*, 10 vols. and index vol. 4to. 193 hand-
coloured engravings.
German edition *Allgemeine Übersicht der Vögel*. 4 vols.
4to ed. J. M. Bechstein.
Nuremberg 1793–1812.
183 hand-coloured engravings.

LATHAM, JOHN and HUGH DAVIES
FAUNULA INDICA ID EST CATALOGUS ANIMALIUM
INDIAE ORIENTALIS QUAE HACTENUS NATURAE
CURIOSIS INNOTUERUNT; . . .
Folio.
Halle 1795, in new ed. Johann Reinhold Forster,
whom see.

LATHAM, JOHN, see PENNANT 1769, PHILLIP 1789

LATREILLE, PIERRE ANDRE, see CUVIER 1817

LAUDER, THOMAS DICK and THOMAS BROWN
PARROTS
8vo.
Edinburgh 1833.
35 coloured plates.

LAUGIER de CHARTROUSE, MEIFFREN, see
TEMMINCK 1820

LAWRENCE, GEORGE NEWBOLD, see BAIRD 1858,
1860

LAYARD, EDGAR LEOPOLD and RICHARD
BOWDLER SHARPE
THE BIRDS OF SOUTH AFRICA
8vo.
London 1875–1884.
The second edition of a book by Layard first published
without plates in Cape Town 1867, 12 coloured
lithographs by John Gerrard Keulemans.

LEACH, WILLIAM ELFORD
THE ZOOLOGICAL MISCELLANY; BEING
DESCRIPTIONS OF NEW, OR INTERESTING ANIMALS
3 vols. 4to (8vo size).
London 1814–1817.
150 hand-coloured engravings, some showing birds,
by Leach and Richard P. Nodder.
A continuation of Shaw and Nodder's *Naturalist's Miscellany*, but much more uncommon.

**LEAR, EDWARD
ILLUSTRATIONS OF THE FAMILY OF PSITTACIDAE, OR
PARROTS: THE GREATER PART OF THEM SPECIES
HITHERTO UNFIGURED, . . .
Large folio.
London 1830–1832.
42 hand-coloured lithographs printed by C. Hull-
mandel, drawn and lithographed by Lear.
Issued in 12 parts.

LEAR, EDWARD, see BOURJOT SAINT-HILAIRE
1837, GOULD 1832, 1833, J. E. GRAY 1846

LEFEVRE, AUGUSTE ALFRED
AN ATLAS OF THE EGGS OF THE BIRDS OF EUROPE
Royal 8vo.
Paris and London 1844–*c.* 1845.
136 hand-coloured lithographs of eggs.
Reissue in French and English.
Paris 1848.

LEGGE, WILLIAM VINCENT
A HISTORY OF THE BIRDS OF CEYLON
1 vol. in 2. Large 4to.
London 1878–1880.
34 hand-coloured lithographs by John Gerrard
Keulemans.
2nd edition 1880, with appendix 1881.

LEHMANN, OSKAR
UNSERE VÖGEL
8vo.
Stuttgart 1895.
12 coloured plates.

LEISLER, JOHANN PHILIPP ACHILLES
NACHTRÄGE ZU BECHSTEINS NATURGESCHICHTE
DEUTSCHLANDS
Demy 8vo.
Hanua 1812–1813.
Only two parts issued; two coloured plates by C.
Westermayr.

LELAND, CHARLES GODFREY
LEGENDS OF THE BIRDS
8vo.
Philadelphia 1864.
12 'coloured illustrations, about 1½ inches square,
pasted in the centre of floral designs occupying a
whole page. The book is very scarce'. (Wood 1931, p.
431.)

LEMAIRE, C. L.
(BIBLIOTHEQUE ZOOLOGIQUE) HISTOIRE NATURELLE
DES OISEAUX D'EUROPE. PREMIERE PARTIE.
PASSEREAUX
Royal 8vo.
Paris 1835–1837.
80 hand-coloured engravings and coloured title-page
by the Pauquet brothers.
Second edition 1846; third 1864, by Florent Prévost
and Lemaire.

LEMAIRE, C. L.
BIBLIOTHEQUE ZOOLOGIQUE. HISTOIRE NATURELLE
DES OISEAUX EXOTIQUES
4to (size of 8vo).
Paris 1836.
80 hand-coloured engravings by Pauquet.
Second edition 1837; third edition by Florent Prévost
and Lemaire 1879.

LeMAOUT, JEAN EMMANUEL MARIE see
BERNARD 1842

LeMAOUT, JEAN EMMANUEL MARIE
LES TROIS REGNES DE LA NATURE REGNE ANIMAL
HISTOIRE NATURELLE DES OISEAUX . . . (part of LES
TROIS REGNES DE LA NATURE)
4to.
Paris 1853.
35 plates, of which 16 (or more?) coloured by William
Henry Freeman.
Rare.
Second edition 1855; 34 plates of which 15 coloured.

LEMBEYE, JUAN
AVES DE LA ISLA DE CUBA
4to.
Havana 1850.
20 coloured lithographs copied from Audubon by
Lauro Ferrod. Rare.

Imp Lemercier Paris

62

La Pie rousse Grandeur naturelle

Dendrocitta vagabunda (Gould)

DE LA CHINE

Paris Ledot ainé Edit Rue de Rivoli 174

London E GAMBART & C° 25 Berners S¹ Oxf S¹

LEMBKE, GEORG, see BORKHAUSEN 1800

LENZ, HARALD OTHMAR and OTTO BURBACH
GEMEINNÜTZIGE NATURGESCHICHTE . . . DIE
VÖGEL
Post 8vo.
Gotha 1891.
Fifth edition of a volume first published in 1851.
Twelve coloured plates.

LESKE, NATHANIEL GOTTFRIED, see WIRSING
1767

LESSON, RENE PRIMEVERE
MANUEL D'ORNITHOLOGIE OU DESCRIPTION DES
GENRES ET DES PRINCIPALES ESPECES D'OISEAUX,
AND ATLAS DES OISEAUX
Together 3 vols. 18mo.
Paris 1828.
129 coloured plates, all in the atlas.

LESSON, RENE PRIMEVERE
HISTOIRE NATURELLE GENERALE ET PARTICULIERE
DES MAMMIFERES ET DES OISEAUX NOUVELLES OU
RARES, DECOUVERTS DEPUIS 1788 JUSQU'A NOS
JOURS
10 vols. text, and atlas of plates. 8vo.
Paris 1828–1837.
131 coloured plates by Antoine Germain Bévalet, Paul
Louis Oudart, Jean Gabriel Prêtre, Vauthier and
Edouard Traviès.

*LESSON, RENE PRIMEVERE
HISTOIRE NATURELLE DES OISEAUX-MOUCHES,
OUVRAGE ORNE DE PLANCHES DESSINEES ET
GRAVEES PAR LES MEILLEURS ARTISTES, ET DEDIE A
S.A.R. MADEMOISELLE
1 vol. in 2. 8vo.
Paris 1828–1830.
86 plates, printed in colour and finished by hand, by
Bessa, Antoine Germain Bévalet, Mlle Zoë Dumont,
Mme Lesson, Jean Gabriel Prêtre and Vauthier.
Originally issued in 17 parts. Continued as *Colibris*
1830–32, *Trochilidées* 1832–33 and *Oiseaux de Paradis*
1834–35, which see.

LESSON, RENE PRIMEVERE
TRAITE D'ORNITHOLOGIE, OU TABLEAU
METHODIQUE DES ORDRES, SOUS-ORDRES,
FAMILLES, TRIBUS, GENRES, SOUS-GENRES ET RACES
D'OISEAUX
2 vols. 8vo.
Paris 1830–1831.
119 coloured plates by Jean Gabriel Prêtre, all in vol. II.

*LESSON, RENE PRIMEVERE
HISTOIRE NATURELLE DES COLIBRIS, SUIVIE D'UN
SUPPLEMENT A L'HISTOIRE NATURELLE DES
OISEAUX-MOUCHES
1 vol. in 2. 8vo.
Paris 1830–1832.
66 plates, printed in colour and finished by hand, by
Jean Gabriel Prêtre and Antoine Germain Bévalet.
Originally issued in 13 parts.
Reissued 1847.

LESSON, RENE PRIMEVERE
CENTURIE ZOOLOGIQUE OU CHOIX D'ANIMAUX
RARES, NOUVEAUX OU IMPARFAITEMENT CONNUS
8vo and 4to.
Paris 1830–1832.
80 coloured plates (42 of birds) by Jean Gabriel Prêtre.
Originally issued in 16 parts.

*LESSON, RENE PRIMEVERE
LES TROCHILIDEES; OU, LES COLIBRIS ET LES
OISEAUX-MOUCHES, SUIVIS D'UN INDEX GENERAL
8vo.
Paris 1832–1833.
66 coloured plates by Jean Gabriel Prêtre and Antoine
Germain Bévalet.

LESSON, RENE PRIMEVERE
ILLUSTRATIONS DE ZOOLOGIE, OU RECUEIL DE
FIGURES D'ANIMAUX PEINTES D'APRES NATURE, . . .
Royal 8vo.
Paris 1832–1835.
Issued in 20 parts: 60 plates, printed in colour and
finished by hand, by Jean Gabriel Prêtre, Bessa, An-
toine Germain Bévalet and Lesson of which 40 illus-
trate birds.

*LESSON, RENE PRIMEVERE
HISTOIRE NATURELLE DES OISEAUX DE PARADIS ET
DES EPIMAQUES; . . .
8vo.
Paris 1834–1835.
43 plates, printed in colour and finished by hand, by
Jean Gabriel Prêtre and Paul Louis Oudart.
Originally issued in parts (probably 16).

PLATE 37
Edouard Traviès illustrated many exotic ornithologies
with minutely detailed, static scientific drawings. "Pie Rousse" from the artist's
Les oiseaux les plus remarquables *(Paris 1845–c. 1857)*
is animated and confidently drawn,
showing his love of nature and of art.

LESSON, RENE PRIMEVERE
VOYAGE AUTOUR DU MONDE ENTERPRIS PAR ORDRE
DU GOUVERNEMENT SUR LA CORVETTE LA
COQUILLE
2 vols. 8vo.
Paris 1839.
10 coloured plates of birds by Jean Gabriel Prêtre,
Antoine Germain Bévalet and Alphonse Prévost.

LESSON, RENE PRIMEVERE, see de
BOUGAINVILLE 1837, DUPERREY 1826

**LEVAILLANT, FRANÇOIS
HISTOIRE NATURELLE DES OISEAUX D'AFRIQUE
6 vols. Large 4to or large folio (the latter often found
with duplicate sets of plates, coloured and plain).
Paris 1796–1808.
300 plates drawn by Johann Friedrich Leberecht Rein-
old [Reinhold] and engraved by Fissart and Perée.
Printed in colour and finished by hand.
Originally published in 51 parts, 4to [Zimmer (1926,
p. 391) has no evidence of the folio ed. before
1805–08]. A seventh volume with 52 plates was never
published, and 115 further drawings were to have been
used for a continuation of the book.
Incomplete German editions, Nuremberg 1797–1802,
48 plates, ed. Johann Matthaeus Bechstein; and Halle
1798, 18 plates.
Also an incomplete Dutch edition (no details obtain-
able) 1812.

**LEVAILLANT, FRANÇOIS
HISTOIRE NATURELLE D'UNE PARTIE D'OISEAUX
NOUVEAUX ET RARES DE L'AMERIQUES ET DES
INDES
Vol. 1 (all published). Large 4to or large folio, the
latter as similar edition in Oiseaux d'Afrique (see
above).
Paris 1801–1802.
49 engravings, printed in colours and finished by
hand.
These plates were printed by Langlois who did almost
all the colour-printing for Levaillant; books, as well as
much other work at this time. French colour-printing
of this period, which includes all the reproductions of
Redouté's flower paintings, has never been surpassed.
Originally published in 8 parts.

***LEVAILLANT, FRANÇOIS
HISTOIRE NATURELLE DES PERROQUETS
2 vols. Folio and large folio (the latter a large-paper
edition as Oiseaux d'Afrique, see above).
Paris 1801–1805.
145 engravings, drawn by Jacques Barraband, printed
in colours and touched up by hand.
Originally published in 24 parts.
Anker (1938, p. 157) gives a large 4to edition also, but

this is probably a cut down copy of the Folio edition.
Copies of the small-paper editions of Levaillant's
books are sometimes found with duplicate plates plain
and coloured. Large-paper copies are usually printed
on 'papier velin', i.e., paper with a glossy vellum
finish on the printed side.
See also Bourjot Saint-Hilaire 1837–38, de Souancé
1857–58.

***LEVAILLANT, FRANÇOIS
HISTOIRE NATURELLE DES OISEAUX DE PARADIS ET
DES ROLLIERS, SUIVIE DE CELLE DES TOUCANS ET
DES BARBUS
2 vols. Folio and large folio (the latter a large-paper
edition as Oiseaux d'Afrique, see above).
Paris 1801–1806.
114 engravings, drawn by Jacques Barraband, engraved by Pérée, Grémillier and Bouquet, and printed
in colours by Langlois and Rousset and finished by
hand.
Originally published in 19 parts.
This book is usually regarded as incomplete unless the
Histoire naturelle des Promerops, etc. (see under) is with
it.

**LEVAILLANT, FRANÇOIS
HISTOIRE NATURELLE DES PROMEROPS, DES
GUEPIERS, ET DES COUROUCOUS
1 vol. Folio.
Paris 1807–c. 1816.
85 engravings drawn by Jacques Barraband, engraved
by Grémillier, Guyard Fils, Bouquet and Barrière.
Printed in colours by Millevoy, Langlois, Bousset and
Bourlier and finished by hand.
Originally published in 14 parts.
This is generally considered as a third volume of the
Oiseaux de Paradis, see above.
The collation of the plates in some of Levaillant's
books demands care. Anker (1938, pp. 156–58) is par-
ticularly useful to those who would pursue the subject.
Levaillant was until exceeded by Gould (and until now
only by him) the producer of the most comprehensive
series of works on exotic birds.

LEVAILLANT, JEAN, see LOCHE 1849

*LEWIN, JOHN WILLIAM
THE BIRDS OF NEW HOLLAND
Small folio.
London 1808.
18 hand-coloured engravings by Lewin.
Second edition as:
THE BIRDS OF NEW SOUTH WALES
As above, but
Sydney 1813.
Third edition as:

A NATURAL HISTORY OF THE BIRDS OF NEW SOUTH WALES, . . .
An enlarged edition of the two former.
Folio.
London 1822.
26 hand-coloured etchings by Lewin.
Fourth edition London 1838, folio (same plates as 3rd ed.).

***LEWIN, WILLIAM
THE BIRDS OF GREAT BRITAIN WITH THEIR EGGS ACCURATELY FIGURED
7 vols. Folio.
London 1789–1794.
Limited to 60 copies.
The illustrations are, in each set, drawings by Lewin coloured by hand and this is in our experience unique among bird books, its only companion among natural history books being Mrs Bowdich's *British Fresh Water Fishes*.
The plates have a stencilled border and a stamp W. Lewin 1789 in the bottom left-hand corner (outside the stencil) on Plates 1–18 and I–III only, and No. 1, 2, etc., stamped at the top left or right-hand corner inside the border. There is a frontispiece in Vol. 1, unnumbered, but stamped 'Frontispiece' and in addition Vol. 1 has 41 plates plus 7 of eggs stamped in Roman numerals in the top right-hand corner.
The following plates run:
Vol. II   (1790)   42–86 plus VIII–XIII of Eggs.
Vol. III   (1791)   87–127 plus XIV–XVIII.
Vol. IV   (1792)   128–165 plus XIX–XXVIII.
Vol. V   (1792)   166–201 plus XXIX–XXXVII.
Vol. VI   (1793)   202–235 plus XXXVIII–XLVII.
Vol. VII (1794)   236–265 plus XLVIII–LII.
In all 324 plates.
The rarest of all English bird books. The workmanship of the earlier plates is superior to that of the later ones; this is not to be wondered at since Lewin must have been exhausted by his extraordinary task.
*Second edition:
8 vols. 4to.
London 1795–1801.
336 hand-coloured engravings.
This book of course bears no comparison with the previous edition.
Further editions 1812 and 1838.

LICHTENSTEIN, ANTON AUGUST HEINRICH
BEITRAG ZUR ORNITHOLOGISCHEN FAUNA VON CALIFORNIEN, NEBST BEMERKUNGEN ÜBER DIE ARTKENNZEICHEN DER PELICANE UND ÜBER EINIGE VÖGEL VON DEN SANDWICH-INSELN
Folio.
Berlin 1838.
5 coloured plates.

LICHTHAMMER, J. W., see BORKHAUSEN 1800

LILFORD, THOMAS LYTTELTON POWYS fourth Baron and OSBERT SALVIN
COLOURED FIGURES OF THE BIRDS OF THE BRITISH ISLES
7 vols. Large 8vo.
London 1885–1898.
421 plates in 36 parts many drawn by Archibald Thorburn, some by John Gerrard Keulemans, George Edward Lodge and William Foster. Chromolithographed.
Second edition 1891–98, of first 28 parts, thereafter same as 1st ed.

LINDNER, FRIEDRICH WILHELM
MALERISCHE NATURGESCHICHTE DER DREI REICHE, FÜR SCHULE UND HAUS . . . [part] VÖGEL
Large 4to.
Brunswick 1840–1844.
4 coloured lithographs by C. W. F. Krämer.

LLOYD, LLEWELYN
THE GAME BIRDS AND WILD FOWL OF SWEDEN AND NORWAY ETC.
Royal 8vo.
London 1867.
52 lithographs, 47 hand-coloured, of which 33 of birds, by Magnus Peter Körner, Wilhelm von Wright and Joseph Wolf.
2nd ed. 1867 with 48 chromolithographs.

LOCHE, VICTOR and JEAN LEVAILLANT
EXPLORATION SCIENTIFIQUE DE L'ALGERIE . . .
1840–42, . . . ZOOLOGIE, VOL. IV [BIRDS]
Folio.
Paris 1849–1867.
15 colour-printed engravings, retouched by hand, after Auguste Nicolas Vaillant and Johann Carl Werner.

LORD, THOMAS
LORD'S ENTIRE NEW SYSTEM OF ORNITHOLOGY
Folio.
London 1791.
111 hand-coloured engravings.

LORENZ, THEODOR [FEDOR] KARLOVIČ
BEITRAG ZUR KENNTNISS DER ORNITHOLOGISCHEN FAUNA AN DER NORDSEITE DES KAUKASUS
Large 4to.
Moscow 1887.
5 hand-coloured photogravures by Lorenz.

LUCAS, JOHN
THE PLEASURES OF A PIGEON-FANCIER
Crown 8vo.
New York 1887.
3 coloured plates.
New edition London 1899, 2 coloured plates.

LUTZ, K. G.
DIE RAUBVÖGEL DEUTSCHLANDS, NEBST EINEM
ANHANG ÜBER VOGELSCHUTZ
8vo.
Stuttgart [1888].
16 coloured lithographs.

LYDON, C., see SHARPE 1898

MacGILLIVRAY, WILLIAM, see CUVIER 1817 (1840)

McMULLIN, S. H., see H. E. JONES 1879

M'MURTRIE, H. M. see CUVIER 1817 (1831)

MacPHERSON, HUGH ALEXANDER, see BUTLER
1896

MADARÁSZ, GYULA [JULIUS von]
MAGYAROSZÁG MADARAI . . . [THE BIRDS OF
HUNGARY]
Large 8vo (4to size).
Budapest 1899–1903.
6 coloured plates (4 by 1900).

MADARÁSZ, GYULA, see von PELZELN 1887

**MALHERBE, ALFRED
MONOGRAPHIE DES PICIDEES, OU HISTOIRE
NATURELLE DES PICIDES, PICUMNINES, YUNCINES
OU TORCOLS . . .
4 vols. Large folio.
Metz 1859–1862.
Issued in 24 parts; 123 lithographs coloured by hand,
by Delahaye, Mesnel and Paul Louis Oudart.
Limited to 100 copies.

MALO, CHARLES
LA VOLIERE DES DAMES
12mo.
Paris 1816.
Frontispiece and 11 plates, all engravings coloured by
hand.

***MANETTI, XAVIERO and GIOVANNI GERINI
ORNITHOLOGIA METHODICE DIGESTA ATQUE
ICONIBUS AENEIS AD VIVUM ILLUMINATIS ORNATA
(STORIA NATURALE DEGLI UCCELLI)
5 vols. Large folio.
Florence 1767–1776.
'Illustrated by 600 costly copper plates colored from
nature. Not only each volume but each plate has a
separate dedication.' (Wood, 1931, p. 450). The drawings were by Violante Vanni, Lorenzo Lorenzi and
Manetti. Zimmer (1926, p. 241) regards them as 'ex-
ecrable', but many are colourful and spirited, and
some of the foretitles are lively. But ornithologically

this book served only to create confusion. In spite of
this Manetti's *Ornithologia* is one of the half-dozen or
so Great Bird Books in the collector's sense.

MARSHALL, CHARLES HENRY TILLSON and
GEORGE FREDERICK LEYCESTER MARSHALL
A MONOGRAPH OF THE CAPITONIDAE, OR
SCANSORIAL BARBETS
Large 4to.
London 1870–1871.
73 coloured lithographs by John Gerrard Keulemans.

MARSHALL, CHARLES HENRY TILLSON, see
HUME 1879

MARSHALL, WILLIAM ADOLF LUDWIG
DIE PAPAGEIEN
8vo.
Leipzig 1889.
63 coloured plates.

MARTIN, WILLIAM CHARLES LINNAEUS
A GENERAL HISTORY OF THE HUMMING-BIRDS, OR
THE TROCHILIDÆ: WITH ESPECIAL REFERENCE TO
THE COLLECTION OF J. GOULD, F. R. S. ETC. . . .
Foolscap 8vo.
London 1852.
17 hand-coloured engravings.
Sometimes regarded as belonging to Jardine's *Natu-
ralist's Library*, which see.

MARTIN, WILLIAM CHARLES LINNAEUS, see
MUDIE 1834 (1853)

MARTORELLI, GIACINTO
MONOGRAFIA ILLUSTRATA DEGLI UCCELLI DI RAPINA
IN ITALIA
Large 4to.
Milan, 1895.
4 coloured plates.

MARTYN, WILLIAM FREDERIC
A NEW DICTIONARY OF NATURAL HISTORY
2 vols. Folio.
London 1785.
100 hand-coloured engravings, many of birds.

MATHEW, MURRAY ALEXANDER, see BUTLER
1896, D'URBAN 1892

MAYNARD, CHARLES JOHNSON
THE BIRDS OF FLORIDA
4to.
Newtonville, Mass. 1872–1879.
Never completed: 9 parts published, with 16 coloured
plates. Very rare.
This work was continued and extended as:

THE BIRDS OF EASTERN NORTH AMERICA; WITH ORIG-
INAL DESCRIPTIONS OF ALL THE SPECIES WHICH OC-
CUR EAST OF THE MISSISSIPPI RIVER, BETWEEN THE
ARCTIC CIRCLE AND THE GULF OF MEXICO, . . .
4to.
Newtonville 1879–1881.
28 coloured plates. Very rare.
Of this a revised edition, 1881, with 32 coloured plates.
A further completely revised edition, Imperial 4to.,
1889–1896, numerous coloured plates and text-fig-
ures. Rare. For a good account of this highly complex
publication see Zimmer (1926, pp. 423–24).

MAYNARD, CHARLES JOHNSON
THE NATURALIST'S GUIDE IN COLLECTING AND
PRESERVING OBJECTS OF NATURAL HISTORY, WITH A
COMPLETE CATALOGUE OF THE BIRDS OF EASTERN
MASSACHUSETTS
8vo.
Salem, Massachusetts 1877.
This, the third edition, has two coloured plates of
birds (the first and second eds., Boston 1870, 1871 had
none).

MAYNARD, CHARLES JOHNSON
EGGS OF NORTH AMERICAN BIRDS
8vo.
Boston 1890.
10 hand-coloured plates of eggs.

MAYNARD, CHARLES JOHNSON
HANDBOOK OF THE SPARROWS, FINCHES, ETC., OF
NEW ENGLAND
8vo.
Newtonville, Mass. 1896.
18 coloured lithographs.

MEISNER, CARL FRIEDRICH AUGUST and
HEINRICH RUDOLF SCHINZ
DIE VÖGEL DER SCHWEIZ, SYSTEMATISCH
GEORDNET UND BESCHRIEBEN, MIT BEMERKUNGEN
ÜBER IHRE LEBENSART UND AUFENTHALT
8vo.
Zürich 1815.
Coloured plates.
An enlarged edition of Meisner's *Systematisches Ver-
zeichniss der Vögel*, Berne 1804, which had no plates.

MELVILLE, ALEXANDER GORDON, see
STRICKLAND 1848

MENZBIR, MIKHAIL ALEKSANDROVICH
ORNITOLOGICHESKAYA GEOGRAFIYA EVROPEISKOI
ROSSII
Royal 8vo.
Moscow 1882.
8 chromolithographs by N. Severtsov.
Second edition 1892.

MENZBIR, MIKHAIL ALEKSANDROVICH
ORNITHOLOGIE DU TURKESTAN ET DES PAYS
ADJACENTS
6 vols. Large 4to.
Moscow 1888–1894.
15 coloured plates by Atchouev, Martinov and Menzbir.

MERIAN, MATTHÆUS (Jr) see JONSTON 1756

MERREM, BLASIUS
BEYTRÄGE ZUR BESONDERN GESCHICHTE DER
VÖGEL GESAMMELT
2 parts. Folio.
Göttingen and Leipzig 1784–1786.
12 hand-coloured engravings by Merrem, Christian
Eberhard Eberlein and Johann Christoph Berken-
kamp. Very rare.
Also as edition in Latin 1786.

MEYEN, FRANZ JULIUS FERDINAND
NOVORUM ACTORUM ACADEMÆ CÆSARÆ
LEOPOLDINO-CAROLINÆ NATURÆ CURIOSORUM.
VOL. XVI. SUPPLEMENT I, SISTENS F. J. F. MEYENII
OBSERVATIONES ZOOLOGICAS, IN ITINERE CIRCUM
TERRAM INSTITUTAS, . . . VÖGEL
4to
Bratislava 1834.
21 hand-coloured lithographs of birds by C. L.
Müller.

MEYER, ADOLF BERNHARD
UNSER AUER-, RACKEL- UND BIRKWILD UND SEINE
ABARTEN
2 vols. Large 4to text, elephant folio atlas.
Vienna 1887.
17 lithographs by G. Mützel coloured by hand.

MEYER, ADOLF BERNHARD and LIONEL
WILLIAM WIGLESWORTH
THE BIRDS OF CELEBES AND THE NEIGHBOURING
ISLANDS
2 vols. Large 4to.
Berlin 1898.
45 lithographs by Bruno Geisler, of which 42 colo-
ured.

**MEYER, BERNHARD and JOHANN WOLF
NATURGESCHICHTE DER VOGEL DEUTSCHLANDS IN
GETREUEN ABBILDUNGEN UND BESCHREIBUNGEN
2 vols, 4to text, folio atlas.
Nuremberg 1799–1807.
180 hand-coloured engravings by Ambrosius Gabler,
J. M. Hergenröder and Johann Carl Bock.

MEYER, BERNHARD and JOHANN WOLF
TASCHENBUCH DER DEUTSCHEN VÖGELKUNDE, . . .
8vo.

Edouard Travriès

Le Hobereau (Buffon) ⅔ nature

Falco Subbuteo (Linnee)

EUROPE

Paris,Ledot ainé Edit. Rue de Rivoli 174

Frankfurt-am-Main 1810.
77 hand-coloured engravings by J. M. Hergenröder and Gustav Philipp Zwinger.
Supplement (no plates) 1822. Rare.

*MEŸER, HENRY LEONARD
ILLUSTRATIONS OF BRITISH BIRDS
4 vols. Folio.
London 1835–1841.
313 hand-coloured lithographs.
2nd issue (1837–44), 320 hand-coloured lithographs.
The method of issue, most confused, is analysed by Wood (1931, p. 462).

MEŸER, HENRY LEONARD
COLOURED ILLUSTRATIONS OF BRITISH BIRDS, AND THEIR EGGS
7 vols. 8vo.
London 1841–1850 (later issue 1852–57).
432 hand-coloured lithographs by Mëyer.
New edition 1853–57 with 411 hand-coloured lithographs.

**MEYER, JOHANN DANIEL
ANGENEHMER UND NÜTZLICHER ZEIT-VERTREIB MIT BETRACHTUNG CURIOSER VORSTELLUNG ALLERHAND KRIECHENDER, FLIEGENDER UND SCHWIMMENDER, . . .
2 vols. Large folio.
Nuremberg 1748–1752.
240 copper engravings by Meyer, hand-coloured, of which about a hundred are of birds.
A very rare and unusual book which has a plate of each bird, and underneath or on a succeeding page a plate of its anatomy.

von MIDDENDORFF, ALEXANDER THEODOR
REISE IN DES ÄUSSERSTEN NORDEN UND OSTEN SIBIRIENS . . . 1843 UND 1844 . . . VOL. II. ZOOLOGIE. PART II. SÄUGETHIERE, VÖGEL UND AMPHIBIEN. . . . B. VÖGEL
4to.
St. Petersburg 1853 (whole report 4 vols. 1847–75).
13 coloured lithographs of birds by Wilhelm Georg Pape.

MILLAIS, JOHN GUILLE
GAME BIRDS AND SHOOTING-SKETCHES; . . .
4to.

2nd edition London 1894.
34 lithographs, 16 coloured (the first edition, 1892, has no coloured plates).

MILLER, Mrs HARRIET
FIRST BOOK OF BIRDS
8vo.
Boston 1899.
8 coloured plates.

MILLER, JOHN FREDERICK
VARIOUS SUBJECTS OF NATURAL HISTORY WHEREIN ARE DELINEATED BIRDS, ANIMALS AND MANY CURIOUS PLANTS, ETC. . . .
1776–1792.
Folio.
London.
60 hand-coloured copper engravings.
Very rare.
The first edition of the *Cimelia Physica*, see below.

*MILLER, JOHN FREDERICK and GEORGE SHAW
CIMELIA PHYSICA, FIGURES OF RARE AND CURIOUS QUADRUPEDS, BIRDS & C. TOGETHER WITH SEVERAL OF THE MOST ELEGANT PLANTS
Large folio.
London 1796.
60 copper engravings (41 birds) by Miller, hand-coloured.
Printed by Bensley and Lance, attractive typographically, notably the title page. The second edition of the previous work.

MILNE-EDWARDS, ALPHONSE
RECHERCHES ANATOMIQUES ET PALEONTOLOGIQUES POUR SERVIR A L'HISTOIRE DES OISEAUX FOSSILES DE LA FRANCE
4 vols. Medium 4to.
Paris 1867–1871.
6 coloured plates.

MILNE-EDWARDS, ALPHONSE and ALFRED GRANDIDIER
RECHERCHES SUR LA FAUNE ORNITHOLOGIQUE ETEINTE DES ILES MASCAREIGNES ET DE MADAGASCAR
Large 4to.
Paris 1866–1874 (in *Ann. Sci. Nat*, (5) 6–19).
38 coloured plates: reprinted as a whole 1874, with only 33 plates, of which 3 coloured.

PLATE 38
*This striking falcon illustrates Edouard Traviès's
collection of lithographs,* Les oiseaux les plus remarquables *(Paris 1845–c. 1857).
Traviès executed this portfolio of about eighty lithographs
in a style all his own. The images show his genius for portraying birds
in naturalistic settings.*

MILNE-EDWARDS, ALPHONSE and EMILE
OUSTALET

    NOTICE SUR QUEL QUES ESPECES D'OISEAUX
    ACTUELLEMENT ETEINTES QUI SE TROUVENT
    REPRESENTEES DANS LES COLLECTIONS DU
    MUSEUM D'HISTOIRE NATURELLE
    Folio.
    Paris 1893.
    5 hand-coloured lithographs by John Gerrard
    Keulemans.

MILNE-EDWARDS, ALPHONSE, see GRANDIDIER
1876

MITCHELL, DAVID WILLIAM, see JOSEPH WOLF
1861

MITCHELL, FREDERICK SHAW

    THE BIRDS OF LANCASHIRE
    Post 8vo.
    London 1885.
    2 coloured lithographs by John Gerrard Keulemans.
    The second edition (1892, ed. Howard Saunders) has
    no coloured plates.

MITTERPACHER, LUDWIG, see PILLER 1783

MIVART, ST GEORGE

    A MONOGRAPH OF THE LORIES, OR BRUSH-
    TONGUED PARROTS, COMPOSING THE FAMILY
    LORIIDÆ
    Large 4to.
    London 1896.
    61 hand-coloured lithographs by John Gerrard Keu-
    lemans.

MÖBIUS, KARL AUGUST, see REICHENOW 1894

MONTAGU, GEORGE

    SUPPLEMENT TO THE ORNITHOLOGICAL
    DICTIONARY, OR SYNOPSIS OF BIRDS
    8vo.
    London 1813.
    Wood (1931, p. 470) points out that there is a rare
    Appendix of 24 coloured engravings by Eliza Dorville
    issued with some copies of this *Supplement*.

de MONTBEILLARD, PHILIB. GUENEAU, see de
BUFFON 1749, 1770

MONTES de OCA, RAFAEL

    ENSAYO ORNITOLOGICO DE LOS TROQUILIDEOS O
    COLIBRIES DE MEXICO
    Folio.
    Mexico City 1875.
    12 coloured plates.

MOORE, JOHN, see EATON 1858.

MOQUIN-TANDON, ALFRED, see WEBB 1841

MORRIS, BEVERLY ROBINSON

    BRITISH GAME BIRDS AND WILD FOWL
    4to.
    London 1855.
    60 hand-coloured and color printed wood-engravings
    by Benjamin Fawcett.
    New editions 1873, 1891 and 1895, the last 2 volumes,
    enlarged by William Bernhard Tegetmeier.

MORRIS, FRANCIS ORPEN

    A HISTORY OF BRITISH BIRDS
    6 vols. Royal 8vo.
    London 1851–1857.
    358 hand-coloured wood engravings by Benjamin
    Fawcett. Some from drawings by Richard Alington.
    Reissues 1856–62, 1863–64, 1865–66.
    New editions 1870, 1891, 1895–96, the last with 394
    col. pl.
    Also a much inferior Crown 8vo 'cabinet' edition n.d,
    [1863–67], reprinted in 1888.

MORRIS, FRANCIS ORPEN

    A NATURAL HISTORY OF THE NESTS AND EGGS OF
    BRITISH BIRDS
    3 vols. Royal 8vo.
    London 1853–1856.
    223 hand-coloured wood engravings.
    Later editions 1870–71, reissued 1875 (232 col. pl.),
    1892, 1896, the last revised by William Bernhard
    Tegetmeier (248 col. pl.).

MORRIS, FRANCIS ORPEN, see DesMURS 1886

MOSLEY, SETH LISTER

    A HISTORY OF BRITISH BIRDS, THEIR NESTS, AND
    EGGS
    3 vols. 8vo.
    Huddersfield 1881–1892.
    277 coloured lithographs. Book unfinished, but 50 of
    its plates used in:

PLATE 39

Many fine bird books were written for the scientific identification
of newly discovered species. Fancy fowl breeding prompted a genre of bird books
exemplified by Ferguson's Illustrated Series of Rare and Prize Poultry (London 1854).
C. J. Culliford has drawn "White-crested Black Polands"
and "Partridge Shanghaes" to illustrate author George Ferguson's breeding success.

MOSLEY, SETH LISTER
ANNOTATED CATALOGUE OF BRITISH BIRDS, NESTS
AND EGGS
8vo.
Huddersfield 1896.
50 coloured plates (see above).

MOTLEY, JAMES and LEWIS LLEWELLYN
DILLWYN
CONTRIBUTIONS TO THE NATURAL HISTORY OF
LABUAN, AND THE ADJACENT COASTS OF BORNEO
Royal 8vo.
London 1855.
5 coloured plates of birds by Joseph Wolf.

MUDIE, ROBERT
THE FEATHERED TRIBES OF THE BRITISH ISLANDS
2 vols. Foolscap 8vo.
London 1834.
2 coloured Baxtertypes as frontispieces, and 18 coloured lithographs. Second edition 1835.
3rd edition, 1841, as above but frontispieces no longer
in Baxtertype. Fourth edition ed. William Charles
Linnaeus Martin 1853–54 reissued 1861, with plain
plates, and again 1878, etc.

von der MÜHLE, HEINRICH
MONOGRAPHIE DER EUROPÄISCHEN SYLVIEN
2 vols. 8vo text and 4to plates.
Regensburg 1856.
4 coloured plates.

MÜLLER, ADOLF and KARL
THIERE DER HEIMATH; DEUTSCHLANDS
SÄUGETHIERE UND VÖGEL, . . . ZWEITES BUCH.
WESEN UND WANDEL DER VÖGEL. DRITTE AUFLAGE
2 vols. 4to.
Cassel 1882–1883.
24 coloured plates by C. F. Deiker and Müller.
Another edition 1897.

MÜLLER, JOHANNES
DIE VORZÜGLICHSTEN SING-VÖGEL TEUTSCHLANDS
MIT IHREN NESTERN UND EYERN NACH DER NATUR
ABGEBILDET UND AUS EIGENER ERFAHRUNG
BESCHRIEBEN. . . .
4to.
Nuremberg 1799–1800.
26 hand-coloured engravings.

von MÜLLER, JOHANN WILHELM
DESCRIPTION DE NOUVEAUX OISEAUX D'AFRIQUE,
DECOUVERTS ET DESSINEES D'APRES NATURE, POUR
SERVIR DE SUITE AUX PLANCHES ENLUMINEES DE
BUFFON AUX PLANCHES COLORIEES DE TEMMINCK
ET LAUGIER DE CHARTROUSE ET AU NOUVEAU
RECUEIL GENERAL DE PLANCHES PEINTES

D'OISEAUX DE O. DES MURS
Folio.
Stuttgart 1853.
16 coloured plates.

MÜLLER, OTTO FRIDERICH
ZOOLOGIA DANICA . . . VOL. IV
Folio.
Copenhagen 1806.
4 coloured plates of birds.
For early editions and discussion of this work, which
began in 1777, see Anker (1938, p. 167).

MÜLLER, SALOMON and HERMANN SCHLEGEL,
ed. COENRAAD JACOB TEMMINCK
VERHANDELINGEN OVER DE NATUURLIJKE
GESCHIEDNIS DER NEDERLANDSCHE OVERZEESCHE
BEZITTINGEN, DOOR DE LEDEN DER
NATUURKUNDIGE COMMISSIE IN INDIË EN ANDERE
SCHRIJVERS
Folio.
Leiden 1839–1844.
14 hand-coloured lithographs from drawings by
Joseph Wolf, Schlegel and A. S. Mulder.

MULSANT, MARTIAL ETIENNE
LETTRES A JULIE SUR L'ORNITHOLOGIE
Royal 8vo.
Paris 1868.
16 coloured plates by Edouard Traviès.

MULSANT, MARTIAL ETIENNE and EDOUARD
VERREAUX
HISTOIRE NATURELLE DES OISEAUX-MOUCHES OU
COLIBRIS CONSTITUANT LA FAMILLE DES
TROCHILIDES
4 vols. and supplement. Large 4to.
Lyons etc. 1873–1879.
120 coloured lithographs by Antoine Germain Bévalet
and Mesplis.

MURRAY, JAMES A.
THE AVIFAUNA OF BRITISH INDIA AND ITS
DEPENDENCIES. . . .
2 vols. 4to.
London and Bombay 1887–1890.
19 coloured plates.

NASH, JOSEPH
A PRACTICAL TREATISE ON BRITISH SONG BIRDS; IN
WHICH IS GIVEN EVERY INFORMATION RELATIVE TO
THEIR NATURAL HISTORY, INCUBATION, &C.
TOGETHER WITH THE METHOD OF REARING AND
MANAGING BOTH OLD AND YOUNG BIRDS
12mo.
London 1824.
8 coloured plates.
Another edition 1872.

**NAUMANN, JOHANN ANDREAS and JOHANN FRIEDRICH NAUMANN

NATURGESCHICHTE DER LAND- UND WASSER-VÖGEL DES NÖRDLICHEN DEUTSCHLANDS UND ANGRÄNZENDER LÄNDER, NACH EIGENEN ERFAHRUNGEN ENTWORFEN

(alternative title)

AUSFUHRLICHE BESCHREIBUNG ALLER WALDFELD- UND WASSER-VÖGEL, WELCHE SICH IN DEN ANHALTISCHEN FÜRSTENTHÜMERN UND EINIGEN UMLIEGENDEN GEGENDEN AUFHALTEN UND DURCH-ZIEHEN

Demy 8vo.

Leipzig and Cöthen 1795–1817.

Published originally in 21 parts and a supplement of 8 further parts. The 21 parts formed 4 volumes, so the complete text is 4 volumes (bound as 8) and a supplement, octavo. With the 21 parts and the first 3 supplemental parts there were issued 8 folio hand-coloured engravings, forming 192 coloured plates in all by Johann Friedrich Naumann and Friedrich Osterloh. Only 3 complete sets of these are believed to exist. With the last 5 supplemental parts there issued 8 octavo hand-coloured engravings while at the same time the original 192 folio plates were re-issued in 8vo size, requiring 193 plates since one folio plate became two in the smaller edition.

New edition by Johann Friedrich Naumann (son) under the title.

*NATURGESCHICHTE DER VÖGEL DEUTSCHLANDS. NACH EIGENEN ERFAHRUNGEN ENTWORFEN. . . .

13 vols. in 15. Post 8vo. The thirteenth volume being a supplement by J. F. N. (1847) with second (posthumous) supplement (1860) by Johann Heinrich Blasius, August Carl Edouard Baldamus and Johann Heinrich Christian Friedrich Sturm.

Leipzig and Stuttgart 1822–1860.

396 hand-coloured engravings (5 title pages and 391 plates) by Naumann and Strum.

The text entirely rewritten.

Re-issued again under the title:

NATURGESCHICHTE DER VÖGEL MITTEL-EUROPAS, ed. Carl Richard Hennicke and many others.

12 vols. Folio.

Gera-Untermhaus 1896–1905.

439 chromolithographs from entirely new drawings; and the text entirely rewritten to become the most scholarly and complete ornithological text book of its time (perhaps of any time). A very scholarly collation of Naumanniana in Zimmer (1926, pp. 453–61).

NAUMANN, JOHANN FRIEDRICH and CHRISTIAN ADAM ADOLPH BUHLE

DIE EIER DER VÖGEL DEUTSCHLANDS UND DER BENACHBARTEN LÄNDER; . . .

4to.

Halle 1818–1828.

10 hand-coloured engravings. Grässner's *Die Vögel Deutschlands und ihre Eier*, 1860, which see, derives much (including plates) from this.

NAUMANN, JOHANN FRIEDRICH

ÜBER DEN HAUSHALT DER NORDISCHEN SEEVÖGEL EUROPAS

Oblong 4to.

Leipzig 1824.

2 hand-coloured engravings.

NAUMANN, JOHANN FRIEDRICH, see GRÄSSNER 1860, J. A. NAUMANN

NEHRKORN, ADOLPH

KATALOG DER EIERSAMMLUNG NEBST BESCHREIBUNGEN DER AUSSER EUROPÄISCHEN EIER

Royal 8vo.

Brunswick 1899.

4 coloured plates of eggs.

NEHRLING, HEINRICH

DIE NORDAMERIKANISCHE VOGELWELT

4to.

Milwaukee, Wis. 1889–1891.

Appeared in 13 parts, 36 coloured lithographs by Robert Ridgway, A. Göring and Gustav Mützel.

English edition Milwaukee 1889–1896 as:

NORTH AMERICAN BIRDS

changing after a few parts to:

OUR NATIVE BIRDS OF SONG AND BEAUTY, . . .

Appeared in 16 parts, 2 vols., same plates.

NELSON, EDWARD WILLIAM

REPORT UPON NATURAL HISTORY COLLECTIONS MADE IN ALASKA BETWEEN THE YEARS 1877 AND 1881

4to.

Washington 1887.

12 coloured plates of birds by Robert and John Livzey Ridgway and Nelson.

NEUMEISTER, GOTTLIEB

DAS GANZE DER TAUBENZUCHT

4to.

Weimar 1837.

15 coloured plates.

NEWBERRY, JOHN STRONG

REPORTS OF EXPLORATIONS AND SURVEYS. . . . FOR A RAILROAD FROM THE MISSISSIPPI RIVER TO THE PACIFIC OCEAN . . . VOLUME VI . . . REPORT UPON THE BIRDS

4to.

Washington 1857.

2 hand-coloured lithographs.

NEWBERRY, JOHN STRONG, see BAIRD 1859

NEWTON, ALFRED, see WOLLEY 1864

NILSSON, SVEN
ORNITHOLOGICA SVECICA
2 vols. Post 8vo.
Copenhagen 1817-1821.
12 hand-coloured engravings by Anders Arvid Arvidsson.

NILSSON, SVEN
ILLUMINERADE FIGURER TILL SKANDINAVIENS
FAUNA
2 vols. 4to.
Lund 1829–1840.
200 hand-coloured lithographs (163 of birds) by Magnus Peter Körner, one by Wilhelm von Wright.

NODDER, FREDERICK POLYDORE, see SHAW 1789

NOLAN, J. J.
ORNAMENTAL, AQUATIC AND DOMESTIC FOWL AND
GAME BIRDS
8vo.
Dublin 1850.
50 coloured plates.

NORTH, ALFRED JOHN
A LIST OF THE INSECTIVOROUS BIRDS OF NEW
SOUTH WALES
8vo.
Sydney 1896–1897.
14 plates, of which 12 coloured.

***NOZEMAN, CORNELIS, MARTINUS HOUTTUYN
and JAN CHRISTIAN SEPP
NEDERLANDSCHE VOGELEN; VOLGENS HUNNE
HUISHOUDING, AERT EN EIGENSCHAPPEN
5 vols. Large folio.
Amsterdam 1770–1829.
5 very fine hand-coloured title pages and 250 hand-coloured engravings by Sepp.
The first part of a French edition:
OISEAUX DE HOLLANDE
was published in Amsterdam 1778

NUYENS, A.
DE VOGELWERELD; HANDBOEK VOOR LIEFHEBBERS
VAN KAMER- EN PARKVOGELS

2 vols. Folio.
Gröningen 1886.
266 coloured lithographs.
Rare.

OGILVIE-GRANT, WILLIAM ROBERT
A HAND-BOOK TO THE GAME-BIRDS
2 vols. Crown 8vo.
London 1895–1897.
39 coloured lithographs by John Gerrard Keulemans
and others.
New edition 1896–1897 with 6 more coloured plates.

OGILVIE-GRANT, WILLIAM ROBERT, see SHARPE
1874, WHITEHEAD 1893

OKEN, LORENZ
ABBILDUNGEN ZU OKEN'S ALLGEMEINE
NATURGESCHICHTE FÜR ALLE STANDE . . . XII.
CLASSE. VÖGEL . . . AND ERG. I . . . DIE NESTER
UND EIER DER VÖGEL
Folio.
Stuttgart 1839–1843.
15 hand-coloured lithographs of birds and 8 of eggs
and nests; copied from Daubenton, Levaillant, Temminck, Wilson, etc.

ORBIGNY, see D'ORBIGNY

ORD, GEORGE, see WILSON 1808

OUDART, PAUL LOUIS, see VIEILLOT 1820

OUSTALET, EMILE
MISSION SCIENTIFIQUE DU CAP HORN. 1882–1883.
TOME VI. ZOOLOGIE. OISEAUX
4to.
Paris 1891.
6 coloured lithographs by John Gerrard Keulemans.

OUSTALET, EMILE, see DAVID 1877, MILNE-
EDWARDS 1893

OWEN, RICHARD, see GOULD 1833

PALLAS, PETER SIMON
ZOOGRAPHIA ROSSO-ASIATICA, . . .
3 vols. Small folio, with addenda and plates.
St Petersburg 1811–1842 (plates 1834–42).
26 hand-coloured engravings of birds by Friedrich
Leonhard Lehmann and others.

PLATE 40
The iridescent plumage of hummingbirds fascinated John Gould,
and he collected 5,000 of their skins. His eight-volume
A Monograph of the Trochilidae, or Family of Humming-birds *(London 1849–87),*
completed by Richard Bowdler Sharpe, illustrates hundreds of species,
in the main drawn on stone by Henry C. Richter and colored by William Hart.
"Pterophanes Temmincki" is named for the Dutch ornithologist [q.v.].

J. Daverne col et lith.

P. Bertrand éditeur

Lith. Julioi à Tours.

Evopsitta Wagleri. (Gray.)

PALMEN, JOHANN AXEL, see SUNDMAN 1879

PALMSTRUCH, JOHAN WILHELM, GUSTAV
JOHAN BILLBERG, CONRAD QUENSEL, OLOF
SWARTZ and JOHANN WILHELM DALMAN
SVENSK ZOOLOGI. VOLS. I AND II . . . [AVES]
8vo.
Stockholm 1806–1825.
12 hand-coloured engravings from drawings by Palm-
struch.

PAQUET, HENRI REMI RENE ('NEREE QUEPAT')
MONOGRAPHIE DUE CINI
8vo.
Paris 1875
2 coloured plates.

PÄSSLER, CARL WILHELM GOTTFRIED, see
BÄDEKER 1855–63.

PEARLESS, see PRATT

von PELZELN, AUGUST, JULIUS von [GYULA]
MADARÁSZ and LUDWIG von LORENZ
MONOGRAPHIE DER PIPRIDÆ ODER MANAKIN-
VÖGEL
Small folio.
Budapest 1887.
4 coloured plates by Madarász.

von PELZELN, AUGUST, see HOLUB 1882, von
WÜLLERSTORF-URBAIR 1865

**PENNANT, THOMAS
THE BRITISH ZOOLOGY. CLASS I: QUADRUPEDS.
CLASS II: BIRDS. PUBLISHED UNDER THE INSPECTION
OF THE CYMMRODORION SOCIETY, INSTITUTED FOR
THE PROMOTING OF USEFUL CHARITIES, AND THE
KNOWLEDGE OF NATURE, AMONG THE
DESCENDANTS OF THE ANCIENT BRITONS
Large folio.
London 1761–1766.
132 hand-coloured engravings, 121 of which are of
birds. The title page says, 'illustrated with 107 copper
plates', and as originally issued in 4 parts this is true, 98
being of birds, but in 1766 an appendix with 25 plates,
23 of birds, appeared completing the work. On account of the title page, however, copies with 107 plates
only are not positively held to be imperfect. Engravings designed and coloured mostly by Peter Paillou,

engraved by Peter Mazell; some after F. A. Desmou-
lins, G. Haulner, Charles Collins, Peter Brown and
George Edwards.
Later editions of *The British Zoology* issued in various
formats, none with coloured plates.

PENNANT, THOMAS
INDIAN ZOOLOGY
Small folio.
London 1769.
12 hand-coloured engravings (11 of birds) after Pieter
Cornelis de Bevere.
Part one, all issued.
2nd edition Medium 4to 1790, 16 coloured plates, 14 of
birds, incorporating work of Latham, Davies and
Forster, which see.

PENNANT, THOMAS, see P. BROWN 1776

PERCHERON, GASTON
LE PERROQUET, HISTOIRE NATURELLE, HYGIENE,
MALADIES
8vo.
Paris 1878.
20 coloured plates.

PERRY, GEORGE
ARCANA; OR, THE MUSEUM OF NATURAL HISTORY:
CONTAINING THE MOST RECENT DISCOVERED
OBJECTS, EMBELLISHED WITH COLOURED PLATES
AND CORRESPONDING DESCRIPTIONS; WITH
EXTRACTS RELATING TO ANIMALS, AND REMARKS
OF CELEBRATED TRAVELLERS; COMBINING A
GENERAL SURVEY OF NATURE
8vo and 4to.
London 1810–1811.
84 engravings in (rare) full set, of which 72 coloured.
Scarce.

du PETIT-THOUARS, ABEL AUBERT, FLORENT
PREVOST and MARC ATHANESE PARFAIT
OEILLET DesMURS
VOYAGE AUTOUR DU MONDE SUR LA FREGATE LA
VENUS . . . ZOOLOGIE MAMMAIFERES, OISEAUX,
REPTILES ET POISSONS
2 vols. 8vo text, Large folio atlas.
Paris 1846–1855.
9 coloured plates of birds by Paul Louis Oudart.

———

PLATE 41
Iconographie des perroquets *(Paris 1857–58) by Charles de Souancé et al*
pictures parrots discovered since the publication of earlier monographs by Levaillant (plates 14 and 15)
and Bourjot Saint-Hilaire (plate 34).
Artist J. Daverne has breathed life into his lithograph, "Evopsitta Wagleri,"
painted from a birdskin at the Musée de Paris.

PHILLIP, ARTHUR, HENRY LIDGBIRD BALL,
JOHN WATTS and JOHN LATHAM
THE VOYAGE OF GOVERNOR PHILLIP TO BOTANY
BAY; . . .
4to.
London 1789.
19 coloured engravings of birds, mostly by Peter
Mazell.
Second and third editions 1790; abridged German edi-
tion 1790; German and French editions 1791; part in
German edition 1793.

PIDGEON, EDWARD, see CUVIER 1817 (1827)

PIESCH, DAVID, see WIRSING 1767

PILLER, MATHIAS and LUDWIG MITTERPACHER
ITER PER POSEGANAM SCLAVONIÆ PROVINCIAM
4to.
Budapest 1783.
2 coloured figures of birds.

PLESKE, THEODOR DMITRIEVICH
ORNITHOGRAPHIA ROSSICA . . .
4to.
St Petersburg 1889–1892.
4 coloured plates by Gustav Mützel.

PLESKE, THEODOR DMITRIEVICH and VALENTIN
L'VOVICH BIANCHI
WISSENSCHAFTLICHE RESULTATE DER VON N.M.
PZEWALSKI NACH CENTRAL-ASIEN
UNTERNOMMENEN REISEN . . . VOL. II VÖGEL . . .
4to.
St Petersburg 1889–1905.
10 hand-coloured lithographs by Gustav Mützel and
John Gerrard Keulemans, of which two published
after 1900.

du PLESSIS, J., see EDWARDS 1758

POLLEN, FRANÇOIS P. L., D. C. van DAM and
HERMANN SCHLEGEL
RECHERCHES SUR LA FAUNA DE MADAGASCAR ET
DE SES DEPENDANCES, . . . 2ME PARTIE . . .
MAMMIFERES ET OISEAUX
Large 4to.
Leiden 1867–1868.
30 hand-coulored lithographs of birds by John Ger-
rard Keulemans.

POPE, ALEXANDER and ERNEST INGERSOLL
UPLAND GAME BIRDS AND WATER FOWL OF THE
UNITED STATES
Oblong elephant folio.
New York 1877–1878.
20 chromolithographs.

PORTLOCK, NATHANIEL
A VOYAGE ROUND THE WORLD; BUT MORE
PARTICULARLY TO THE NORTH-WEST COAST OF
AMERICA: PERFORMED IN 1785, 1786, 1787, AND
1788, IN THE KING GEORGE AND QUEEN
CHARLOTTE
4to.
London 1789.
5 hand-coloured engravings of birds.

POYNTING, FRANK
EGGS OF BRITISH BIRDS, WITH AN ACCOUNT OF
THEIR BREEDING-HABITS. LIMICOLÆ
4to.
London 1895–1896.
54 chromolithographs of eggs after designs by Poynting and M. Horman-Fisher

PRATT, ANNE (Mrs PEARLESS)
OUR NATIVE SONGSTERS
12mo.
London 1852.
72 coloured lithographs.
Other editions 1853 and 1857.

PREVOST, FLORENT see BONAPARTE 1857, KNIP
1809, LEMAIRE 1836 (1879), du PETIT-THOUARS 1846

PRÜTZ, GUSTAV and H. DIETZ
ILLUSTRIRTES MUSTERTAUBEN-BUCH; ENTHALTEND
DAS GESAMMTE DER TAUBENZUCHT
2 vols. in 1. 4to.
Hamburg 1887.
81 chromolithographs by J. F. Richter.

PUCHERAN, JACQUES, see DUMONT D'URVILLE
1842

QUENSEL, CONRAD, see PALMSTRUCH 1806

QUOY, JEAN RENE CONSTANT, see DUMONT
D'URVILLE 1830, de FREYCINET 1824

RADDE, GUSTAV FERDINAND RICHARD
REISEN IM SÜDEN VON OST-SIBERIEN IN DEN
JAHREN 1855–1859 INCL. . . . BAND II. DIE
FESTLANDS-ORNIS DES SÜDOSTLICHEN SIBERIENS
Large 4to.
St Petersburg 1863.
15 chromolithographs from drawings by Radde.

RADDE, GUSTAV FERDINAND RICHARD
ORNIS CAUCASICA. DIE VOGELWELT DES KAUKASUS
SYSTEMATISCH UND BIOLOGISCH-GEOGRAPHISCH
4to.
Cassel 1884.
26 chromolithographs from drawings by Radde.

RAINE, WALTER
> BIRD-NESTING IN NORTH-WEST CANADA
> 8vo.
> Toronto 1892.
> 6 coloured plates of eggs.

RAMBERT, EUGENE and LEO PAUL SAMUEL ROBERT
> LES OISEAUX DANS LA NATURE; DESCRIPTIONS
> PITTORESQUE DES OISEAUX UTILES
> Folio.
> Paris 1878.
> 110 plates, of which 60 coloured.

RAMSAY, ROBERT GEORGE WARDLAW, see TWEEDDALE 1881

RATHBUN, FRANK R.
> BRIGHT FEATHERS OR SOME NORTH AMERICAN
> BIRDS OF BEAUTY
> Large 4to.
> Auburn, New York 1880–1882.
> 5 hand-coloured plates and 2 hand-coloured text figures.

RATHKE, MARTIN HEINRICH, see ESCHSCHOLZ 1829

RAUSCH, MATHIAS
> DIE GEFIEDERTEN SÄNGERFÜRSTEN DES
> EUROPÄISCHEN FESTLANDES
> 8vo.
> Magdeburg 1899.
> The second edition, 3 coloured plates.

**RAY, JOHN and FRANÇOIS SALERNE
> L'HISTOIRE NATURELLE, ECLAIRCIE DANS UNE DE
> SES PARTIES PRINCIPALES, L'ORNITHOLOGIE. . . .
> 4to.
> Paris 1767.
> Ray's *Synopsis Methodica Avium* of 1713 translated and much edited by Salerne.
> 31 hand-coloured plates drawn and engraved by François Nicolas Martinet, the illustrator of the great Sonnini edition of Buffon's birds (1799, see Buffon) and coloured by Jacques de Sève. H. B. has seen this scarce book in very handsome French morocco bindings.

REICHENBACH, ANTON BENEDICT
> PRAKTISCHE NATURGESCHICHTE DER VÖGEL, FÜR
> GEBILDETE ALLER STÄNDE
> 4to.
> Leipzig 1850.
> 89 coloured steel engravings.

REICHENBACH, HEINRICH GOTTLIEB LUDWIG
> DIE VOLLSTÄNDIGSTE NATURGESCHICHTE DER
> VÖGEL DES IN- UND AUSLANDES, ETC. ABT. II.
> VÖGEL
> 11 vols. 4to.
> Dresden 1845–63.
> 922 coloured plates, 'mostly copied from Gould. Naumann, etc.' (Nissen, 1936, p. 45.) Zimmer (1926, p. 505) says 'The entire work is extremely puzzling as to arrangement and method of appearance and I can find no complete and accurate collation of the various components'. But he then proceeds to give one! (pp. 505–14). Several parts of this work were separately published under various different titles.

REICHENOW, ANTON
> VOGELBILDER AUS FERNEN ZONEN; ABBILDUNGEN
> UND BESCHREIBUNGEN DER PAPAGEIEN
> Folio.
> Cassel 1878–1883.
> 33 coloured lithographs by Gustav Mützel.

REICHENOW, ANTON, ed. KARL AUGUST MÖBIUS
> DIE VÖGEL DEUTSCH-OST-AFRIKAS, from VOL. I of
> DER THIERWELT OST-AFRIKAS UND DER NACHBAR
> GEBIETE
> Large 8vo (4to size).
> Berlin 1894–1896.
> 108 plates, of which 44 coloured.

von REIDER, JAKOB ERNST and CARL WILHELM HAHN
> FAUNA BOICA ODER GEMEINNÜTZIGE
> NATURGESCHICHTE DER THIERE BAYERNS. . . .
> ZWEITE ABT . . . DEUTSCHLANDS VÖGEL IN
> ABBILDUNGEN NACH DER NATUR
> 2 vols. Post and demy 8vo.
> Nuremberg 1830–1835.
> 182 hand-coloured plates, some engravings, some lithographs.

REINHARDT, JOHANNES CHRISTOPHER HAGEMANN, see WALTER 1828

REISER, OTHMAR
> MATERIALIEN ZU EINER ORNIS BALCANCIA. II.
> BULGARIEN. . . .
> Large 8vo (4to size).
> Vienna 1894.
> 3 coloured plates.

REISER, OTHMAR and LUDWIG von FÜHRER
> MATERIALIEN ZU EINER ORNIS BALCANCIA IV.
> MONTENEGRO
> Large 8vo (4to size).
> Vienna 1896.
> 2 coloured plates (Vols. I and III not fully issued by 1900).

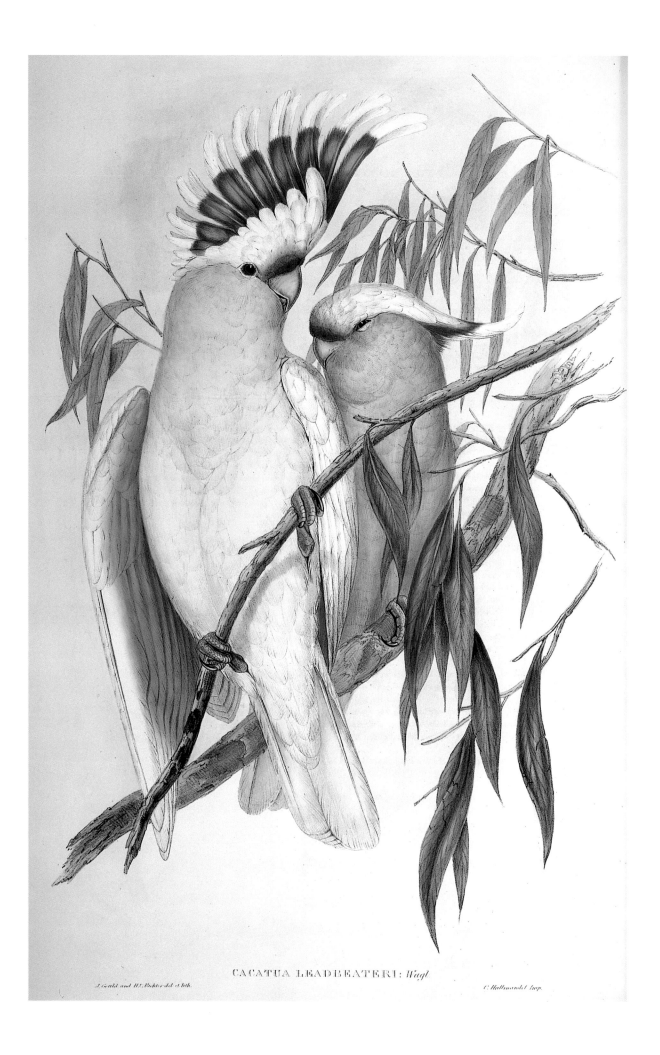

CACATUA LEADBEATERI: *Wagl*

J. Gould and H.C. Richter del. et lith.

C. Hullmandel. Imp.

REY, JEAN GUILLAUME CHARLES EUGENE
DIE EIER DER VÖGEL MITTELEUROPAS
2 vols. 8vo.
Gera-Untermhaus 1889–1905.
128 chromolithographs of eggs by Alexander Reichert.

RICHARD, ACHILLE, see de BUFFON 1749 (1825, 1851)

RICHARDSON, JOHN and WILLIAM SWAINSON
FAUNA BOREALI-AMERICANA; OR THE ZOOLOGY OF THE NORTHERN PARTS OF BRITISH AMERICA: CONTAINING DESCRIPTIONS OF THE OBJECTS OF NATURAL HISTORY COLLECTED ON THE LATE NORTHERN LAND EXPEDITIONS UNDER COMMAND OF CAPTAIN SIR JOHN FRANKLIN, R.N. PART SECOND, THE BIRDS
4to.
London (possibly 1831) 1832 (Vol. 2 of 4 vols. 1829–37).
50 hand-coloured lithographs by Swainson.

RICHARDSON, JOHN, JOHN EDWARD GRAY, GEORGE ROBERT GRAY and RICHARD BOWDLER SHARPE
THE ZOOLOGY OF THE VOYAGE OF H.M.S. EREBUS AND TERROR, UNDER THE COMMAND OF CAPTAIN SIR JAMES CLARK ROSS, R.N., F.R.S., DURING THE YEARS 1839 TO 1843 . . .
2 vols. Large 4to.
London 1844–1875.
37 coloured lithographs of birds by Joseph Wolf and others.

RICHARDSON, JOHN, see DALLAS 1868

RIDGWAY, ROBERT, see BAIRD 1874

RIEDEL, GOTTLEIB FRIEDRICH
SAMMLUNG VON FEDER-VIEH, BESONDERS HAUSGEFLÜGEL
Small folio.
Augsburg 1773.
26 hand-coloured engravings.

von RIESENTHAL, OSKAR
DIE RAUBVÖGEL DEUTSCHLANDS UND DES ANGRENZENDEN MITTELEUROPAS
2 vols. 8vo text, folio plates.

Cassel 1876–1878.
60 chromolithographs from paintings by von Riesenthal.

von RIESENTHAL, OSKAR, see ROBERT 1880

ROBERT, LEO PAUL SAMUEL and OSKAR von RIESENTHAL
GEFIEDERTE FREUNDE. BILDER ZUR NATURGESCHICHTE ANGENEHMER UND NÜTZLICHER VÖGEL MITTEL-EUROPAS . . .
2 vols. Folio plates and royal 8vo text.
Leipzig 1880–1883.
60 chromolithographs by Robert.
Plates issued in 3 parts.
20 of the plates were issued in London 1880 under the title *Glimpses of Bird Life* with text by Harting, whom see.

ROBERT, LEO PAUL SAMUEL, see HARTING 1880, RAMBERT 1878

de ROCHEBRUNE, ALPHONSE TREMEAU
FAUNE DE LA SENEGAMBIE. VOL. I. VERTEBRES [PART 3]. OISEAUX
2 vols. Large 8vo.
Paris 1883–1885.
30 hand-coloured lithographs drawn by J. Terrier.

von ROSENBERG, C. B. HERMANN
REISTOCHTEN NAAR DE GEELVINKBAAI OP NIEUW-GUINEA IN 1869–70
4to.
The Hague 1875.
20 plates of birds, some coloured.

ROTHSCHILD, WALTER
THE AVIFAUNA OF LAYSAN AND THE NEIGHBOURING ISLANDS: WITH A COMPLETE HISTORY TO DATE OF THE BIRDS OF THE HAWAIIAN POSSESSIONS
1 vol. in 2. Large 4to
London, 1893–1900.
83 lithographs, 55 coloured; mostly by John Gerrard Keulemans.

ROUX, JEAN LOUIS FLORENT POLYDORE
ORNITHOLOGIE PROVENÇALE; OU, DESCRIPTION AVEC FIGURES COLORIEES, DE TOUTES LES OISEAUX QUI HABITENT CONSTAMMENT LA PROVENCE, OU QUI N'Y SONT QUE DE PASSAGE: SUIVI D'UN

PLATE 42
This beautiful Leadbeater's Cockatoo illustrates
John Gould's The Birds of Australia *(London 1840–69),*
the fruit of his great journey to that continent. Gould explored Australia for two years,
identifying some 300 new Australasian birds,
most of which were drawn for his book by Henry C. Richter.

Mesnel del et Lith

A Malherbe dirext

MELAMPIC LEWIS (Wils) fig.1.vieux mâle; f.2. id femelle;
f.3. mâle, ad. f.4 femelle ad
f.5. jeune femelle

MELAMPICUS TORQUATUS (Audub)

Lith.Compan rue Rousselot, Nº.15.

ABREGE DES CHASSES, DE QUELQUES
INSTRUCTIONS DE TAXIDERMIE ETC.
2 vols. 4to.
Paris and Marseilles 1825–1830.
425 hand-coloured lithographs drawn by Roux.
Originally published in 56 parts. Rare.

ROWLEY, GEORGE DAWSON (ed).
ORNITHOLOGICAL MISCELLANY
3 vols. Large 4to.
London 1875–1878.
108 hand-coloured lithographs (104 of birds or their
eggs) from drawings by John Gerrard Keulemans.

RÜPPELL, WILHELM PETER EDUARD SIMON and
PHILLIP JAKOB CRETZSCHMAR
ATLAS ZU DER REISE IM NÖRDLICHEN AFRIKA. . . .
ERST ABTHEILUNG ZOOLOGIE
Small folio.
Frankfurt-am-Main 1826–1828.
119 hand-coloured lithographs, 36 of birds by F. C.
Vogel and Friedrich Heinrich von Kittlitz.

RÜPPELL, WILHELM PETER EDUARD SIMON
NEUE WIRBELTHIERE ZU DER FAUNA VON
ABYSSINIEN GEHÖRIG
Folio.
Frankfurt-am-Main 1835–1840.
95 hand-coloured lithographs, 42 of birds by F. C.
Vogel.
Both these books are rare: it is said that only 60 sub-
scribers were obtained by Rüppel.

RÜPPELL, WILHELM PETER EDUARD SIMON
SYSTEMATISCHE ÜBERSICHT DER VÖGEL NORD-OST-
AFRIKA'S, . . .
Royal 8vo.
Frankfurt-am-Main 1845.
50 hand-coloured lithographs, from drawings by
Joseph Wolf.

RUSS, KARL FRIEDRICH OTTO
DIE FREMLÄNDISCHEN STUBENVÖGEL, IHRE
NATURGESCHICHTE, PFLEGE UND ZUCHT
4 vols. 8vo.
Hanover and Magdeburg 1879–1899.
36 coloured plates from drawings by Emil Schmidt.

RUSS, KARL FRIEDRICH OTTO
THE SPEAKING PARROTS: A SCIENTIFIC MANUAL

Crown 8vo.
London 1884.
Transl. by Leonora Schultze of *Die sprechenden Papageien*, Berlin 1882 (no plates).
8 coloured plates by A. F. Lydon.

RUSSELL, ALEXANDER
THE NATURAL HISTORY OF ALEPPO, AND PARTS
ADJACENT. . . .
4to.
London 1756.
16 coloured engravings, of which 3 of birds.
Second edition 1794.

RUSSELL, WILLIAM HOWARD, see TWEEDDALE,
1881

de la SAGRA, RAMON and ALCIDE DESSALINES
D'ORBIGNY
HISTOIRE PHYSIQUE, POLITIQUE ET NATURELLE DE
L'ILE DE CUBA
3 vols. in 2. 8vo text, folio atlas.
Paris 1839–1843.
41 coloured copper-plates, of which 33 of birds by
Jean Gabriel Prêtre and Edouard Traviès.

de la SAGRA, RAMON
ALBUM D'OISEAUX DE CUBA. . . .
2 vols. Folio.
Paris 1843.
Same plates as previous work, with minor modifica-
tions.

SALERNE, FRANÇOIS, see RAY 1767
A translation of a posthumous work by John Ray,
published in 1713. As Salerne has, however put a great
deal of his own into the book, and as the engravings,
which represent its present interest, are French, it
should perhaps be attributed to the Frenchman.

SALVADORI, Count TOMMASO, see SHARPE 1874,
THOMSON 1881

SALVIN, FRANCIS HENRY and WILLIAM
BRODRICK
FALCONRY IN THE BRITISH ISLES
4to.
London 1855.
24 coloured lithographs by Brodrick.
2nd (better) edition 1873: 28 coloured plates (all re-
drawn).

PLATE 43
Alfred Malherbe's Monographie des picidées *(Metz 1859–62)*
is a lavish scientific treatise illustrated with fine,
hand-colored lithographs by Delahaye, Mesnel, Oudart and others.
Alexander Wilson named "Melampic Lewisii" to honor its discoverer, Meriwether Lewis,
who found it on his trans-American journey of 1804–06.

SALVIN, OSBERT and FREDERICK DuCANE
GODMAN
BIOLOGIA CENTRAL-AMERICANA. AVES
4 vols. Large 4to.
London 1879–1904.
84 coloured lithographs by John Gerrard Keulemans
(a few by Edward Neale), of which 68 had appeared by
the end of 1900.

SALVIN, OSBERT, see LILFORD 1885, P. L. SCLATER
1866, SHARPE 1874, THOMSON 1881

SAMUELS, EDWARD AUGUSTUS
ORNITHOLOGY AND OOLOGY OF NEW ENGLAND
8vo.
Boston 1867.
4 coloured plates of eggs.
Later editions, with more coloured plates, 1868,
1869(23), 1870(8).

SAMUELS, EDWARD AUGUSTUS and WILLIAM
COUPER
OUR NORTHERN AND EASTERN BIRDS
Royal 8vo.
New York 1883.
7 coloured plates by Alexander Pope and after Au-
dubon.

SAUNDERS, HOWARD, see SHARPE 1874,
THOMSON 1881

de SAVIGNY, MARIE JULES-CESAR LELORGNE
HISTOIRE NATURELLE ET MYTHOLOGIQUE DE L'IBIS.
8vo.
Paris 1805.
10 coloured engravings from drawings by Henri
Joseph Redouté (younger brother of the famous
flower painter), and Jacques Barraband.
Rare.

de SAVIGNY, MARIE JULES-CESAR LELORGNE.
Ed. JEAN VICTOR AUDOUIN
SYSTEME DES OISEAUX DE L'EGYPTE ET DE LA
SYRIE . . .
4to.
Paris 1810.
14 plates, printed in colour and finished by hand, by
Jacques Barraband, Jean Gabriel Prêtre and Henri
Joseph Redouté.
Part of a larger work, *Description de l'Egypte*, issued
1809–1830, based on observations during the French
expedition 1798–1801.

SCHÄFFER, JACOB CHRISTIAN
ELEMENTA ORNITHOLOGICA ICONIBVS VIVIS
COLORIBVS EXPRESSIS ILLVSTRATA
4to.

Regensburg 1774.
70 hand-coloured engravings from drawings by Joh.
Jos. Rotermundt.
Reissue 1779.

SCHÄFFER, JACOB CHRISTIAN
MUSEVM ORNITHOLOGICVM, EXHIBENS
ENVMERATIONEM ET DESCRIPTIONEM AVIVM QVAS
NOVA PRORSVS RATIONE SIBI PARATAS IN MVSEO
SVO ASSERVAT
4to.
Regensburg 1789.
52 hand-coloured engravings, after Franck, von
Reicheln and others, by Johann Sebastian Leitner,
Johann Christoph Pemsel, Johann Adam Fridrich
(Friedrich) and J. M. Mansinger.

SCHINZ, HEINRICH RUDOLF
BESCHREIBUNG UND ABBILDUNG DER
KÜNSTLICHEN NESTER UND EYER DER VÖGEL, . . .
Large 4to.
Zurich 1819–1830.
73 hand-coloured engravings of eggs by Johann
Daniel Wilhelm Hartmann.
French edition: *Histoire naturelle des Nids, Ouvrages et
des Oeufs des Oiseaux* 1820–1830.

*SCHINZ, HEINRICH RUDOLF, see CUVIER 1817
(1821, 1830, 1846), MEISNER 1815

SCHLEGEL, HERMANN
ABHANDLUNGEN AUS DEM GEBIETE DER ZOOLOGIE
UND VERGLEICHENDEN ANATOMIE
Folio.
Leiden 1841–1851.
6 coloured plates of birds.

**SCHLEGEL, HERMANN, and A. H. VERSTER de
WÜLVERHORST
TRAITE DE FAUCONNERIE
Double-elephant folio.
Leiden and Düsseldorf 1844–1853.
Lithograph title page, 2 lithograph views, and 14 col-
oured lithographs of falcons or falconry, by J. B. Son-
derland, Portman, van Wouw, J. Wolf, C. Scheuren
and G. Saal.

SCHLEGEL, HERMANN and JANUS ADRIAN
HERKLOTS
FAUNA VAN NEDERLANDS—VOGELS
2 vols. in 3. Crown 8vo (all that was published of the
projected *Fauna*).
Leiden 1854–1858.
Issued in 45 parts, 362 hand-coloured lithographs
from drawings by Schlegel.
Re-issued Leiden 1859 and Amsterdam-Haarlem
1877–88 as *De vogels van Nederland*. . . .

SCHLEGEL, HERMANN and GERARDUS
FRIEDRICH WESTERMAN
  DE TOERAKO'S
  Double elephant folio.
  Amsterdam 1860.
  17 hand-coloured lithographs from drawings by
  Schlegel.
  ? new edition Leiden 1868.

SCHLEGEL, HERMANN
  NATUURLIJKE HISTORIE VAN NEDERLAND. DE
  DIEREN VAN NEDERLAND. GEWERVELDE DIEREN.
  . . . DE VOGELS
  Post 8vo.
  Haarlem 1860.
  51 hand-coloured lithographs of birds from drawings
  by Schlegel.
  Second edition Haarlem 1868 (18 col. pl.).
  Not to be confused with *Fauna van Nederlands* series,
  above.

SCHLEGEL, HERMANN
  DE VOGELS VAN NEDERLANSCH INDIË
  3 vols. in 1. Large 4to.
  Leiden and Amsterdam 1863–1866.
  50 hand-coloured lithographs, some by Joseph Smit.

SCHLEGEL, HERMANN, see BONAPARTE 1850, S.
MULLER 1839, POLLEN 1867, von SIEBOLD 1844,
SUSEMIHL 1839 (1845)

von SCHRENK, PETER LEOPOLD
  REISEN UND FORSCHUNGEN IM AMUR-LANDE . . .
  VOL. I . . . PART II VÖGEL DES AMUR-LANDES. . . .
  4to.
  St Petersburg 1860 (whole work 4 vols. and appendix
  1858–95).
  7 hand-coloured lithographs from drawings by
  Wilhelm Georg Pape.

von SCHUBERT, GOTTHILF HEINRICH
  NATURGESCHICHTE DER VÖGEL
  Folio.
  Esslingen n.d.
  30 coloured plates.

SCLATER, PHILIP LUTLEY
  A MONOGRAPH OF THE BIRDS FORMING THE
  TANAGRINE GENUS CALLISTE
  8vo.
  London 1857–1858.
  45 hand-coloured lithographs by Paul Louis Oudart.

SCLATER, PHILIP LUTLEY
  CATALOGUE OF A COLLECTION OF AMERICAN BIRDS
  BELONGING TO PHILIP LUTLEY SCLATER
  Post 8vo.

London 1861–1862.
20 hand-coloured lithographs by John Jennens.
Only 100 copies issued.

SCLATER, PHILIP LUTLEY
  LIST OF THE SPECIES OF PHASIANIDÆ
  8vo.
  London 1863.
  Originally published in *Proc. Zool. Soc. Lon. 1863*
  with 13 coloured plates, but here reissued with 19.
  Rare.

SCLATER, PHILIP LUTLEY and OSBERT SALVIN
  EXOTIC ORNITHOLOGY, CONTAINING FIGURES AND
  DESCRIPTIONS OF NEW OR RARE SPECIES OF
  AMERICAN BIRDS
  Small folio.
  London 1866–1869.
  100 hand-coloured lithographs by Joseph Smit.

SCLATER, PHILIP LUTLEY
  A MONOGRAPH OF THE JACAMARS AND PUFF-BIRDS,
  OR FAMILIES GALBUILDÆ & BUCCONIDÆ
  Large 4to.
  London 1879–1882.
  55 hand-coloured lithographs by John Gerrard Keu-
  lemans.

SCLATER, PHILIP LUTLEY and WILLIAM HENRY
HUDSON
  ARGENTINE ORNITHOLOGY. A DESCRIPTIVE
  CATALOGUE OF THE BIRDS OF THE ARGENTINE
  REPUBLIC
  2 vols. Royal 8vo.
  London 1888–1889.
  20 hand-coloured lithographs by John Gerrard Keu-
  lemans.
  Limited to 200 copies.

SCLATER, PHILIP LUTLEY see SHARPE 1874,
THOMSON 1881, JOSEPH WOLF 1861

SCLATER, WILLIAM LUTLEY, see SHELLEY 1896

***SEBA, ALBERTUS
  LOCUPLETISSIMI RERUM NATURALIUM THESAURI
  ACCURATA DESCRIPTIO, ET ICONIBUS
  ARTIFICIOSISSIMIS EXPRESSIO, PER UNIVERSAM
  PHYSICES HISTORIAM
  4 vols. Large folio.
  Amsterdam 1734–1765.
  451 magnificent engravings by Pieter Tanjé, 227 being
  of birds. H. B. has only seen one copy of this book
  with hand-colouring, but feels certain that it was published in this state.
  In the early part of the century many books were
  issued both plain and coloured.

Bubo maximus. Sibb.

Vol. I 1734; II 1735; III 1758; IV 1765.
Plates reissued, Paris and Strasbourg 1827–30 as *Planches du Cabinet de Seba*, ed. Félix Edouard Guérin-Méneville.

SEEBOHM, HENRY and CHARLES DIXON
A HISTORY OF BRITISH BIRDS, WITH COLOURED ILLUSTRATIONS OF THEIR EGGS
4 vols. 8vo.
London 1882–1885.
68 chromolithographs of eggs printed by Hanhart.
2nd edition 1896.

SEEBOHM, HENRY
THE GEOGRAPHICAL DISTRIBUTION OF THE FAMILY CHARADRIIDÆ, OR THE PLOVERS, SANDPIPERS, SNIPES, AND THEIR ALLIES
Large 4to.
London 1887–1888.
21 hand-coloured lithographs by John Gerrard Keulemans.

SEEBOHM, HENRY and RICHARD BOWDLER SHARPE
COLOURED FIGURES OF THE EGGS OF BRITISH BIRDS, WITH DESCRIPTIVE NOTICES
Royal 8vo.
Sheffield 1896.
60 chromolithographs.

SEEBOHM, HENRY and RICHARD BOWDLER SHARPE
A MONOGRAPH OF THE TURDIDÆ, OR FAMILY OF THRUSHES
2 vols. Large 4to.
London 1898–1902.
149 hand-coloured lithographs by John Gerrard Keulemans, of which 120 published by end 1900.

SEEBOHM, HENRY, see SHARPE 1874, WHITEHEAD 1893

**SELBY, PRIDEAUX JOHN
(PLATES TO SELBY'S) ILLUSTRATIONS OF BRITISH ORNITHOLOGY
2 vols. Double elephant folio.
Text see William Jardine 1826.
Edinburgh 1821–1834.
222 engravings, 222 or 218 hand-coloured, many coloured by Daniel McNee (copies vary).

Published in 19 parts.
Reissued irregularly, and often in part; thus different copies of Vol. I have been found on paper watermarked 1832 and 1839, the former reissued in 1833. Reissued in 1841 by Henry G. Bohn (Bohn's reprint) with the titles coloured.

SELBY, PRIDEAUX JOHN, see JARDINE 1826, 1833, 1835, 1836

**SELIGMANN, JOHANN MICHAEL, see EDWARDS 1743 (1749, 1768, 1772)

SEPP, JAN CHRISTIAN, see NOZEMAN 1770

*SHARPE, RICHARD BOWDLER
A MONOGRAPH OF THE ALCEDINIDÆ: OR, FAMILY OF KINGFISHERS
3 vols. 4to.
London 1868–1871.
120 lithographs coloured by hand from drawings by John Gerrard Keulemans.
Anker (1938, p. 194) 'the printing and colouring sometimes leave much to be desired'.

*SHARPE, RICHARD BOWDLER (editor), with HANS GADOW, EDWARD HARGITT, ERNST HARTERT, WILLIAM ROBERT OGILVIE-GRANT, Count TOMMASO SALVADORI, OSBERT SALVIN, HOWARD SAUNDERS, PHILIP LUTLEY SCLATER, HENRY SEEBOHM and GEORGE ERNEST SHELLEY
CATALOGUE OF THE BIRDS IN THE BRITISH MUSEUM
27 vols. 8vo.
London 1874–1898.
387 hand-coloured and chromolithographs by William Hart, John Gerrard Keulemans, Joseph and Peter Smit.
While this is not a Great Bird Book on the strength of its illustrations, it is certainly one from the Ornithological point of view. A full collation of the volumes and plates, with authors, artists and dates of publication is given by J. T. Zimmer (1926, pp. 95–98). There is an index to species and genera in Sharpe and Ogilvie-Grant (1899–1912), and to genera in *Bull. Brit. Orn. Cl. 9* (1899).

*SHARPE, RICHARD BOWDLER and CLAUDE WILMOTT WYATT
A MONOGRAPH OF THE HIRUNDINIDÆ OR FAMILY OF SWALLOWS

———

PLATE 44
Eugenio Bettoni's Storia naturale degli uccelli *(Milan 1865–71)*
depicts the birds of northern Italy in 126 chromolithographs. Artist Oscar Dressler drew
directly on the stones that printed the various colors for this lifelike rendering
of a nesting Eagle Owl.

2 vols. in 1. 4to.
London 1885–1894.
104 coloured lithographs by Wyatt.

SHARPE, RICHARD BOWDLER
BIRDS IN NATURE
4to.
London and Boston 1888.
39 coloured lithographs by Léo Paul Samuel Robert.
300 copies issued.

SHARPE, RICHARD BOWDLER
SCIENTIFIC RESULTS OF THE SECOND YARKAND
MISSION; BASED UPON THE COLLECTIONS AND
NOTES OF THE LATE FERDINAND STOLICZKA, PH.D.
AVES
Large 4to.
London 1891.
24 coloured lithographs by John Gerrard Keulemans
and William Hart.

**SHARPE, RICHARD BOWDLER
A MONOGRAPH OF THE PARADISEIDÆ, OR BIRDS OF
PARADISE, AND PTILONORHYNCHIDÆ OR BOWER-
BIRDS
2 vols. Small folio.
London 1891–1898.
70 hand-coloured lithographs engraved by John Ger-
rard Keulemans and William Hart, some after plates of
Gould and Sharpe 1875–88 which see.
A continuation of Gould's *Birds of New Guinea*, which
was itself completed by Bowdler Sharpe.

SHARPE, RICHARD BOWDLER
ALLEN'S NATURALIST'S LIBRARY . . . A HAND-BOOK
TO THE BIRDS OF GREAT BRITAIN
4 vols. Crown 8vo.
London 1894–1897.
128 chromolithographs by John Gerrard Keulemans.
Reissued 1896–97 in *Lloyd's Natural History*.

SHARPE, RICHARD BOWDLER
A CHAPTER ON BIRDS . . . RARE BRITISH VISITORS
Crown 8vo.
London 1895.
18 chromolithographs by John Gerrard Keulemans.

SHARPE, RICHARD BOWDLER and C. LYDON
SKETCH-BOOK OF BRITISH BIRDS
8vo.
London 1898.
306 coloured figures.

SHARPE, RICHARD BOWDLER, see DRESSER 1871,
GOULD 1849, 1850, 1875, 1880, LAYARD 1875,
RICHARDSON 1844, SEEBOHM 1896, 1898,
WHITEHEAD 1893

SHAW, GEORGE and FREDERICK POLYDORE
NODDER
THE NATURALISTS MISCELLANY: OR COLOURED
FIGURES OF NATURAL OBJECTS; DRAWN AND
DESCRIBED IMMEDIATELY FROM NATURE
24 vols. 8vo.
London 1789–1813.
1064 hand-coloured engravings, 284 of them of birds,
some by Richard P. Nodder.
See also Leach 1814.

*SHAW, GEORGE
MUSEUM LEVERIANUM, CONTAINING SELECT
SPECIMENS FROM THE MUSEUM OF THE LATE SIR
ASHTON LEVER, KT.; WITH DESCRIPTIONS IN LATIN
AND ENGLISH
Vol. I (all published). 4to.
London 1792–1796.
6 parts; 72 hand-coloured engravings.

SHAW, GEORGE and JAMES SOWERBY
ZOOLOGY OF NEW HOLLAND
Folio.
London 1794.
Various coloured plates of 'mammals and birds inter-
spersed. . . . This must be an extremely rare work'.
(Wood 1931, p. 566).

SHAW, GEORGE, see J. F. MILLER 1796

SHELLEY, GEORGE ERNEST
A HANDBOOK TO THE BIRDS OF EGYPT
Royal 8vo.
London 1872.
14 hand-coloured lithographs from drawings by John
Gerrard Keulemans.

*SHELLEY, GEORGE ERNEST
A MONOGRAPH OF THE NECTARINIIDÆ
(CINNYRIDÆ), OR FAMILY OF SUN-BIRDS
Large 4to.
London 1876–1880.
121 hand-coloured lithographs by John Gerrard
Keulemans.

*SHELLEY, GEORGE ERNEST and WILLIAM
LUTLEY SCLATER
THE BIRDS OF AFRICA, COMPRISING ALL THE SPECIES
WHICH OCCUR IN THE ETHIOPIAN REGION
5 vols. in 7. Large 8vo.
London 1896–1912.
57 hand-coloured lithographs by Henrik Gronvold,
14 published in or before 1900.

SHELLEY, GEORGE ERNEST, see SHARPE 1874

SHIELD, GEORGE
ORNITHOLOGIA BRITANNICA
Large folio.
c. 1840.
6 hand-coloured plates. No text. 'Excessively rare'
(Wood, 1931, p. 567).

von SIEBOLD, PHILIPP FRANZ, COENRAAD
JACOB TEMMINCK and HERMANN SCHLEGEL
FAUNA JAPONICA . . . [AVES]
Folio.
Leiden 1844–1850 (whole work 6 vols. 1833–50).
120 hand-coloured lithographs, some from drawings
by Joseph Wolf and Schlegel.
The second volume of a six-volume work with text
by Temminck and Schlegel published 1833–50.

SLATER, HENRY HORROCKS, see BUTLER 1896

SMELLIE, WILLIAM, see de BUFFON 1749 (1792)

SMITH, Sir ANDREW
ILLUSTRATIONS OF THE ZOOLOGY OF SOUTH
AFRICA; . . .
5 vols. in 4. Large 4to.
London 1839–1849.
279 coloured plates, 114 of birds (in Vol. II) by Ford.

SMITH, C. W. and Sir C. D'OYLY
ORIENTAL ORNITHOLOGY
Folio.
Behar, India 1829.
12 coloured plates, no text; but published.

SMITH, FRANCIS
THE CANARY; ITS VARIETIES, MANAGEMENT, AND
BREEDING . . .
Crown 8vo.
London 1868.
Reprint 1872.
12 coloured plates.

SNELLEMANN, JOH. F., see VETH 1886

SONNINI de MANONCOUR, CHARLES NICOLAS
SIGISBERT, see de BUFFON 1749 (1799)

*de SOUANCE, CHARLES, Prince CHARLES LUCIEN
JULES LAURENT BONAPARTE and EMILE
BLANCHARD
ICONOGRAPHIE DES PERROQUETS NON FIGURES
DANS LES PUBLICATIONS DE LEVAILLANT ET DE M.
BOURJOT SAINT-HILAIRE
4to and Large folio.
Paris 1857–1858.
48 lithographs coloured by hand, by Emile Blanchard
and J. Daverne. Originally intended to be published in

30 parts, publication stopped at part 12. The plate
XLVIII was published separately in 1866. The book is
a supplement to Levaillant's *Histoire des Perroquets*
1801–05, and to Bourjot Saint-Hilaire 1837–38, both
of which see.

SOULEYET, FRANÇOIS LOUIS AUGUSTE, see
VAILLANT 1841

SOUTHWELL, THOMAS, see STEVENSON 1866

SOWERBY, JAMES
THE BRITISH MISCELLANY: OR COLOURED FIGURES
OF NEW, RARE, OR LITTLE KNOWN ANIMAL
SUBJECTS; MANY NOT BEFORE ASCERTAINED TO BE
INHABITANTS OF THE BRITISH ISLES; AND CHIEFLY IN
THE POSSESSION OF THE AUTHOR
2 vols. in 1. 8vo.
London 1804–1806.
7 hand-coloured engravings of birds by Sowerby.

SOWERBY, JAMES, see SHAW 1794

SPALOWSKY, JOACHIM JOHANN NEPOMUK
ANTON
BEITRAG ZUR NATURGESCHICHTE DER VÖGEL
Folio.
Vienna 1790–1795.
271 hand-coloured engravings.

SPARRMAN, ANDREAS
MUSEUM CARLSONIANUM, IN QUO NOVAS ET
SELECTAS AVES, COLORIBUS AD VIVUM BREVIQUE
DESCRIPTIONE ILLUSTRATAS, . . .
Small folio.
Stockholm 1768–1789.
100 hand-coloured engravings from drawings by
Jonas Carl Linnerhielm.

SPARRMAN, ANDREAS
SVENSK ORNITHOLOGIE MED EFTER NATUREN
COLORERADE TEKNINGAR
Folio.
Stockholm 1806–1817.
68 hand-coloured engravings (from the previous
work).
Anker (1938, p. 199) refers to a copy with 70 plates and
Nissen (1936) gives 72.

von SPIX, JOHANNES BAPTIST
AVIUM SPECIES NOVÆ, QUAS IN ITINERE PER
BRASILIAM ANNIS 1817–1820 JUSSU ET AUSPICIIS
MAXIMILIANI JOSEPH I. BAVARIÆ REGIS SUSCEPTO
COLLEGIT ET DESCRIPSIT
2 vols. Large 4to.
Munich 1824–1825.
222 hand-coloured lithographs by Matthias Schmidt.
Revised edition 1840, ed. Karl Friedrich Philipp von
Martius.
Rare.

GALLINULA CHLOROPUS.

J. Wolf and H C Richter del et lith.   Walter & Cohn, Imp.

SPRATT, Mrs G.
THE LANGUAGE OF BIRDS, COMPRISING POETIC AND
PROSE ILLUSTRATIONS OF THE MOST FAVOURITE
CAGE BIRDS. WITH TWELVE HIGHLY-COLOURED
PLATES
12mo.
London 1837.
12 hand-coloured lithographs. 'The plates are cer-
tainly "highly coloured" ' (Wood, 1931, p. 580).
Another edition 1851

STERLAND, W. J.
THE BIRDS OF SHERWOOD FOREST. WITH NOTES ON
THEIR HABITS, NESTING, MIGRATIONS, ETC. BEING A
CONTRIBUTION TO THE NATURAL HISTORY OF THE
COUNTY
Crown 8vo.
London 1869.
3 hand-coloured lithographs by Sterland.

STEVENSON, HENRY and THOMAS SOUTHWELL
THE BIRDS OF NORFOLK, WITH REMARKS ON
THEIR HABITS, MIGRATION, AND LOCAL
DISTRIBUTION. . . .
3 vols. Post 8vo.
London and Norwich 1866–1890.
5 coloured lithographs by Joseph Wolf and Joseph
Smit.

STRACK, FRIEDRICH
NATURGESCHICHTE IN BILDERN MIT
ERLAUTERNDEM TEXT
4to.
Dusseldorf 1819–1821.
150 hand-coloured engravings (72 of birds).

STREUBEL, AUG. VOLLR., see CUVIER 1817 (1846)

STRICKLAND, HUGH EDWIN and ALEXANDER
GORDON MELVILLE
THE DODO AND ITS KINDRED; OR THE HISTORY,
AFFINITIES, AND OSTEOLOGY OF THE DODO,
SOLITAIRE, AND OTHER EXTINCT BIRDS OF THE
ISLANDS MAURITIUS, RODRIGUEZ, AND BOURBON
Folio.
London 1848.
2 coloured lithographs.

STUDER, JACOB HENRY and THEODORE JASPER
STUDER'S POPULAR ORNITHOLOGY, . . . THE BIRDS
OF NORTH AMERICA: DRAWN AND COLOURED FROM
LIFE
Folio.
Columbus, Ohio 1874–1875.
First published in 40 parts; 119 chromolithographs
from drawings by Jasper.
Other editions Columbus 1878, New York 1881, 1882,
1888, 1894, 1895, 1897.

STUDER, THEOPHIL
DIE FORSCHUNGSREISE S.M.S 'GAZELLE' . . .
1874–76 . . . VOL. III. ZOOLOGIE UND GEOLOGIE
4to.
Berlin 1889 (whole report 5 vols. 1888–90).
5 chromolithographs from drawings by O. Bay and
Gustav Mützel.

STURM, JAKOB, JOHANN HEINRICH CHRISTIAN
FRIEDRICH STURM and JOHANN WILHELM
STURM
DEUTSCHLANDS FAUNA IN ABBILDUNGEN NACH
DER NATUR MIT BESCHREIBUNGEN. II.
ABTHEILUNG. DIE VÖGEL
Post 8vo.
Nuremberg 1829–1834.
18 hand-coloured engravings of birds, by J.H.C.F
Sturm.

STURM, JOHANN HEINRICH CHRISTIAN
FRIEDRICH, see NAUMANN 1795 (1860)

STURT, CHARLES
TWO EXPEDITIONS INTO THE INTERIOR OF
SOUTHERN AUSTRALIA, DURING 1828–31
2 vols. 8vo.
London 1833.
4 coloured plates of birds.

SUCHETET, ANDRE
HISTOIRE DU BIMACULATED DUCK DE PENNANT
4to.
Lille 1894.
2 coloured plates.

SUCKLEY, GEORGE, see BAIRD 1859, J. C. COOPER
1859

PLATE 45
This Moorhen illustrates John Gould's
The Birds of Great Britain *(London 1862–73).*
Joseph Wolf details the plumage of fledglings, generally not shown,
in a lively group. Lithographer Henry C. Richter has perfected the background,
a waterlily nursery. Many of the plates in this work show nestlings,
the product of Wolf's field study.

SUNDEVALL, CARL JACOB and JOHAN GUSTAV HJALMAR KINBERG
SVENSKA FOGLARNA
4 vols. text and atlas of plates all oblong folio.
Stockholm 1856–1886 (plates issued between 1856–1869).
Issued originally in 40 parts, the first 21 alone containing plates.
84 hand-coloured lithographs by Peter Åkerlund and Paulina Sjöholm. Rare.

SUNDMAN, GÖSTA and JOHANN AXEL PALMÉN
FINSKA FOGELÄGG (SUOMEN LINTUIN MUNIA)
Small folio.
Helsingfors 1879–1888.
25 chromolithographs of eggs by Sundman.

SUSEMIHL, JOHANN CONRAD and ERWIN EDUARD see BORKHAUSEN 1800

SUSEMIHL, JOHANN CONRAD, ERWIN EDUARD SUSEMIHL and HERMANN SCHLEGEL
ABBILDUNGEN DER VOGEL EUROPAS IN STAHL GESTOCHEN
8vo. and 4to.
Darmstadt (and Stuttgart) 1839–1851.
108 hand-coloured engravings by the Susemihls and 11 hand-coloured lithographs by Joseph Wolf.
Also with French title Histoire naturelle des Oiseaux d'Europe.
Diurnal bird-of-prey material offprinted with 44 plates by Hermann Schlegel in 1845 as Die Europäischen Tag-Raubvögel.

SWAGERS, E.
COLLECTION COMPLETE DES OISEAUX D'EUROPE, DESSINES ET COLORIES D'APRES NATURE
8vo.
Amiens 1833.
400 coloured plates.

SWAINSON, WILLIAM
ZOOLOGICAL ILLUSTRATIONS, OR ORIGINAL FIGURES AND DESCRIPTIONS OF NEW, RARE, OR OTHERWISE INTERESTING ANIMALS, SELECTED CHIEFLY FROM THE CLASSES OF ORNITHOLOGY, ENTOMOLOGY, AND CONCHOLOGY. . . .
1st series 3 vols.
2nd series 3 vols.
8vo.
London 1st series 1820–1823, 2nd series 1829–1833.
334 hand-coloured lithographs (1st series 198; 2nd series 136) by Swainson.
For collation and evidence of reissue in 1840's see Zimmer (1926, pp. 613–14).

SWAINSON, WILLIAM
A SELECTION OF THE BIRDS OF BRAZIL AND MEXICO (also called ORNITHOLOGICAL DRAWINGS, ETC.)
8vo.
London 1834–1841.
78 hand-coloured lithographs by Swainson.
Originally issued in 7 parts under the alternative title.

SWAINSON, WILLIAM see CUVIER 1817 (1827), JARDINE 1833, 1837, 1838, RICHARDSON 1832

SWARTZ, OLOF, see PALMSTRUCH 1806

SWAYSLAND, WALTER see BLAKSTON 1877

SWAYSLAND, WALTER and RICHARD KEARTON
FAMILIAR WILD BIRDS
4 vols. Crown 8vo.
London etc. 1883–1888.
160 chromolithographs, mostly by Archibald Thorburn, some A. F. Lydon.

*SWEET, ROBERT
THE BRITISH WARBLERS, AN ACCOUNT OF THE GENUS SYLVIA; . . .
Royal 8vo.
London 1823.
6 hand-coloured engravings by E. D. Smith.
Further additions and editions; 11 plates by 1828; 16 by 1829.
New edition 1832 with 16 coloured plates.
In 1853 incorporated in English ed. Johann Matthäus Bechstein's Naturgeschichte der Stubenvögel, which see.

SWEET, ROBERT, see BECHSTEIN 1795 (1860)

SYME, PATRICK
A TREATISE ON BRITISH SONG BIRDS. INCLUDING OBSERVATIONS ON THEIR NATURAL HABITS, MANNER OF INCUBATION, &C. WITH REMARKS ON THE TREATMENT OF THE YOUNG AND MANAGEMENT OF THE OLD BIRDS IN A DOMESTIC STATE
8vo.
Edinburgh and London 1823.
15 hand-coloured engravings by R. Scott. Scarce.

TACHANOVSKIY (TACZANOWSKI), LADISLAS (WLADYSLAW)
KONSTANTEGO TYZENHAUZA OOLOGIA PTAKÓW POLSKICH WYSTAWIONA NA 170 TABLICACH . . . DO KTÓRYCH OPISY UTOZYT W. TACZANOWSKI
1 vol. and atlas. 8vo.
Warsaw 1862.
170 coloured plates of eggs.

TEGETMEIER, WILLIAM BERNHARD
> THE POULTRY BOOK: COMPRISING THE BREEDING
> AND MANAGEMENT OF PROFITABLE AND
> ORNAMENTAL POULTRY, THEIR QUALITIES AND
> CHARACTERISTICS; . . .
> Royal 8vo.
> London and New York 1866–1867.
> 30 chromolithographs by Harrison Weir.
> Later editions London 1867 and 1873.
> See also Wingfield 1853

TEGETMEIER, WILLIAM BERNHARD
> PIGEONS: THEIR STRUCTURE, VARIETIES, HABITS
> AND MANAGEMENT
> Royal 8vo.
> London 1868.
> 16 chromolithographs by Harrison Weir.

TEGETMEIER, WILLIAM BERNHARD, see BLYTH
1881, BUTLER 1896, F. O. MORRIS, 1853 (1896)

**TEMMINCK, COENRAAD JACOB and MEIFFREN
LAUGIER de CHARTROUSE
> NOUVEAU RECUEIL DE PLANCHES COLORIEES
> D'OISEAUX, POUR SERVIR DE SUITE ET DE
> COMPLEMENT AUX PLANCHES ENLUMINEES DE
> BUFFON, . . .
> 5 vols. in 6. Folio and 4to. The former a large paper
> edition.
> Paris 1820–1839.
> 600 engravings coloured by hand, by Nicolas Huet
> and Jean Gabriel Prêtre.
> A sequel to the great edition of Buffon's *Natural History* (birds 1770–83) with plates by François Nicolas
> Martinet, which see, also DesMurs's *Iconographie Ornithologique* 1845–49, which is in turn a supplement to
> this work.
> Good collation in Zimmer (1926, pp. 626–28).

TEMMINCK, COENRAAD JACOB, see
BONAPARTE 1857, BOURJOT SAINTE-HILAIRE
1837, DesMURS 1849, KNIP 1809, S. MÜLLER 1839,
von SIEBOLD 1844, WERNER 1826

THEURIET, ANDRE
> NOS OISEAUX
> 4to.
> Lille 1894.
> 41 coloured plates.
> New edition Lille and Paris 1895.

THIENEMANN, FRIEDRICH AUGUST LUDWIG,
CHRISTIAN LUDWIG BREHM and GEORGE
AUGUST WILHELM THIENEMANN
> SYSTEMATISCHE DARSTELLUNG DER
> FORTPFLANZUNG DER VÖGEL EUROPAS MIT
> ABBILDUNGEN DER EIER. . . .
> 4to.
> Leipzig 1825–1838.
> 28 hand-coloured engravings by F. A. L. Thienemann.

THIENEMANN, FRIEDRICH AUGUST LUDWIG
> EINHUNDERT TAFELN COLORIRTER ABBILDUNGEN
> VON VOGELEIERN ZUR FORTPFLANZUNGS-
> GESCHICHTE DER GESAMMTEN VÖGEL
> 2 vols. Large 4to.
> 1845–1856.
> 100 lithographs, of which 89 hand-coloured.

THOMSON, CHARLES WYVILLE, OTTO FINSCH,
WILLIAM ALEXANDER FORBES, ALFRED HENRY
GARROD, TOMMASO SALVADORI, OSBERT
SALVIN, HOWARD SAUNDERS, PHILIP LUTLEY
SCLATER and ARTHUR HAY Marquess of
TWEEDDALE
> REPORT ON THE SCIENTIFIC RESULTS OF THE
> VOYAGE OF H.M.S. CHALLENGER. . . . ZOOLOGY
> VOL. II. PART VIII–REPORT ON THE BIRDS
> Large 4to.
> London 1881.
> 30 hand-coloured lithographs by Joseph Smit.

TIRPENNE, JEAN LOUIS, see TRAVIES 1845.

*TRAVIES, EDOUARD and JEAN LOUIS TIRPENNE
> LES OISEAUX LES PLUS REMARQUABLES
> Folio.
> Paris 1845–c.1857.
> 79 hand-coloured lithographs by Traviès.
> Nissen (1936, pp. 50–51) also gives:—

TRAVIES, EDOUARD
> COLLECTION PITTORESQUE DES PLUS JOLIS OISEAUX
> DES QUATRE PARTIES DU MONDE
> Paris n.d.
> 47 coloured plates by Traviès.

TRAVIES, EDOUARD
> OISEAUX ET PAPILLONS
> Paris n.d.
> 93 coloured plates by Traviès.

TRISTRAM, HENRY BAKER
> THE SURVEY OF WESTERN PALESTINE. THE FAUNA
> AND FLORA OF PALESTINE
> 4to.
> London 1884.
> 7 coloured plates of birds by Joseph Smit.

TROUESSART, EDOUARD LOUIS
> LES OISEAUX UTILES
> Folio.
> Paris 1891.
> 44 coloured plates.

FALCO ÆSALON, *Linn.*

von TSCHUDI, JOHANN JACOB and JEAN LOUIS
CABANIS
UNTERSUCHUNGEN ÜBER DIE FAUNA PERUANA
Large 4to.
St Gallen 1844–1846.
36 hand-coloured lithographs of birds (publ. mostly
in 1846) from drawings by Joseph Dinkel, Schmidt
and Johann Carl Werner.

TUCKER, ANDREW G. C.
ORNITHOLOGIA DANMONIENSIS: OR, AN HISTORY
OF THE HABITS AND ECONOMY OF DEVONSHIRE
BIRDS
4to.
London 1809.
Two parts only publ. 12 plates by W. R. Jordan, of
which 6 coloured.

TURNBULL, WILLIAM PATTERSON
THE BIRDS OF EAST LOTHIAN AND A PORTION OF
THE ADJOINING COUNTIES
8vo and Large 4to.
Glasgow 1867.
First published (no plates) Philadelphia 1863. Glasgow
ed. (only 150 copies 8vo and 50 4to—all but 12 of latter
burned) has coloured frontp. by Edwin Sheppard and
12 coloured text-figures by William Sinclair.
Rare.

TURNER, LUCIEN McSHAN
CONTRIBUTIONS TO THE NATURAL HISTORY OF
ALASKA. RESULTS OF INVESTIGATIONS MADE
CHIEFLY IN THE YUKON DISTRICT AND THE
ALEUTIAN ISLANDS; CONDUCTED UNDER THE
AUSPICES OF THE SIGNAL SERVICE, UNITED STATES
ARMY, EXTENDING FROM MAY, 1874, TO AUGUST,
1881 . . . NO. II
4to.
Washington 1886.
11 chromolithographs from drawings by Robert and
John Livzey Ridgway.

TWEEDDALE, ARTHUR HAY Marquess of and
WILLIAM HOWARD RUSSELL, ed., ROBERT
GEORGE WARDLAW RAMSAY
THE ORNITHOLOGICAL WORKS OF ARTHUR, NINTH
MARQUIS OF TWEEDDALE . . . REPRINTED FROM
THE ORIGINALS, BY THE DESIRE OF HIS WIDOW
4to.
London 1881.

22 hand-coloured lithographs of birds by Joseph Smit
and John Gerrard Keulemans (from *Trans. Zool. Soc.
Lond.* and Rowley 1875–78 which see).
Previously Viscount Walden, whom see.

TWEEDDALE, ARTHUR HAY Marquess of
(WALDEN), see DRESSER 1871, THOMSON 1881.

TYAS, ROBERT, see COTTON 1854

VAILLANT, AUGUSTE NICOLAS, JOSEPH
FORTUNE THEODORE EYDOUX, FRANÇOIS
LOUIS AUGUSTE SOULEYET and HENRI MARIE
DUCROTAY de BLAINVILLE
VOYAGE AUTOUR DU MONDE EXECUTE PENDANT
LES ANNEES 1836 ET 1837 SUR LA CORVETTE LA
BONITE. . . . ZOOLOGIE
2 vols. Royal 8vo.
Paris 1841–1852.
10 engravings of birds by Alphonse Prévost and
Johann Carl Werner printed in colour.

VERREAUX, EDOUARD see MULSANT 1873

VERREAUX [VERRAUX], JULES, see CHENU 1862,
DesMURS 1886

VETH, PIETER JAN and JOH. F. SNELLEMANN
MIDDEN-SUMATRA. REIZEN EN ONDERZOEKINGEN
DER SUMATRA-EXPEDITIE, MITGERUST DOOR HET
(AARDRIJKSKUNDIG) GENNOTSCHAP, 1877–1879 . . .
NATUURLIJKE HISTOIRE. EERSTE AFDEELING.
ZOOGDIEREN EN VOGELS
4to.
Amsterdam 1886.
4 coloured plates of birds, by John Gerrard Keule-
mans.

**VIEILLOT, LOUIS JEAN PIERRE
HISTOIRE NATURELLE DES PLUS BEAUX OISEAUX
CHANTEURS DE LA ZONE TORRIDE
Large folio.
Paris 1805–c. 1809.
72 engravings by Louis Bouquet (printed by Langlois)
from drawings by Jean Gabriel Prêtre, coloured by
hand, numbered I–LXX, XXVIII*, XXVIII**.

**VIEILLOT, LOUIS JEAN PIERRE
HISTOIRE NATURELLE DES OISEAUX DE L'AMERIQUE
SEPTENTRIONALE, CONTENANT UN GRAND

PLATE 46
*Joseph Wolf's aptitude for drawing birds of prey
and his interest in nestlings are here combined to great advantage.
This Merlin illustrates John Gould's
The Birds of Great Britain (London 1862–73),
one of the author's most popular works.*

CALOPHASIS ELLIOTI.

NOMBRE D'ESPECES DECRITES OU FIGURES POUR LA PREMIERE FOIS
2 vols. Large folio.
Paris 1807–*c.* 1809.
131 plates (printed in colour by Langlois) by Jean Gabriel Prêtre, finished by hand.
Numbered: Vol. I: 1–57, 2 bis, 3 bis, 10 bis, 14 bis. Vol. II: 57 bis, 53–124, 68 bis, 90 bis.
A small number of copies of a large Columbier folio *papier velin* edition were also published.

**VIEILLOT, LOUIS JEAN PIERRE and PAUL LOUIS OUDART
LA GALERIE DES OISEAUX, . . .
2 vols. 4to.
Paris 1820–1826.
324 hand-coloured lithographs from drawings by Oudart and 35 plain plates.

*VIEILLOT, LOUIS JEAN PIERRE
ORNITHOLOGIE FRANÇAISE, OU HISTOIRE NATURELLE, GENERALE ET PARTICULIERE DES OISEAUX DE FRANCE
4to.
Paris 1823–1830.
Issued only in parts, no title page. Nissen (1936, p. 51) gives 8 parts, 48 plates, 1823–26. Anker (1938, p. 207) mentions 12 parts, the last 4 appearing in 1830, but gives a collation of the first 8 only (48 plates). 100 plates were the complete intended number, and all were reissued in 1907. The plates are lithographs coloured by hand by Charles Etienne Pierre Motte from drawings by Paul Louis Oudart.

VIEILLOT, LOUIS JEAN PIERRE, see AUDEBERT 1802

VIGORS, NICHOLAS AYLWARD, see BEECHEY 1839, GOULD 1831

VIREY, JULES JOSEPH, see de BUFFON 1749 (1799)

VÖGEL, BENEDICT CHRISTOPH, see DIETZSCH 1772

VOIGT, FRIEDRICH SIEGFRIED, see CUVIER 1817 (1831)

VOSMAER, ARNOUT
(REGNUM ANIMALE) NATUURKUNDIGE BESCHRYVING EENER UITMUNTENDE VERZAMELING VAN ZELDSAAME GEDIERTEN, BESTAANDE IN

OOST- EN WESTINDISCHE VIERVOETIGE DIEREN, VOGELEN EN SLANGEN, . . .
4to.
Amsterdam 1766–1804 (bird parts 1768–1804).
A curious miscellany, also including animals from Africa, issued in 34 parts, with 35 hand-coloured engravings, of which 10 are of birds, and an illuminated title page 'Regnum Animale'.
The same plates appear to have been also published in Amsterdam in 1804 with a text in French.

WAGLER, JOHANN GEORG
MONOGRAPHIA PSITTACORUM
4to.
Munich 1832.
6 coloured plates.

WALDEN, ARTHUR HAY Viscount (later Marquess of TWEEDDALE, whom see)
A LIST OF BIRDS KNOWN TO INHABIT THE PHILIPPINE ARCHIPELAGO
4to.
Boston 1875 (*Trans. Zool. Soc. Boston, 9*).
11 coloured lithographs by Joseph Smit.

WALDEN, ARTHUR HAY Viscount (= TWEEDDALE), see DRESSER 1871, THOMSON 1881

WALLACE, ROBERT L.
THE CANARY BOOK: . . .
Crown 8vo.
London 1879.
5 coloured plates by A. F. Lydon, T. W. Wood and J. W. Ludlow. Enlarged and revised eds. 1884, and 1893, latter 2 vols., 13 plates.

WALLACE, ROBERT L.
BRITISH CAGE BIRDS . . .
8vo.
London 1886.
32 coloured plates.

WALLENGREN, HANS THURE SIGURD and KNUD JANSEN
VÅRA VANLIGASTE NYTTIGA FÅGLAR OCH DERAS ÄGG
8vo.
Lund 1896.
20 chromolithographs.
Danish edition 1896.

PLATE 47
Artist Joseph Wolf provided the large,
stunning prints for Daniel Elliot's A Monograph of the Phasianidae, or Family of Pheasants
(New York 1870–72). "Calophasis ellioti" was named in recognition of
Elliot's great contribution to ornithology.
The artist on stone is Joseph Smit, whose collaboration with Wolf
illustrated many fine bird books.

THAUMALEA AMHERSTIÆ.

WALTER, JOHANN ERNST CHRISTIAN
VÖGEL AUS ASIEN, AFRICA, AMERICA UND
NEUHOLLAND IN (COLORIRTEN) ILLUMINIERTEN
ABBILDUNGEN, . . .
4to.
Copenhagen 1828–1842.
144 hand-coloured engravings copied from Audebert,
Temminck and Levaillant by Walter. Published in 18
parts.

WALTER, JOHANN ERNST CHRISTIAN
NORDISK ORNITHOLOGIE, . . .
Folio.
Copenhagen 1828–1841.
Published in 48 parts; 288 hand-coloured engravings
by Walter.

WALTER, JOHANN ERNST CHRISTIAN and
JOHANNES CHRISTOPHER HAGEMANN
REINHARDT
PRAGTFUGLE OG PATTEDYR I COLOREREDE
AFBILDNINGER. . . .
Folio.
Copenhagen 1828–1841.
36 hand-coloured engravings, of which 23 of birds,
mostly copied from Temminck and Levaillant by
Walter.

WARING, S., Mrs
THE MINSTRELSY OF THE WOODS; OR, SKETCHES
AND SONGS CONNECTED WITH THE NATURAL
HISTORY OF SOME OF THE MOST INTERESTING
BRITISH AND FOREIGN BIRDS
Post 8vo.
London 1832.
17 hand-coloured woodcuts.

WARREN, BENJAMIN HARRY
REPORT ON THE BIRDS OF PENNSYLVANIA, WITH
SPECIAL REFERENCE TO THE FOOD-HABITS,
BASED ON OVER THREE THOUSAND STOMACH
EXAMINATIONS
8vo.
Harrisburg 1888.
49 coloured lithographs after Audubon.
2nd edition 1890: 99 coloured lithographs after Au-
dubon.

WATTS, JOHN, see PHILLIP 1789

WEBB, PHILIP BARKER, see BARKER-WEBB

WEBBER, CHARLES WILKINS
WILD SCENES AND SONG-BIRDS
Royal 8vo.
New York and London 1854.
20 coloured plates, 13 of birds, by Mrs Webber and
Alfred J. Miller.
Reissue 1858.

WEBBER, CHARLES WILKINS, see H. G. ADAMS
1856

WERNER, JOHANN-CARL and COENRAAD JACOB
TEMMINCK
ATLAS DES OISEAUX D'EUROPE, POUR SERVIR DE
COMPLEMENT AU MANUEL D'ORNITHOLOGIE DE M.
TEMMINCK (ATLAS DES OISEAUX D'EUROPE D'APRES
C. J. TEMMINCK)
3 vols. Post 8vo.
1826–1842.
530 hand-coloured lithographs after Werner.
Reissue 1848 in 2 vols. 526 coloured plates
To illustrate C. J. Temminck (1820–40). Manuel d'Or-
nithologie.
Paris, second ed.

WESTERMAN, GERARDUS FRIEDRICH, see
SCHLEGEL 1860

WESTWOOD, JOHN OBADIAH, see CUVIER 1817
(1851, 1863)

WHEELER, GEORGE MONTAGUE and HENRY
WEATHERBEE HENSHAW
REPORT UPON UNITED STATES GEOGRAPHICAL
SURVEYS . . . WEST OF THE ONE HUNDREDTH
MERIDIAN, . . . REPORT UPON THE
ORNITHOLOGICAL COLLECTIONS . . .
Vol. 5 of 8 vols. 4to.
Washington 1875.
15 chromolithographs by Robert Ridgway.

WHEELWRIGHT, HORACE WILLIAM [AN OLD
BUSHMAN]
A SPRING AND SUMMER IN LAPLAND
Crown 8vo.
London 1871.
Second edition (first, no plates, 1864) with 6 coloured
plates of birds.

PLATE 48
Lady Amherst's Pheasant is prized for its
"strikingly contrasting colours," as Daniel Elliot states in its description.
Joseph Wolf has drawn the pheasant and John Keulemans
has masterfully redrawn it on stone to illustrate Elliot's A Monograph of the Phasianidae, or Family of Pheasants
(New York 1870–72). The author commends the colorist of this volume,
J. D. White, in his Preface.

WHITE, ADAM

A POPULAR HISTORY OF BIRDS COMPRISING A
FAMILIAR ACCOUNT OF THEIR CLASSIFICATION AND
HABITS
16mo.
London 1855.
20 hand-coloured plates.

WHITE, GILBERT

THE NATURAL HISTORY AND ANTIQUITIES OF
SELBORNE, IN THE COUNTY OF SOUTHAMPTON
4to.
London 1788 (1789 on title page).
No coloured plates in first edition, but several or
many of birds in several of the very numerous (over
150 by 1950) subsequent editions, e.g. 1861, 1876.

WHITE, JOHN

JOURNAL OF A VOYAGE TO NEW SOUTH WALES . . .
4to.
London 1790.
65 coloured plates, some after Thomas Watling, by
Miss S. Stone, Catton, Frederick Polydore Nodder
and others, of which 29 of birds.

WHITEHEAD, JOHN, RICHARD BOWDLER
SHARPE, WILLIAM ROBERT OGILVIE-GRANT and
HENRY SEEBOHM

EXPLORATION OF MOUNT KINA BALU, NORTH
BORNEO
4to.
London 1893.
11 hand-coloured lithographs, 6 of birds, by
Whitehead.

zu WIED-NEUWIED, Prince MAXIMILIAN
ALEXANDER PHILIP

ABBILDUNGEN ZUR NATURGESCHICHTE BRASILIENS
Large folio.
Weimar 1822–1831.
90 coloured copper-engravings, of which 5 of birds by
H. Hessen.

WIENER, AUGUST F., see BLAKSTON 1877

WIESE, VALDEMAR HEINRICH FERDINAND

TROPEFUGLENES LIV I FANGENSKAB. HAANDBOG I
FUGLENES RØGT, PLEJE OG OPDRÆT
2 vols. Large 8vo.
Aarhus 1894–1896.
22 plates, of which 18 chromolithographs after Wiese.

WIGLESWORTH, LIONEL WILLIAM, see A. B.
MEYER 1898

WILHELM, GOTTLIEB TOBIAS

UNTERHALTUNGEN AUS DER NATURGESCHICHTE
(parts 4 and 5: VÖGEL)
8vo.
Augsburg and Vienna 1792–1828 (birds 1810).
90 hand-coloured engravings.

WILKES, CHARLES and JOHN CASSIN

UNITED STATES EXPLORING EXPEDITION DURING
THE YEARS 1838, 1839, 1840, 1841, 1842. . . .
2 vols. Folio and large folio.
Philadelphia 1858.
42 coloured plates of birds by George G. White, Tit-
ian Ramsay Peale, William E. Hitchcock and Edwin
Sheppard.
First published 1848 without plates by Peale.

WILLIBALD, E.

DIE NESTER UND EIER DER IN DEUTSCHLAND UND
DEN ANGRENZENDEN LÄNDERN BRÜTENDEN
VÖGEL
12mo.
Luckau 1854.
8 coloured plates.
Reissued unchanged, 1874; third (enlarged) edition
Leipzig 1886.

**WILSON, ALEXANDER and GEORGE ORD

AMERICAN ORNITHOLOGY; OR, THE NATURAL
HISTORY OF THE BIRDS OF THE UNITED STATES
9 vols. Folio.
Philadelphia 1808–1814.
76 hand-coloured engravings by Alexander Lawson,
J. G. Warnicke, G. Murray and Benjamin Tanner
from original drawings by Wilson.
This book antedates Audubon by some years and is
the first American Bird Book with coloured plates,
published in America. Catesby's *Natural History of
Carolina*, etc. London 1731–43, and Levaillant's
Oiseaux de l'Amérique, Paris 1801–02 are both less
comprehensive.
So, although the plates are not very exciting, the book
is of considerable importance. Vols. VII–IX, revised
by George Ord, were reissued in 1824–25; and the
whole again in 1828–29, ed. Ord with the plates coloured better. But the work is not nowadays considered complete without the continuation in 4 vols.,

PLATE 49
A Monograph of the Paradiseidae, or Birds of Paradise *(London 1873), by the American,
Daniel Elliot, was printed at London, the center of natural history publishing.
The frolicsome family of the Little King Bird of Paradise is the product of artist Joseph Wolf
and lithographic artist Joseph Smit. Both men emigrated from Germany
to pursue prolific careers in London, and they collaborated on many fine bird books.*

BUCEROS RHINOCEROS.

1825–33, by Prince Charles Lucien Jules Laurent Bonaparte, which see. Later editions, below, are a combination of the two:

Edinburgh 1831, 4 vols. Cap. 8vo., ed. Robert Jameson, with some extraneous textual matter and no coloured plates.

London and Edinburgh 1832, 3 vols. 8vo., ed. Sir William Jardine, the 76 Wilson plates and 21 others from Bonaparte by Titian Ramsay Peale and A. Rider re-engraved by William Home Lizars. As Bonaparte's final volume, 1833, had not yet been published, this edition has fewer coloured plates than its successors. The 'Jardine Edition'.

Boston 1840, 1 vol. 12mo., ed. Thomas Mayo Brewer, no coloured plates. The 'Brewer Edition'.

New York ?1852, 1853, 1854 reissues of the 'Brewer edition' with a coloured title-page. No coloured plates.

Philadelphia 1871, 5 vols. (3 text, 2 plates) Super-royal 8vo. The Ord revised edition of 1828–29 with the material from all four volumes of Bonaparte 1825–33, and combined index, 103 coloured plates (being the full 76 of Wilson and 27 of Bonaparte) in all. The 'Philadelphia Edition'.

London 1876, 3 vols. Medium 4to. As Jardine Edition with material from Bonaparte's fourth volume added, including the 6 coloured plates, making thus the full 103, the other 97 from the Lizars engravings of the Jardine edition; adorned by hand with exaggerated colours. The 'Chatto and Windus Edition' (publisher).

New York 1877, 3 vols. Post 8vo. Text from same plates as Chatto and Windus Edition but plates chromolithographs of Lizars engravings. The 'Bouton Edition' (publisher).

Philadelphia 1878, 3 vols. in 1, Super-royal 8vo., a reprint of the Philadelphia Edition with uncoloured, reduced, zinc etchings from original plates, often 4 to a page.

WILSON, ALEXANDER, see BONAPARTE 1825, T. BROWN 1831

WILSON, SCOTT BARCHARD, ARTHUR HUMBLE EVANS and HANS GADOW
AVES HAWAIIENSES: THE BIRDS OF THE SANDWICH ISLANDS
Large 4to.
London 1890–1899.
64 hand-coloured lithographs by Frederick William Frohawk.

W. WINGFIELD & G. W. JOHNSON
THE POULTRY BOOK
4to.
London 1853.
22 chromolithographs by H. Weir.
Another edition rearranged and edited by W. B. Tegetmeier.
Royal 8vo.
London 1856.
16 chromolithographs by H. Weir.
(See also Tegetmeier 1866–7).

WIRSING, ADAM LUDWIG, FRIEDRICH CHRISTIAN GÜNTHER, NATHANIEL GOTTFRIED LESKE and DAVID PIESCH
SAMMLUNG VON NESTERN UND EYERN VERSCHIEDENER VÖGEL AUS DEN CABINETTEN DES HERRN GEHEIMEN HOFRATH SCHMIDELS UND DES HERRN VERFASSERS
Folio.
Nuremberg (1767) 1772(–1786).
101 hand-coloured engravings.
Originally published in 4 parts (no text to parts 3 and 4).
French translation of Part I only in 1777.

WIRSING, ADAM LUDWIG, see DIETZSCH 1772

WOLF, JOHANN
ABBILDUNGEN UND BESCHREIBUNGEN MERKWÜRDIGER NATURGESCHICHTLICHER GEGENSTÄNDE
2 vols. 4to.
Nuremberg 1816–1822.
72 hand-coloured engravings, 20 of birds by Johann Wolf, Ludwig Christof Tyrof, Ambrosius Gabler and Carl Wilhelm Hahn.

WOLF, JOHANN and JOHANN FRIEDRICH FRAUENHOLZ
ABBILDUNGEN UND BESCHREIBUNGEN DER IN FRANKEN BRÜTENDER VÖGEL
Folio.
Nuremberg 1799.
18 hand-coloured engravings by Ambrosius Gabler.

WOLF, JOHANN and JOHANN FRIEDRICH FRAUENHOLZ
ABBILDUNGEN DER VÖGEL EUROPAS, IN STAHL GESTOCHEN

PLATE 50
The Rhinoceros Hornbill is one of fifty-seven hand-colored lithographs
illustrating Daniel Elliot's A Monograph of the Bucerotidae, or Family of Hornbills *(London 1877–82).*
The artist on stone, John Keulemans,
has artfully incorporated the birds within foliage surroundings,
and created a great depth of field imitating their native jungle.

8vo and 4to.

Darmstadt 1839–1852.

Issued in parts; 108 hand-coloured engravings and hand-coloured lithographs.

(Also with French title *Histoire naturelle des Oiseaux d'Europe*).

WOLF, JOHANN, see B. MEYER 1799, 1810

WOLF, JOSEPH

THE POETS OF THE WOODS

4to.

London 1853

12 chromolithographs by Wolf.

WOLF, JOSEPH

FEATHERED FAVOURITES

8vo.

London 1854.

12 chromolithographs by Wolf.

*WOLF, JOSEPH, DAVID WILLIAM MITCHELL and PHILIP LUTLEY SCLATER

ZOOLOGICAL SKETCHES, MADE FOR THE ZOOLOGICAL SOCIETY OF LONDON FROM ANIMALS IN THEIR VIVARIUM IN THE REGENTS PARK

2 vols. Folio.

London 1861–1867.

100 hand-coloured and chromolithographs, 39 being of birds, by Wolf.

WOLLEY, JOHN and ALFRED NEWTON

OOTHECA WOLLEYANA: AN ILLUSTRATED CATALOGUE OF THE COLLECTION OF BIRDS' EGGS, BEGUN BY THE LATE JOHN WOLLEY, JUN., M.A., F.Z.S., AND CONTINUED WITH ADDITIONS BY THE EDITOR ALFRED NEWTON

2 vols. Royal 8vo.

London 1864–1907.

2 coloured plates of birds after Joseph Wolf, one published after 1900; and 21 coloured plates of eggs by J. T. Balcomb and Henrik Gronvold, the 8 by Gronvold published after 1900.

WOLSTENHOLME, DEAN

PIGEONS, FANCY AND FOREIGN

8vo.

London 1858.

30 coloured plates.

WRIGHT, LEWIS

THE ILLUSTRATED BOOK OF POULTRY

4to.

London 1873.

50 chromolithographs by J. W. Ludlow

Another ed. with 18 plates, 1893.

von WRIGHT, MAGNUS

SVENSKA FOGLAR EFTER NATUREN OCH PÅ STEN RITADE

Oblong folio.

Stockholm 1828–1837.

179 hand-coloured lithographs (a final part with 5 more was never issued).

von WÜLLERSTORF-URBAIR, Baron BERNHARD and AUGUST von PELZELN

REISE DER ÖSTERREICHISCHEN FREGATTE 'NOVARA' UM DIE ERDE, IN DEN JAHREN 1857, 1858, 1859, . . . VÖGEL

4to.

Vienna 1865.

6 coloured plates by Theodor Franz Zimmermann.

de WÜLVERHORST, A. H. VERSTER, see SCHLEGEL 1844

WYATT, CLAUDE WILMOTT

BRITISH BIRDS: BEING COLOURED ILLUSTRATIONS OF ALL THE SPECIES OF PASSERINE BIRDS RESIDENT IN THE BRITISH ISLES, . . .

Small folio.

London 1894.

25 hand-coloured lithographs by Wyatt.

WYATT, CLAUDE WILMOTT

BRITISH BIRDS: WITH SOME NOTES IN REFERENCE TO THEIR PLUMAGE

Small folio.

London 1899.

42 hand-coloured lithographs by Wyatt. Often regarded as Vol. 2 of previous work, but not so by publishers.

WYATT, CLAUDE WILMOTT, see SHARPE 1885

ZAMBRINI, FRANCESCO

SCELTA DI CURIOSITA LETTERARIE INEDITE O RARE DAL SECOLO XIII AL XVII IN APPENDICE ALLA COLLEZIONE DI OPERE INEDITE O RARE. DISPENSA CXL. CON FIGURE IN CROMOLITOGRAFIA A FAC-SIMILE DEL CODICE. TRATTATELLO DI FALCONERIA. LIBRO DELLE NATURE DEGLI UCCELLI FATTO PER LO RE DANCHI TESTO ANTICO TOSCANO MESSO IN LUCE DA F. Z.

8vo.

Bologna 1874.

Tuscan codex of 1444, faithful reproduction in chromolithography.

Original had 31 coloured figures.

ZETTERSTEDT, JOHAN WILHELM

RESA GENOM SWERIGES OCH NORRIGES LAPPMARKER, FÖRRÄTTAD ÄR 1821

2 vols. in 1. Crown 8vo.

Lund 1822.

2 coloured plates of birds by B. F. Fries.

ZORN von PLOBSHEIM, Baron FRIEDRICH AUGUST, see FRISCH 1733

Allen, Elsa Guerdrum. *The History of American Ornithology before Audubon.* (Orig. pub.: American Philosophical Society. *Transactions* ns Vol. 41: 3. Philadelphia, 1951.) Facsimile. King of Prussia, PA: Arader, 1979.

Anker, Jean. *Bird Books and Bird Art: An Outline of the Literary History and Iconography of Descriptive Ornithology.* (Orig. pub. Copenhagen, 1938.) Lochem, The Netherlands: Antiquariaat Junk B. V., 1973.

Bannon, Lois Elmer, and Taylor Clark. *Handbook of Audubon Prints.* Gretna, LA: Pelican Publishing Co., 1980. (Another ed. 1985.)

Boddaert, Pieter. *Table des* Planches enluminéez d'histoire naturelle. (Orig. pub. Utrecht, 1783) Reprint. Ed. W. B. Tegetmeier. London, 1874.

British Museum (Natural History). *Catalogue of the Books, Manuscripts, Maps and Drawings.* 8 vols. London, 1903–40.

Buchanan, Handasyde. *Nature into Art: A Treasury of Great Natural History Books.* London: Weidenfeld & Nicolson, 1979.

Carus, Julius V., and Wilhelm Engelmann. *Bibliotheca zoologica . . . 1846–1860.* Leipzig, 1861. [Continuation of Engelmann.]

Coues, Elliott. *Faunal Publications Relating to British Birds.* U.S. National Museum. *Proceedings.* Vol. 2: pp. 359–482. Washington, D.C.: G.P.O., 1880.

Coues, Elliott. *Faunal Publications Relating to North America.* U.S. Geological Survey. *Miscellaneous Publications.* No. 11: pp. 567–748. Washington, D.C.: G.P.O., 1878.

Coues, Elliott. *Faunal Publications Relating to the Rest of America.* U.S. Geological and Geographical Survey. *Bulletin.* No. 5: pp. 239–330. Washington, D.C.: G.P.O., 1879.

Coues, Elliot. *Systematic Publications Relating to American Species, Arranged According to Families.* U.S. Geological and Geographical Survey. *Bulletin.* No. 5: pp. 521–1072. Washington, D.C.: G.P.O., 1879.

Dance, S. Peter. *The Art of Natural History: Animal Illustrators and Their Work.* Woodstock, NY: Overlook Press; London: Cameron & Tayleur Ltd., 1978.

Engelmann, Wilhelm. *Bibliotheca historico-naturalis . . . 1700–1846.* Leipzig, 1846.

Fries, Waldemar H. *The Double Elephant Folio: The Story of Audubon's* Birds of America. Chicago: American Library Association, 1973.

Giebel, Christoph G. *Thesaurus ornithologiæ. Repertorium der . . . Arten der Vögel. . . .* Leipzig, 1872–77.

Harting, James E. *Bibliotheca accipitraria.* London, 1891.

Jackson, Christine E. *Bird Etchings: The Illustrators and Their Books, 1655–1855.* Ithaca and London: Cornell University Press, 1985.

Jackson, Christine E. *Bird Illustrators: Some Artists in Early Lithography.* London: H. F. & G. Witherby, 1975.

Jackson, Christine E. *Wood Engravings of Birds.* London: H. F. & G. Witherby, 1978.

Keulemans, Tony, and Jan Coldewey. *Feathers to Brush: The Victorian Bird Artist John Gerrard Keulemans, 1842–1912.* Epse, The Netherlands, 1982.

Lambourne, Maureen. *John Gould's Birds.* Secaucus, NJ: Chartwell Books, 1980.

Lysaght, A. M. *The Book of Birds: Five Centuries of Bird Illustration.* London: Phaidon Press, 1975.

Mullens, W. H., and H. Kirke Swann. *A Bibliography of British Ornithology from the Earliest Times to the End of 1912.* (Orig. pub. London: MacMillan and Co., 1917.) Facsimile. Codicote, Hitchin, Herts.: Wheldon & Wesley Ltd., 1986.

Newton, Alfred. "Ornithology." *Encyclopedia Britannica.* Vol. 18: pp. 2–50. 9th ed. London, 1884.

Newton, Alfred, et al. *A Dictionary of Birds.* London, 1896.

Nissen, Claus. *Die Illustrierten Vogelbücher.* Stuttgart: Hiersemann Verlag, 1953.

Ronsil, Rene. *Bibliographie ornithologique française: Travaux publiés en langue française et en latin, en France et dans les Colonies Françaises de 1473 à 1944.* 2 vols. Paris: Paul Lechevalier, 1948–49.

Ronsil, Rene. *La française dans le livre d'oiseaux.* Paris, 1957.

Sauer, Gordon C. *John Gould, the Bird Man: A Chronology and Bibliography.* Lawrence, KS: University Press of Kansas, 1982.

Sharpe, Richard Bowdler. *An Analytical Index to the Works of the Late John Gould.* London, 1893.

Sharpe, Richard B., and W. R. Ogilvie-Grant. *Hand-List of the Genera and Species of Birds in the British Museum.* 6 vols. London, 1899–1912.

Skipwith, Peyton. *The Great Bird Illustrators and Their Art, 1730–1930.* London: Hamlyn, 1979.

Sotheby's. *Bibliothèque Marcel Jeanson, deuxième partie, ornithologie.* Monaco: Sotheby's Holdings, Inc., 1988.

Stone, Witmer. *A Bibliography and Nomenclator of the Ornithological works of John James Audubon.* American Ornithologist's Union. *The Auk.* Vol. 23: pp. 298–312. Cambridge, MA: A.O.U., 1906.

Streseman, Ernst, *Ornithology: From Aristotle to the Present.* (orig. pub. *Die Entwicklung der Ornithologie von Aristoteles bis zur Gegenwart.* Berlin: F. W. Peters, 1951.) Cambridge, MA: Harvard University Press, 1975.

Taschenberg, Ernst O. W. *Bibliotheca zoologica . . . 1861–1880.* 8 vols. Leipzig, 1887–1930. [Continuation of Carus.]

Tate, Peter. *A Century of Bird Books.* London: H. F. & G. Witherby, 1979.

Thayer, Evelyn, and Virginia Keyes. *Catalogue of a Collection of Books on Ornithology in the Library of John E. Thayer.* Boston, 1913.

Waterhouse, F. H. *The Dates of Publication of Some of the Zoological Works of the Late John Gould.* London, 1885.

Whittell, Hubert Massey. *The Literature of Australian Birds.* Perth, 1954.

Wood, Casey A. *An Introduction to the Literature of Vertebrate Zoology . . . [in the Libraries of] . . . McGill University, Montreal.* (Orig. pub. London: Oxford University Press, 1931) Facsimile. Hildesheim and New York: Georg Olms Verlag, 1974.

Zimmer, J. T. *Catalogue of the Edward E. Ayer Ornithological Library.* Field Museum of Natural History. *Publications (Zoology).* Vol. 16 (in 2 parts). Chicago: Field Museum, 1926.

Zoological Society of London. *Catalogue of the Library.* 5th ed. London, 1902.

J.Smit del & lith.

Hanhart imp

EPIMACHUS ELLIOTI.

LIST OF THE PLATES

Elizabeth Braun

The List of Plates records each illustration's collaborating artists, printmakers, authors, and publishers. The first line of each description is the title of the print; italic letters identify the source of the title as either the print itself or its text; titles in roman letters signify modern common names. The title and edition given is that of the actual volume from which we photographed the print; following is a description of the print medium, and the names of the artists who collaborated on it when known. A few sentences give additional information on the creation of the print, or about the particular volume from which we photographed it. Locations of original watercolor models for the prints are given when known; current locations are as of July 1989.

All quotes whose sources are not cited are taken from the texts of the works illustrated; in many instances, page numbers are given. Citations noted in parentheses are to be found in the Reference Bibliography, which lists sources for further reading. Definitions of printmaking terms may be found in Buchanan's Appendix. Gavin Bridson's article "The Treatment of Plates in Bibliographical Description" (Society for the Bibliography of Natural History, *Journal*, 7: 4, 1976) was an inspiration for this List, as were many model publications by the Hunt Institute.

1
Figured half title
Etching made by Jan Christian Sepp and Jan Sepp, after their watercolor, and hand colored.
Nozeman, Cornelis. *Nederlandsche vogelen*. Amsterdam 1770–1829. Vol. 3, title page.
Our frontispiece is the decorative half title that serves as title page to the third volume of this first comprehensive Dutch ornithology. Visible are a hoopoe, bullfinch, quail and nest, and other birds, artificially posed together in a charming vignette. In the copy once owned by Marcel Jeanson, "IV" substitutes for the "III" of this example (Sotheby's, 1988, p. 55). The example pictured here exists complete as issued, uncut and unbound, in portfolios with ribbon ties. An illustration appears as our plate 8.
Courtesy of W. Graham Arader III Gallery, New York.

2
The Cock Hoopoe
Etching with engraving, after the painting by Eleazar Albin, and hand colored by the artist or his daughter, Elizabeth.

Albin may have etched the plate himself or with the aid of his daughter, according to David Knight (*Zoological Illustration*, Folkstone, 1977, p. 99).
Albin, Eleazar. *A Natural History of Birds*. London 1738. Second issue of vol. 2, pl. 42.
Albin observed and collected familiar birds in the field for this first colorplate English bird book. Two plates are signed H. Fletcher and G. Thornton, but otherwise no printmaker is identified; as Knight suggests, the artist and his daughter may have made the fairly coarse etchings. Albin's text advises that "Nature is so uniform . . . that the Picture of an Individual will, to an human Eye, at least serve for a Representation of the Species." It was later known that birds show great variance in coloration, and therefore Albin's portraits of individuals may or may not typify a species.
Courtesy of Sotheby's, H. Bradley Martin collection.

3
Largest White Bill'd Woodpecker   Ivory-billed woodpecker
Etching with engraving by Mark Catesby after his own painting, and hand colored by George Edwards.

PLATE 51
"Epimachus ellioti" illustrates Charles Cory's
The Beautiful and Curious Birds of the World *(Boston 1880–83). This image expands*
on an illustration to Elliot's 1870–72
Monograph of the Paradiseidae *[q.v.], for which Joseph Smit drew Wolf's design on stone.*
Smit composed this image alone, adding a third bird, lush foliage,
and an increased illusion of space.

Catesby, Mark. *The Natural History of Carolina*. London 1754. Second edition. Vol. 1, pl. 16.

Catesby discovered and named this large and beautiful woodpecker, now extinct. His description includes an ethnographic detail: "The Bills of these Birds are much valued by the Canada Indians, who make Coronets of 'em for their Princes and great warriors, by fixing them round a Wreath, with their points outward. The Northern Indians, having none of these Birds in their cold country purchase them of the Southern People at the price of two, and sometimes three Buck-skins a Bill" (p. 16). Johann Seligmann translated the text into German, and recreated the plates in smaller format for *Sammlung . . . Vögel* (Nürnberg 1749–76). This compilation included contemporary work by Edwards (plate 4).
Courtesy of New York Public Library.

4
The Dodo
Etching by George Edwards after his own design, and hand colored.
Edwards, George. *Gleanings of Natural History*. London 1806. Second edition. Vol. 2, pl. 294.

For this plate Edwards copied a reputedly accurate oil painting of a living dodo, which had become extinct in the late 1600s. In the painting it stood a hefty thirty inches high, and he put the "Guiney Pig" next to the dodo "only to give a true idea of its magnitude" (p. 181). In the Introduction, Edwards bows out of any controversy over the painting's authenticity, asserting that *Gleanings* "consists of hints and informations received from friends," which they expected him to publish. Despite this unrigorous examination of sources, Edwards's work was hugely popular and has an enduring appeal. It was translated into German with copied plates by Johann Seligmann for *Sammlung . . . Vögel* (Nürnberg 1749–76), and thence into many European languages.
Courtesy of New York Public Library.

5
Bubo Noctua Maxima   Owl
Etching and engraving, probably made by Ferdinand Helfreich Frisch after a painting by himself or by his brother Philipp Jacob Frisch, and hand colored, with gum arabic applied to eyes and talons.
Frisch, Johann L. *Vorstellung der Vögel in Teutschland*. Berlin 1733–63. Vol. 1, pl. 93.

This work's 255 etchings are modeled on the author's collection of mounted birdskins. This first book of German birds, including some domestic fowl and North American species, spanned thirty years and three generations. The etchings show the hands of several members of the artistic Frisch family. Their style is exuberant and the plates deeply bitten, with variances in quality and style among them. In 1938, Anker located about half the original watercolors at Mainz in the library of Jacob Moyat.
Courtesy of Sotheby's, H. Bradley Martin collection.

6
Heath Hen
Engraving by Mark Catesby after his own painting, and hand colored by George Edwards.
Catesby, Mark. *The Natural History of Carolina*. London 1754. Second edition. Appendix, pl. 1.

This late production from Catesby's burin is exclusively engraved, though most of his plates are etched: "I undertook, and was initiated in the way of, etching them myself, which I have not done in a Graver-like manner, choosing rather to omit their method of cross-Hatching, and to follow the humour of the Feathers, which is more laborious, and I hope has proved more to the purpose" (Vol. 1, p. xi). Catesby did not paint this bird during his travels in America, but rather at an English estate. Like his Ivory-billed woodpecker (plate 3), the Heath Hen became extinct early in the twentieth century. This Appendix was completed in 1747, after the body of the work, and passed on to subscribers; the book is incomplete without it.
Courtesy of a private collection.

7
Anatra d'Estate   Wood duck
Etching possibly by Violante Vanni after his own painting or that of Lorenzo Lorenzi or Xaverio Manetti, printed in olive ink, and hand colored.
Manetti, Xaverio. *Ornithologia methodice*. Florence 1767–76. Vol. 5, pl. 579.

This monumental bird book presents a contrast to the contemporary works by Nozeman (plates 1 and 8) and Pennant (plate 9). Its 600 folio etchings convey a stunning lack of veracity in color and proportion, yet its engaging figures are irresistible. As Dance proposes, "their real-life counterparts would surely disown them" as dandified fops animating the foibles of humans (1978. p. 70). The engraved text at the bottom of the plate inscribes this image to the illustrious Dottore Grazio Traversari, perhaps a patron of the work; similar dedication lines appear on each plate.
Courtesy of Donald Heald Fine Art, New York.

8
Merganser
Engraving made by Jan Christian Sepp or Jan Sepp in 1797, after their artwork, and hand colored.
Nozeman, Cornelis. *Nederlandsche vogelen*. Amsterdam 1770–1829. Vol. 3, pl. 125.

The 250 plates illustrate comprehensively the birds of the Netherlands, and are animated in a naturalistic manner that contrasts with those of Manetti's contemporary work (plate 7). They are meticulously drawn, and accurate coloring extends to landscape vignettes often more intricate than in this example. On occasion watercolor paintings used as models for this work come onto the market, and they reveal a minute delineation only slightly diminished by the translation into engraving.
Courtesy of W. Graham Arader III Gallery, New York.

9

The Heron

Etching by Peter Mazell, after the watercolor by Peter Paillou, and hand colored by the latter.

Pennant, Thomas. *The British Zoology*. London 1761–66. Part 2, opposite page 116.

Almost all of the 132 plates of this work represent birds, making it the most comprehensive British bird book since the 1676 *Ornithologiae* of Francis Willughby and John Ray. Produced in the folio format of the contemporary books by Nozeman (plates 1 and 8) and Manetti (plate 7), Pennant's work has similarly animated figures, brightly colored, with some sacrifice of naturalism for the sake of composition. Paillou painted most of the bird portraits. Mazell illustrated many other bird books in this era, including Pennant's important *Arctic Zoology* and *Indian Zoology*. He also contributed three plates of marine mammals to the atlas volume of Captain Cook's *Voyages*. On occasion, Paillou's watercolors associated with *British Zoology* may be found on the market.

Courtesy of W. Graham Arader III Gallery, New York.

10

Coq hupé

Etching by François Martinet after his own design, and hand colored.

de Buffon, George. *Planches enluminées*. Paris 1765–81. Pl. 49.

Buffon headed the Jardin du Roi from 1738 to 1788, working amongst the myriad natural objects he catalogued for his 44-volume *Histoire naturelle générale* (Paris 1749–1804). He initiated a deluxe set of 973 illustrations "for all those birds which need to be presented in color in order to be identified and whose colors constitute at least half their description." (Quoted in Adams, A. B. *The Eternal Quest*. New York, 1969, p. 104.) The birds are named in French, and later authors published indexes with scientific Latin binomials. The fairly accurate prints are clearly numbered, facilitating the discussion of new, exotic species for which no Latin binomials had been devised. This system spawned useful continuations such as Temminck's *Nouveau recueil* (plate 27).

Courtesy of New York Public Library.

11

Le Faucon Pélerin   Peregrine falcon

Etching by Maddalena Bouchard, and hand colored.

Bouchard, Maddalena. *Recueil de cent-trente-trois oiseaux*. Rome 1771–83. Pl. 26

According to Dance, Bouchard's gesticulating birds copy and exaggerate the posturing of Manetti's figures (plate 7), with various "irreverent touches" added (p. 70). Gold borders distinguish this work from that of Manetti, and the slapdash drawing and coloring alienates it from Martinet's tidy prints, which also have gold borders (plate 10). No text accompanies the prints and they must have been intended by the artist as an attractive, entertaining portfolio. Bouchard executed illustrations of fruit for G. Bonelli's *Hortus romanus* (Rome 1772–93), not seen by us, and one wonders how

animated that orchard became under her influence.

Courtesy of Donald Heald Fine Art, New York.

12

Song Thrush

Etching by James Bolton after his own design, and hand colored by him.

Bolton, James. *Harmonia ruralis*. Stannary 1794–96. Pl. 5.

Bolton describes his model reader as a "lady who gives place in . . . her house to a few pretty songbirds, [and] may wish to be informed of their manners . . . in a wild state, or state of nature; at the same time having no desire to acquaint herself with the history of the vulture, the cormorant . . . &c." He draws feathers with minute accuracy, whereas they "are either wholly disregarded, or else most vilely mangled, most *wickedly* deranged" by his contemporary artists. Bolton felt sympathy for caged birds, admonishing his reader to take "a little pains to provide them with their natural food" and keep their water clean. This thrush feeds on its preferred wild diet, cranberries. (Quotes taken from Bolton's Preface.)

Courtesy of Sotheby's, H. Bradley Martin collection.

13

Le Parkinson   Lyre bird

Engraving by Jean Baptiste Audebert, after the watercolor by Sydenham Edwards, printed in colors and in gold by Langlois, under the direction of Louis Bouquet.

Audebert, Jean. *Les oiseaux dorés*. Paris 1800–02. Vol. 2, pl. 14.

The French applied color-printed engraving to bird illustration in the late 1790s, producing gorgeous, expensive volumes of icons. The books featured exotic birdlife from newly explored territories, in celebration of Napoleon's farflung empire. Their brilliant plumage suits them to the elaborate engraving and printing methods Audebert helped perfect. Audebert has named this bird in honor of Sydney Parkinson, naturalist on Captain Cook's first voyage; although Parkinson died on the return voyage, his excellent drawings and collections survived. Edwards drew this figure from a rare birdskin preserved at London, sending it to Audebert for reproduction in his book. The engraved copper plates, made obsolete by the wholesale adoption of lithography for bird illustration, were offered for sale at the price of scrap copper in the 1860s.

Courtesy of Sotheby's, H. Bradley Martin collection.

14

Le Perroquet Jaune écaillé de rouge   Amazon parrot

Engraving made under the direction of Louis Bouquet, after the gouache by Jacques Barraband, printed in colors by Langlois, and hand colored.

Levaillant, François. *Histoire naturelle des perroquets*. Paris 1801–05. Vol. 2, pl. 137.

Barraband's original gouache figures for Levaillant's works on parrots and on birds of paradise (plate 18) were dispersed at the Sotheby's sale of the Marcel Jeanson collection in 1988.

The original for this engraving is presently owned by Arader. Barraband's skill was greatly esteemed and his name lent *cachet* to the sumptuous folio volumes authored by Levaillant. Similarly, Louis Bouquet is prominently acknowledged for his hand in creating the engravings. Langlois's studio harbored printers expert at carefully inking plates *à la poupée* with brilliant colors, and pulling each print perfectly from the press.
Courtesy of Donald Heald Fine Art, New York.

15

Le Perroquet Aourou-couraou
Engraving made under the direction of Louis Bouquet, after a gouache by Jacques Barraband, printed in colors by Langlois, and hand colored.
Levaillant. *Histoire naturelle des perroquets*. Paris 1801–05. Vol. 2, pl. 110.
Plates for color printing describe each feather with engraved rows of parallel filaments, in imitation of their actual structure. This syntax of lines produces an almost photographic illusion of reality that is enhanced by the saturated colors of the inks. From even a short distance it is difficult to distinguish between the painting and a good example of the print. The original painting has great personality and shows the advantage Barraband enjoyed in painting from live birds, not skins; it is currently owned by Heald.
Courtesy of Donald Heald Fine Art, New York.

16

Golden Eagle
Engravings by Louis Bouquet, with some aquatint etching, after the gouache by Jacques Barraband, printed in colors and hand colored.
de Savigny, Marie Jules-Cesar. *Système des oiseaux de l'Egypte*. Paris 1810. Pl. 12.
Barraband's renown won him a commission to depict select birds uncovered on the Napoleonic army's expedition through Egypt in 1798–1801. This magnificent eagle is one of the few single figure plates among the fourteen in the atlas volume of ornithology prints. It glows with the success of the graphic medium used to reproduce it: color-printed engraving such as Bouquet used for the works of Levaillant (plates 14, 15, and 18). This volume is most often found printed in black, not in colors.
Courtesy of Sotheby's, H. Bradley Martin collection.

17

Colombi-galline à Camail   Nicobarica pigeon
Engraving by César Macret, after a watercolor by Pauline Knip, inked in colors and printed at the press of Millevoy, hand colored with gouache, and highlighted with gum arabic and gold.
Knip, Antoinette. *Les pigeons*. Paris 1809–11. Vol. 1, 3d division *Des Colombi-Gallines*, pl. 2.
Georges Cuvier, the great systematist of animal anatomy, lauded Knip's depictions of the subtle differences between closely related pigeon species and varieties. Two of the original watercolors, currently owned by Arader, show the precision and elegance of her hand. The engravings were inked *à la poupée* in several deep hues and hand colored with gouache, and the metallic feathers of this East Indian species were highlighted with reflective gold. The title page advertises Knip as the pupil of Barraband, and she certainly continues his style, with perhaps greater sophistication in the engraving and inking of the plates.
Courtesy of W. Graham Arader III Gallery, New York.

18

Coq de Roche   Cock-of-the-rock
Engraving by Grémillier, after the gouache by Jacques Barraband, inked in colors and printed at the press of Rousset, and hand colored.
Levaillant, François. *Histoire naturelle des oiseaux de paradis*. Paris 1801–06. Vol. 1, pl. 51.
Levaillant proudly claimed that his illustrations resembled living birds rather than "feathered mannequins" (p. 6). Brilliant species from tropical and temperate climates appear, including a bright-eyed blue jay from North America whose original watercolor is currently owned by Heald. Levaillant's books appeared in several states of issue, one of which pairs color-inked and black-inked prints pulled from the same engraved plates. An examination of such copies, one of which is held by the New York Public Library, reveals the mastery of engravers such as Grémillier.
Courtesy of W. Graham Arader III Gallery, New York.

19

White-headed Eagle
Engraving with etching by Alexander Lawson, after the watercolor by Alexander Wilson, and hand colored.
Wilson, Alexander. *American Ornithology*. Philadelphia 1808–14. Vol. 4 (1811), pl. 36.
Wilson trained himself to observe and draw birds, walking thousands of miles to collect specimens, and eventually producing the first American colorplate bird book. He poses the bald eagle, emblem of the United States, against a vignette of Niagara Falls, wonder of the North American continent. Wilson engraved the plates for the prospectus, traveled widely to gain subscriptions, and colored the prints himself when his colorists failed him. Noting the meager return on his time and effort, he wryly called himself a "volunteer in the cause of Natural History, impelled by nobler views than those of money." (Quoted in Adams, A.B. *The Eternal Quest*. New York, 1969. p. 179.)
Courtesy of New York Public Library.

20

Wild Turkey
Etching by James Johnstone, after a design by Thomas Brown, hand colored, and finished with gum arabic.
Brown, Thomas. *Illustrations*. Edinburgh 1831–35.
This large, rare work by Brown contains 124 etchings modified from those of Alexander Wilson's *American Ornithology* (plate 19) and Charles Bonaparte's continuation of it by the

same title. In 1831 Wilson's text was republished at Edinburgh, and Brown issued a set of deluxe plates which could serve as illustrations. These adult turkeys are copied from plate 9 of Bonaparte's work, and the female's small wattle and breast plumes are taken from plate 4 of John Audubon's *The Birds of America*. The chicks have audubonesque, animated poses taken from the many figures in the same plate 4. William Lizars co-published the work and must have been an apt collaborator. Lizars had etched Audubon's print in 1827, as well as octavo copies of Wilson's and Bonaparte's plates for an 1832 edition of the *Ornithology*. Despite the dubious footing of the male bird, the feathers are etched with a dazzling complexity of fine lines, especially notable of the male's wing.
Courtesy of Sotheby's, H. Bradley Martin collection.

21
Red Necked Grebe
Etching by Prideaux John Selby after his own watercolor, printed by William Lizars, and hand colored under the direction of Patrick Syme.
Selby, Prideaux John. *Illustrations of British Ornithology.* Edinburgh 1821–34. Vol. 2, pl. 72.
Like Audubon and Brown, Selby issued his illustrations of birds separately from the printed text. This allowed him to copyright the text without depositing eleven costly sets of prints, as required for copyright under English law. His text volume for land birds first appeared in 1819 (with a second edition in 1825) and for water birds in 1833. Selby drew and etched his own plates, and sent them to Lizars for printing. He enjoyed a gentleman's passion for natural history, investing great energy in the production of his work. Jackson notes that Selby's *Illustrations*, with their intricate, loving lines, embody "copperplate work at its very best," on the eve of being superseded by lithography in the 1830s (1985. p. 212).
Courtesy of Sotheby's, H. Bradley Martin collection.

22
Oiseau-mouche Sapho   Hummingbird
Engraving by Jean Coutant after the watercolor by Antoine Bévalet, inked in colors and printed by Lesauvage, and hand colored.
Lesson, René. *Histoire naturelle des oiseaux-mouches.* Paris 1828–30. Pl. 27.
Lesson applied the quality of craftsmanship evident in the works of Levaillant to a modest octavo format enlarged for our plate. His artists were the best in France, those who painted the *vélins*, or type specimen drawings, at the Muséum d'histoire naturelle. In this period hundreds of exquisite, small engravings were prepared by these artists as specimens from voyages of discovery enhanced the museum collections. Lesson pioneered the description of hummingbirds, found only in the Americas, which John Gould continued later in the century (plate 40).
Courtesy of Sotheby's, H. Bradley Martin collection.

23
Meadow Lark
Engraving with line and aquatint etching by Robert Havell, after the painting by John Audubon with background by George Lehman, and hand colored.
Audubon, John. *The Birds of America.* London 1827–38. Pl. 136.
Audubon designed this composition and painted the highly detailed figures of the Meadowlarks; his companion artist Lehman painted the background wildflowers onto the original watercolor in 1830. Much of the detailed foliage distinctive of Audubon prints was supplied by Lehman, Joseph Mason, and Maria Martin. Lehman traveled the American south with Audubon in 1830–32, painting detailed backgrounds for about thirty of the watercolors made on this journey.
Courtesy of W. Graham Arader III Gallery, New York.

24
Iceland or Jer Falcon
Engraving with line and aquatint etching by Robert Havell, after the watercolor by John Audubon, and hand colored.
Audubon. *The Birds of America.* London 1827–38. Pl. 366.
Audubon observed this northern species on his collecting expedition to Labrador in the summer of 1833, but painted this specimen in England in 1835–36 from a captive bird. Audubon's original watercolor has a dark blue wash for the sky that silhouettes the bird's plummeting form. Havell's aquatint etching imitates the evenly toned dark sky. Audubon used vignettes for other white birds, the pelican, egrets, terns, and his lovely Tropic bird, with great dramatic effect. His contemporary, Bourjot Saint-Hilaire, used it equally well for a white cockatoo (plate 34) through the less painstaking medium of lithography. An alternative method used by bird artists was to pose white birds against dark foliage, or to handcolor the surrounding paper.
Courtesy of Hirschl & Adler Gallery, New York.

25
The Nébuleux, shewing its finery   Twelve-wired bird of paradise
Aquatint etching with engraved lines by Robert Havell, after another print, hand colored with gouache and highlighted with gum arabic.
Havell, Robert. *A Collection of the Birds of Paradise.* London c. 1835. Pl. 14.
Havell used aquatint etching to great advantage in making the 435 plates of Audubon's *The Birds of America*. Despite its effectiveness, it was rarely used for bird prints, though common to flower and landscape prints of the era. It takes excessive patience to describe the fine details of feathers in aquatint, so its exclusion from ornithological illustration is understandable. For this rare work, Havell used aquatint to reproduce twenty-two prints from Levaillant's *Histoire naturelle des oiseaux de paradis* (plate 18), of which this imitates

plate 16 on a smaller scale. The aquatint creates a convincingly soft effect in the display of plumes.
Courtesy of Sotheby's, H. Bradley Martin collection.

26
Roseate Spoonbill
Engraving with aquatint etching by Robert Havell, after the painting by John Audubon or possibly George Lehman, and hand colored.
Audubon, John. *The Birds of America*. London 1827–38. Pl. 321.
This spoonbill was painted during Audubon's 1831–32 journey through the southern United States with his assistant artist, Lehman. Dwight considers it possible that Lehman executed the entire painting, because "Audubon rendered his birds in flatter, less dramatic light"; Audubon would nevertheless have determined its pose. (*The Original Water-color Paintings by John James Audubon.* New York, 1966. Vol. 1, text to pl. 35.) The watercolor shows sketchy pencil trees extending into the distance at left, and Havell has quite admirably transformed these into a swampy landscape in aquatint. Havell owned the book from which this print was photographed; to compile it he chose the best of the prints colored by his artists.
Courtesy of Watkinson Library, Trinity College.

27
Couroucou temnure   Trogon
Engraving made after the watercolor by Jean Gabriel Prêtre, and hand colored.
Temminck, Coenraad. *Nouveau recueil*. Paris 1820–39. Pl. 326.
The 600 engravings were made after the watercolors by Prêtre and Nicolas Huët, both painters at the Muséum d'histoire naturelle at Paris. They were intended to serve as graphic type specimens of newly discovered species, and were of special use to those scientists without access to large collections of actual birdskin specimens. As with de Buffon's work (plate 10), the plates are clearly numbered; thus if the names assigned to these new species became obsolete, their accurate figures could still be referred to by future scholars. They are remarkable for their clarity of line, and accuracy of proportion, feather markings, and coloring.
Courtesy of New York Public Library.

28
Ruffed Grouse
Engraving with etching in line and aquatint by Robert Havell, after the watercolor by John Audubon, and hand colored.
Audubon, John. *The Birds of America*. London 1827–38. Pl. 41.
Audubon spent his years of research not in the library, but in the field, observing birds miles from civilization, traveling in poverty while his wife supported their children. He shot birds to paint, to dissect, to send to his patrons, and to eat. His text on the ruffed grouse opens with a heartfelt discus-

sion of its excellent edibility. Audubon used foliage expertly as a design element, this background being entirely painted by his own hand. However, the trillium at left blooms in the spring, and the grape-like moonseed at right fruits in the fall.
Courtesy of Hirschl & Adler Gallery, New York.

29
Wood Duck
Engraving with aquatint etching by Robert Havell, after the watercolor by John Audubon, and hand colored.
Audubon. *The Birds of America*. London 1827–38. Pl. 206.
The 435 prints of Audubon's great work were prepared by Havell in parts of five prints each. Audubon divided his time between supervising the etching and coloring in England, and collecting and drawing new specimens in America. Audubon perfected old drawings of birds continually during his travels, at times creating compositions with expedient measures. For example, Audubon pasted a cutout of his flying wood duck underneath an otherwise balanced composition painted in 1821; in 1825 he less convincingly incorporated the nesting female. This colorful patchwork created the engraver's model for the print, which was photographed from Havell's personal copy of *The Birds of America*. Audubon's watercolors are owned by the New-York Historical Society.
Courtesy of Watkinson Library, Trinity College.

30
Blue and Yellow Macaw
Lithograph drawn by Edward Lear after his own design, printed by Charles Hullmandel and hand colored under the artist's supervision.
Lear, Edward. *Illustrations of the Family of Psittacidae*. London 1830–32. Pl. 8
Lear's book on parrots signals a profound change in bird illustration, the switch from laboriously incised and printed etching or engraving to the easily drawn and printed lithograph. Lear drew his designs directly on the stone printing surface while looking at the living bird at Regent's Park Zoo in London; in contrast, Audubon gave over his designs to craftsmen who tooled them onto a metal plate. The immediacy of Lear's hand to the final print gave him complete control over artistic and anatomical nuances. The remaining fine bird books shown in our plates were illustrated with lithographs.
Courtesy of New York Public Library

31
Toucan Ariel
Lithograph after the watercolor by Jean Theodore Descourtilz, printed by Callier, and hand colored.
Descourtilz, Jean Theodore. *Oiseaux brillans du Brésil*. Paris 1834. Pl. 48.
This work is fantastically rare, existing in only a handful of examples; a facsimile was published at London in 1969 as *Pageantry of Tropical Birds*. Descourtilz was distinguished as a botanist, and plants are accurately and prominently rendered

in these bird prints. In 1852, the artist's more common *Ornithologie bresilienne* appeared, with beautiful chromolithographed plates by Waterlow & Sons of London. Some of its plates derive from the earlier work, and the two should not be confused despite their similar names. The new medium of lithography, with no entrenched rules of plate composition, freed Descourtilz to draw the birds in the spontaneous attitudes they adopt in nature.
Courtesy of Sotheby's, H. Bradley Martin collection.

32
Culmenated Toucan
Lithograph drawn by Edward Lear as overseen by John Gould, printed by Charles Hullmandel, and hand colored.
Gould, John. *A Monograph of the Ramphastidae.* London 1833–35. Pl. 1.
The folio-format lithographs of Lear's book on parrots (plate 30) opened a world of opportunity to John Gould. For fifty years he applied it to monographs on different families of birds, as well as to multivolume avifaunas of entire continents. Brightly colored toucans, drawn lifesize, comprised this early and popular monograph. Lear drew the stones for a number of these and Gould recognized his effort by allowing his signature to remain in the image.
Courtesy of New York Public Library.

33
Quetzal Trogon
Lithograph drawn by William Hart after the design of John Gould, and hand colored.
Gould, John. *A Monograph of the Trogonidae.* London 1858–75. Second edition. Pl. 1.
Gould sifted through masses of information, comparing birdskins in several European collections to select the one typical of a species and therefore worthy of illustration. He distinguished between species, lumped varieties, featured the male and female of a species on one plate, and listed the various names given to each bird since its discovery. Gould published almost 3,000 prints of birds, and made such evaluations for each one. The second edition of *Trogonidae* featured habitat vignettes, new illustrations, and twelve species not figured in the first edition of 1836–38. Audubon distinguished between Gould, a largely closet naturalist who compiled his works from specimens and books, and himself, a field naturalist who published original, observed data. Both types of scientist were as necessary then as they are today.
Courtesy of the Library of the American Museum of Natural History.

34
White-crested Cockatoo
Lithograph drawn by Johann Carl Werner, of a mount stuffed by Florent Prévost, printed by Benard et Frey, and hand colored by the artist.
Bourjot Saint-Hilaire, Alexandre. *Histoire naturelle des perroquets.* Paris; Strasbourg 1835–39.

This work was styled by the author to be a continuation of Levaillant's work on parrots (plates 14 and 15). This marvelous image is atypical of its prints in both the dramatic pose and the dark vignette, with its cryptic pyramids. The author credits the taxidermist, a curator at the Muséum d'histoire naturelle, for creating the pose of "defense and anger" drawn by Werner, an artist of *vélins* at the same institution. Many of these plates are transfer lithographs derived from Lear's prints and are consequently reversed, making them easily distinguishable from the originals.
Courtesy of New York Public Library.

35
Eagle Owl
Lithograph drawn by Edward Lear under the direction of John Gould, printed by Charles Hullmandel, and hand colored under the direction of Bayfield.
Gould, John. *The Birds of Europe.* London 1832–37.
Lear's contribution to this work, the second of Gould's string of folios, comprises the most memorable images, the complement being drawn by Elizabeth Gould, the author's wife. Hyman has remarked that Lear seems to have drawn many of "the large . . . and eccentric birds, the eagles, vultures, falcons, owls, storks, pelicans, and cranes" (Hyman, S. *Edward Lear's Birds.* New York, 1980, p. 45). Their extraordinary forms enabled him to create images imbued with personality yet not sentimentalized. This owl is accurate, yet his character renders him unforgettable; Hyman thinks Lear projected facets of his own personality into the expressions of his birds. Gould's was the first comprehensive work on European birds, linking the earlier regional studies by Nozeman (plates 1 and 8), Manetti (plate 7), and Pennant (plate 9).
Courtesy of Donald Heald Fine Art, New York.

36
Faucon Groënlandais Gyrfalcon
Lithograph probably drawn by W. Van Wouw, after the watercolor by Joseph Wolf, with glove possibly drawn by C. Scheuren or G. Saal, printed by A. Arnz et Comp., and hand colored.
Schlegel, Hermann. *Traité de fauconnerie.* Leiden and Düsseldorf 1844–53. Pl. 1
This magnificent drawing is one of the first published by the preeminent bird artist of the late nineteenth century, Joseph Wolf. The work it illustrates is a monument to the sport of hawking, which was associated with royalty. The Greenland Falcon was the pride of a hawker's birds for its tractable character, beauty, strength, and the great effort and cost expended to obtain one from Greenland. The text is a fascinating overview of the literature of the sport, complemented by plates that illustrate interesting paraphernalia, scenes of the hunt, and portraits of the most esteemed types of hunting birds.
Courtesy of Sotheby's, H. Bradley Martin collection.

37

Le Pie Rousse Rufous treepie
Lithograph by Edouard Traviès after his own drawing, printed by Bouquet, and hand colored.
Traviès, Edouard. *Les oiseaux.* Paris *c.* 1857. Pl. 62.
An artist of *vélins* at the Muséum d'histoire naturelle at Paris, Traviès painted birds for many highly accurate, jewel-like engravings included in the published narratives of French voyages of discovery. In this work he breaks free of static scientific illustration to draw animated, individualistic bird portraits. They display the spontaneous attitude of wild birds, not the knowing gaze of the captives that Lear used as models (plates 30, 32, and 35). The work is uncommon and precious; Arader currently owns the original watercolor drawing, once the property of Marcel Jeanson.
Courtesy of Sotheby's, H. Bradley Martin collection.

38

Le Hobereau Duck hawk
Lithograph by Edouard Traviès after his own drawing, printed by Bouquet, and hand colored.
Traviès, Edouard. *Les oiseaux.* Paris *c.* 1857. Pl. 18.
Traviès's innovation in the composition of his bird prints is here shown by adopting the point of view of a fellow (luckier) denizen of the meadow. Like the lithographs of his contemporary, Daumier, who painted newsworthy Frenchmen in action, there is an "on the spot," reporter-like quality to these prints. This portfolio of about eighty folio lithographs exemplifies the immediacy the medium conveyed in the hands of a master draftsman. The original drawing, currently owned by Arader, is confidently drawn in broad strokes of soft pencil, lightly washed with watercolor.
Courtesy of Sotheby's, H. Bradley Martin collection.

39

White-crested Black Polands and *Partridge Shanghaes*
Lithographs with two tintstones, drawn on stone by C. J. Culliford, and printed and hand colored by the artist.
Ferguson, George. *Ferguson's Illustrated Series of Rare and Prize Poultry.* London 1854.
The unnumbered plates of this octavo-format book display the fancy fowl cherished by poultry breeders. Culliford probably drew them from life, but idealized the forms without a concern for rigorous ornithological illustration. These are prize specimens from the yard of the author. The tintstones provide the broad areas of colors that enliven the prints, and hand coloring provides the plumage details.
Courtesy of New York Public Library.

40

Temminck's Sapphire-wing Hummingbird
Lithograph drawn on stone by Henry Constantine Richter, after the drawing by John Gould, printed by Hullmandel and Walton, hand colored, and highlighted with gum arabic.
Gould, John. *A Monograph of the Trochilidae.* London 1849–87. Vol. 3, pl. 178.

Of the thousands of birds studied by Gould, none delighted him more than the hummingbirds. He erected a building in Regent's Park Zoo, London, which held glass cases displaying hundreds of tiny mounted birds. An original pencil sketch showing this display in 1851 is in the Ellis Collection of the Spencer Library, University of Kansas. At the Great Exhibition of the same year, Gould maintained a tent which showcased his painstaking method of coloring their distinctive, iridescent patches of feathers, and sold subscriptions. Richter has copied the anatomical details of this flower from plate 4187 of W. Curtis's *Botanical Magazine.*
Courtesy of W. Graham Arader III Gallery, New York.

41

Wagler's Parrot
Lithograph drawn by J. Daverne after his own design, printed by Juliot, and hand colored.
Souancé, Charles de. *Iconographie des perroquets.* Paris 1857–58. Pl. 20.
The author planned this work to complement the monographs on parrots published by Levaillant (plates 14 and 15) and Bourjot Saint-Hilaire (plate 34). It discusses and illustrates species identified since the completion of the latter work in 1839, apparently without duplicating those pictured by Gould in *The Birds of Australia* (1840–48). Souancé notes that the artist has portrayed an individual bird whose symmetrical red feathers are atypical of the species. Specimens for the work were examined at "chez MM. Verreaux, naturalistes," the studio of two brothers at Paris, expert taxidermists, who mounted birdskins for famous ornithologists, and whose establishment was a clearinghouse of information.
Courtesy of New York Public Library.

42

Leadbeater's Cockatoo
Lithograph drawn by Henry C. Richter after his watercolor modeled on a sketch by John Gould, and hand colored.
Gould, John. *The Birds of Australia.* London 1840–69. Vol. 5, pl. 2.
Gould's tens of thousands of prints attained a high level of consistency, due to carefully trained hand colorists. The delicate two-color wash of this cockatoo's crest has been painted by an expert without the aid of guiding lithographed lines. In 1847, the Academy of Natural Sciences at Philadelphia acquired Gould's collection of Australian birdskins, which represented all but five known species and included their nests and eggs. Many preliminary watercolors for this work are at the Spencer Library, University of Kansas, and at the National Library of Australia, Canberra. A facsimile edition of 1,000 sets was published using modern printmaking processes by Lansdowne Press (Melbourne 1972–75). A handy and inexpensive reference to *Australia,* as well as to Gould's works on the birds of New Guinea and the kangaroos and mammals of Australia, was published by Ebes Douwma and Sotheby's (Melbourne 1987). It reproduces

1,213 prints in color, scaled to the size of baseball cards. *Courtesy of the Library of the American Museum of Natural History.*

43
Lewis's Woodpecker
Lithograph drawn by Mesnel after his watercolor and under the direction of Alfred Malherbe, printed by Compan, and hand colored.
Malherbe, Alfred. *Monographie des picidées.* Metz 1859–62. No. 56 of 80 numbered copies. Vol. 3, pl. 96.
The original watercolors reveal that the plate compositions were created by the "cut and paste" method used by Audubon (plate 29); they are currently owned by Arader. The carefully painted figures of birds were attached into a square sheet with a lightly sketched branch, and the artist on stone, Mesnel, perfected the composition. Lewis's Woodpecker was first described by Alexander Wilson (plate 19) from a skin brought back from the American northwest by Meriwether Lewis in 1807. It is distinguished by its beautiful rosy belly feathers and deep green back plumage.
Courtesy of Sotheby's, H. Bradley Martin collection.

44
Eagle Owl
Chromolithograph drawn by Oscar Dressler on several stones after his own design, with some hand coloring.
Bettoni, Eugenio. *Storia naturale degli ucelli.* Milan 1865–71. Pl. 107.
Dressler has recreated the soft, variegated plumage of the owl by printing in several colors of browns, buffs and greys. This print shows off the great potential of chromolithography for picturing the nuances of color in feathers, exactly repeatable in plate after plate. Few other chromolithographed bird books attained this level of sophistication and accuracy in their color printing. The images are notable for showing the nests and nestlings of many birds of prey; some show the chicks at different ages as indicated by the development of their plumage.
Courtesy of Sotheby's, H. Bradley Martin collection.

45
Moorhen
Lithograph drawn by Henry C. Richter, after the watercolor by Joseph Wolf, printed by Walter & Cohn, and hand colored.
Gould, John. *The Birds of Great Britain.* London 1862–73. [Part 2, pl. 2.] Vol. 4, pl. 85.
This most beloved of Gould's works carries his finest compositions, many of which are elegant tableaus featuring adults, nests, and chicks in a landscape vignette. This is particularly true of the waterfowl and gamebirds in which Wolf took a special interest. The horizontal line through the body of the adult at right is the result of a break in the stone. The print therefore exists in two states, with and without this mark.
Courtesy of New York Public Library.

46
Merlin
Lithograph drawn by Henry C. Richter, after the watercolor by Joseph Wolf and Richter, printed by Walter, and hand colored.
Gould. *The Birds of Great Britain.* London 1862–73. [Part 7, pl. 1.] Vol. 1, pl. 19.
This elegant Merlin, a falcon, bears comparison with that drawn by Travies (plate 38). The posture of the bird is typical, and irresistible to the artist for the grace of the tapered wings distinctive of falcons. Richter's manner of drawing on stone is quite different from that of Travies, avoiding the calligraphic flourishes of the latter's style, and in fact minimizing lines and concentrating on tones. Richter drew hundreds of prints for Gould, his style no doubt dictated by the author. *John Gould's Birds,* with an informative introduction by his descendant, Maureen Lambourne, reproduces all the plates in one volume (New York, 1981).
Courtesy of New York Public Library.

47
Calophasis ellioti Elliot's Pheasant
Lithograph drawn by Joseph Smit, after the watercolor by Joseph Wolf, printed by P. W. M. Trap, and hand colored by J. D. White.
Elliot, Daniel G. *A Monograph of the Phasianidae.* New York 1870–72. [Part 6 (Supplement), pl. 1.]
This species was discovered in China in November of 1871 just four months before the plate was printed at London. Robert Swinhoe shot specimens and shipped them to Elliot, who described them, honoring the collector's wish that this sample be named in Elliot's honor. Elliot assigned the bird to its own genus because of physiological differences from known species; "Calophasis" means beautiful pheasant, an apt name for this bird.
Courtesy of New York Public Library.

48
Lady Amherst's Pheasant
Lithograph drawn by John G. Keulemans, after the watercolor by Joseph Wolf, and hand colored by J. D. White.
Elliot. *A Monograph of the Phasianidae.* New York 1870–72. [Part 1, pl. 8.] Vol. 2, pl. 14.
The arrestingly colored Lady Amherst's Pheasant had been in demand as a roaming decoration for English estates for several years. Elliot included its depiction in the first part of his great work on the pheasants. It is named for the woman who brought the first living specimens to England. The lithographs of this work are particularly stunning, all of them meticulously drawn and colored.
Courtesy of New York Public Library.

49
Little King Bird of Paradise
Lithograph drawn by Joseph Smit, after the watercolor by Joseph Wolf, printed by M. & N. Hanhart, and hand colored by J. D. White.

Elliot, Daniel G. *A Monograph of the Paradiseidae.* London 1873. Pl. 16.

Although an American, Elliot looked to London's established wildlife artists and lithographers when publishing his beautiful folios of bird prints. The bird of paradise does not have the jewellike appearance of engravings after Barraband (plate 18), but it is a delightfully animated, naturalistic composition of adults and immature birds. In the main, prints illustrating Elliot's works avoided aggressively active birds in favor of more serene compositions, even when employing the skill of artists such as Wolf, who supplied some of Gould's goriest birds of prey.
Courtesy of New York Public Library.

50
Rhinoceros Hornbill
Lithograph drawn by John G. Keulemans after his watercolor, printed by M. & N. Hanhart, and hand colored by J. D. Smith.
Elliot, Daniel G. *A Monograph of the Bucerotidae.* London 1887–92. Pl. 4.
The author, a gentleman when it came to crediting the many collaborators on his various works, praises Keulemans's success in drawing such strange birds. Hornbills fly and perch in a peculiar manner aptly conveyed by these lithographs. The book from which we photographed this print was once owned by Alan Francis Brooke, commander of the British forces in Europe during World War II, and a great birder.
Courtesy of W. Graham Arader III Gallery, New York.

51
Epimachus ellioti   Elliot's Bird of Paradise
Lithograph drawn by Joseph Smit after his watercolor, printed by M. & N. Hanhart, and hand colored.

Cory, Charles B. *The Beautiful and Curious Birds of the World.* Boston 1880–83.

This relatively unknown work carries twenty lithographs, of which Cory commissioned Joseph Smit to draw about half. These are exceptional in their design and quality of drawn line, as evidenced by this plate. Smit is best known as a lithographic draftsman who copied the paintings of others, such as the famous Joseph Wolf, onto stone (plates 47 and 49). In 1873 he had lithographed Wolf's designs for Elliot's monograph on the birds of paradise. The posture of the main figure may be informed by this previous work, which also figured the species, but the composition is much more elaborate. Smit indulges in carefully drawn foliage, and a detailed background; the passionflower in hot orange leaps into the foreground. This style of drawing bears comparison with Hart's illustration for Sharpe's work on the birds of paradise (plate 52).
Courtesy of W. Graham Arader III Gallery, New York.

52
Prince Rudolph's Bird of Paradise
Lithograph drawn by William Hart after his watercolor, printed by Mintern Bros., and hand colored.
Sharpe, Richard Bowdler. *A Monograph of the Paradiseidae.* London 1891–98. Part 2, pl. 5.
This species from New Guinea, first described in 1885, was represented by few skins in European collections. Sharpe solicited the male bird, a type specimen, from the Royal Museum of Zoology at Dresden, and had John Keulemans draw the figure under the supervision of its director. Hart adapted this beautiful bird to his composition on stone, and drew the female bird from a specimen at the British Museum. The bird was named for a crown prince of Austria.
Courtesy of W. Graham Arader III Gallery, New York.

APPENDIX TO THE NEW EDITION

Handasyde Buchanan

PRINTING TECHNIQUES

NATURAL HISTORY PLATES have been made by a variety of techniques through the centuries, and it is not possible to appreciate their finer points without knowing something of the methods involved and the results that could be achieved. The great age of natural history books can be divided into three periods:

Its Rise, 1700–80 The first books with coloured illustrations began to be produced about 1700. Copper engraving, hand-coloured, was the medium of illustration.

The Grand Era, 1780–1830 The copper engravings continued, but the most important works were illustrated with stipple engravings in France, and with aquatint or mezzotint in Britain. The plates of this period were partly printed in colours, partly coloured by hand.

The Gradual Decline, 1830–60 and later This was the age of the lithograph, originally an interesting method with hand-coloured plates, but one that became ever cheaper, and finally, after the arrival of chromolithography, sometimes very nasty indeed.

TECHNIQUES BEFORE 1700

The wood-cut, first developed around 1400, was the earliest method of all. It had ceased to be used on a large scale by 1700, when our period starts, but it is perhaps worth a mention to point out the basic principles of printing.

The original picture was first copied on to a wood block. Then the space between the drawn lines was cut away with a sharp knife, so that these lines, standing proud of the rest of the block, would receive the ink and in due course print black. The image had to be drawn and carved in reverse, of course, as with all the methods of printing discussed here, so that when the inked block was pressed on to a sheet of paper the print made by it would be the right way round.

Wood engraving is a refinement of the wood-cut, in which the engraver uses a burin, the fine steel cutting tool of copper engravers, to obtain a multitude of fine lines that result in subtle gradations of grey tones.

COPPER ENGRAVING

This method was used throughout the eighteenth century and into the early nineteenth, and a large number of very fine plates were produced in this way. The original drawing was transferred on to a copper plate in reverse, usually by tracing or similar means. Then the lines were cut away with a burin—

PARADISORNIS RUDOLPHI, *Finsch.*

W. Hart del. et lith.

Mintern Bros. imp.

the deeper the cut, the more ink it takes up and the blacker is the eventual printed line. The plate was then inked and the print was taken from it.

Copper engraving, like the wood-cut and wood engraving, was basically a lineal method and did not allow for very much in the way of light and shade. The following methods enabled more sophisticated effects to be achieved.

MEZZOTINT

The mezzotint was invented in Germany in the seventeenth century. To prepare a copper plate for mezzotint printing it was first roughened all over its surface so that it would, if left like this, print completely black. Then the engraver proceeded to reduce the intensity of the blackness where he wanted lighter areas to appear, by scraping off the roughness with a tool called a rocker. He worked from dark to light, rather than from light to dark, as in the preceding methods. The rocker blade consisted of a number of tiny teeth which made zigzag marks on the plates. It was a laborious task, as the rocker had to be used many times in every direction. When the plate was considered to have been rocked sufficiently, the design was transferred on to it, in reverse, with a scraper.

With this method, as with the aquatint described below, the plates wore each time a print was taken from them, so that no two prints were ever exactly the same. Often the plate needed retouching, which made a further difference to the next print, and on occasion the whole plate had to be re-modelled. The best example of this is *The Temple of Flora*.

Mezzotint plates were often colour-printed, since surface printing methods like this were better suited to colour printing than were line processes. Colour printing itself is described below.

STIPPLE ENGRAVING

This was an etching rather than an engraving technique—in other words acid, rather than a tool, was used to cut into the copper plate. The plate was first covered with a substance such as varnish, which was impervious to acid. Using etching needles and punches the design was then copied over in the form of small dots which penetrated this etching ground and went right through to the copper beneath. The dots were larger and close together where the design was to be the darkest, and small and far apart where a light effect was required. When the acid was applied it ate through the copper in which the dots had been punched—more or less deeply, according to the size of dot—leaving intact only the parts covered with the ground. Very fine details were sometimes added by retouching the plate afterwards. A very delicate and varied tone was produced, which was generally used with colour printing on the plate, if necessary retouched by hand later.

———

PLATE 52
"Prince Rudolph's Bird of Paradise" is the showpiece
of Richard Bowdler Sharpe's A Monograph of the Paradiseidae, or Birds of Paradise *(London 1891–98).*
William Hart, a pillar of John Gould's success,
here draws for the man who inherited Gould's mantle
and produced our last fine bird book.

Stipple engraving was the method used for the plates of the great French masters Redouté, Bessa and Prévost in the late eighteenth and early nineteenth centuries. Bartolozzi invented the method in England, but it came to full flower in France, and Langlois was perhaps the greatest French engraver.

AQUATINT

The main difference between the aquatint and the stipple engraving was that in the aquatint the etching ground was porous. Acid was applied to the plate many times; as soon as a particular area was sufficiently bitten into, it was covered with a non-porous ground, and so on until the darkest areas had been dealt with. Any area that was to print pure white was completely covered with the non-porous ground to start with. This method produced a kind of soft half-tone effect. As with mezzotints, the plates wore and had to be continually worked on, so apparently identical prints produced by this method may contain a number of minor differences.

SOFT GROUND ETCHING

Soft ground etching was the method used for the plates of John Edwards' *A Collection of Flowers Drawn After Nature*, and for no other natural history book. These plates, which appeared between 1783 and 1801, used 'light' only for the etched tints, and it is possible to think that one is looking at a pure watercolour.

In this method the etching ground was mixed with tallow, and was therefore softer. The design was drawn or traced on a sheet of paper laid over the ground, and the softness of the ground enabled the etcher to cut the lines through it on to the plate beneath. Acid was then applied, and worked in the same way as with stipple engraving.

COLOUR PRINTING

Some natural history plates were entirely colour-printed, while others, including the great works of Thornton, Redouté and Levaillant, were partially colour-printed and retouched by hand afterwards. There were two ways of colour printing from the plate—applying all the colours on to a single copper plate (the method favoured in England), or making several identical copper plates, applying a different colour to each, and printing them on to the paper one after another. This latter method was the one used in France.

LITHOGRAPHY

The technique of lithography was invented accidentally by an Austrian, Alois Senefelder, in 1796. In a hurry one day, he wrote down his mother's laundry list on a handy stone—he had been conducting etching experiments using various objects as 'plates'—and when he later tried to wash off the writing with acid and water he found he could not, since the ink was greasy. By about 1840 lithography had ousted all other techniques.

In the perfected method a smooth lithographic stone received the design in pen and greasy ink or a greasy lithographic crayon. The softness of the crayon gave a rather imprecise line, and lithographic plates were frequently improved by retouching with a scraper or by various other methods. The stone was then wetted, but the inked parts rejected the moisture. When a greasy ink was passed over the stone, however, it was accepted by the previously inked portions. The lithograph was frequently hand-coloured, which accounts for its superiority to the chromolithograph.

Apart from the difference in appearance, a lithographic print does not have the plate mark which surrounds engravings, so is easily distinguishable.

CHROMOLITHOGRAPHY

This is the name given to colour printing using lithographic methods. The plates could be printed many times over, with blocks of colour overlapping and overprinting to create a range of colours. As many lithographic stones were needed as there were colours to be applied. This multiple printing gave the plates a rather greasy, shiny appearance, suitable for the vivid plumage of tropical birds but much less so for flower prints. The process required considerable skill to do it well, because of the multiple printing. This explains why, especially late in the period, so many bad chromolithographic plates were produced.

ABBREVIATIONS

Natural history plates frequently carry a number of credits to the various people involved in preparing them. Since Latin abbreviations are usually used they can be perplexing to the uninitiated. Below is a brief glossary of these terms.

Del.: stands for *delineavit* or *delineaverunt*—Latin for he (or she) or they drew—and therefore refers to the artist. This is usually found on the bottom left-hand side of the print, after the artist's name.

Dir.: stands for *direxit* or *direxerunt*, and refers to the person(s) who supervised the engraving (i.e. not necessarily the actual engraver). The name precedes it.

Exc.: stands for *excudit* or *excuderunt*, meaning (it always follows a name) engraved by, or sometimes engraved and printed.

Fe. or *Fec.*: stands for *fecit* or *fecerunt*, meaning made by. A less common variant of *del*. The name always precedes it.

Imp.: stands for *impressit* or *impresserunt*, meaning printed by. On French plates it often stands for *imprimé* or *Imprimerie*—it all means the same thing. This information is usually found below the title of the plate.

Lith. or *Lit.*: refers to the lithographer, whose name it follows.

Pinx.: stands for *pinxit* or *pinxerunt*, meaning painted by. In this context it is a less common alternative to *del*. *Pinx.* also sometimes denotes the hand-colourist.

Sc. or *Sculp.*: stands for *sculpsit* or *sculpserunt*, meaning engraved by. It follows the engraver's name and is usually found on the bottom right-hand side of a plate.

BOOK SIZES

The general reader—and the expert will have no need to read this account anyway—wants to know within reason how large a book is, and not to be told this in too technical a way. When a sheet of paper from the printers has been folded once it is called a folio, and produces two leaves, that is four numbered pages. Folded again it is a quarto—four leaves, eight pages. A large number of ordinary books are octavo, with eight leaves and therefore sixteen pages from each original printer's sheet. Smaller books can be 12mo, 16mo, 24mo and 32mo.

The American Century Dictionary gives 30 different sizes of folio, quarto and octavo books. Most readers do not want to know all these details, and do not mind how many times a sheet has been folded. So I have always borne this in mind and written about 'large folio', 'folio', 'small folio', and so on. One problem is that the terms are not used consistently; to me, for instance, a large quarto is a folio, and I call it this! A small quarto is sometimes called an octavo. Quarto books are, however, almost always square or squarish, while folios and octavos are taller than they are wide.

There is one exception to all this—very, very large books, such as Audubon's *The Birds of America*, or the somewhat smaller Thornton's *The Temple of Flora*, must be distinguished somehow, so to me the first is elephant folio (some prefer double elephant folio), and the latter is very large folio. Remember also that most large natural history books came out either in parts, or in their original boards, and the most valuable ones were bound more proudly by their owners afterwards, some in full calf binding, some in half calf, and some in full or half morocco. The best of these bindings are contemporary, but some, less fortunately—for their value at any rate—are modern. In all cases, or very nearly all, this made the original size smaller. If we want to be really fussy, or perhaps it is better to say really accurate, we must give the size of books in inches and centimeters, both in height and breadth. However, since the original sheets from the printers varied in size, this would have to be done for every single book. As an approximate guide we can think of elephant, the largest size encountered, as about 30 x 40 inches (Audubon's *Birds* is actually 29½ × 39½), with folio, quarto and so on correspondingly smaller.

WATERMARKS

Good, hand-made paper such as was used for natural history plates always contained a watermark, made by pressing a wire shape against the paper during the making process. The watermark consisted of the paper-maker's name and usually the date, and was invisible unless held up against the light, when it could, and still can, be seen with a little difficulty. The date is particularly important with mezzotints and aquatints, since every time a print was pressed on to and then pulled off the plate, the plate wore, as described above, so that in fact no two prints were exactly the same.

If a print is dated 1806 and the watermark is dated, say, 1818, the print cannot have been a very early issue. If the watermark says 1802, the chances are high that it will be one of the earliest issues. Anyone with a real interest in the subject should look very carefully at watermarks.

THE INDEX